COLLECTIVE BEHAVIOR

Response to Social Stress

COLLECTIVE BEHAVIOR

Response to Social Stress

Joseph B. Perry, Jr
and Meredith David Pugh

Bowling Green State University

WEST PUBLISHING COMPANY
St. Paul ☐ New York
Los Angeles ☐ San Francisco

Library of Congress Cataloging in Publication Data

Perry, Joseph B.
Collective behavior.

Bibliography: p.
Includes index.
1. Collective behavior. 2. Disaster relief—
Research. 3. Social movements. I. Pugh,
Meredith, joint author. II. Title.
HM281.P394   301.1   78-2574
ISBN 0-8299-0158-2

4th Reprint—1984

ACKNOWLEDGMENTS

The authors are indebted to the following for permission to reproduce copyrighted materials.

Figure 1.2 From *Communities in Disaster: A Sociological Analysis of Stress Situations* by Allen H. Barton. Copyright © 1969 by Allen H. Barton. Used by permission of Doubleday & Company, Inc. **Pp. 26–27** From *The Crowd: A Study of the Popular Mind* by Gustave LeBon. Copyright © 1960 by Macmillan Publishing Co., Inc. Reprinted by permission. **Table 3.1** From "Diffusion and belief in a collective delusion: the Seattle windshield pelting epidemic" by Nathan Z. Medalia and Otto N. Larsen. In the *American Sociological Review* 23 (April 1958): 180–186. Reprinted by permission of the authors and the American Sociological Association. **Figure 3.1** From "A theory of rumor transmission" by H. Taylor Buckner. In *Public Opinion Quarterly* 29 (1965): 54–70. Reprinted by permission of the author and *Public Opinion Quarterly*. **Table 3.2** From "A theory of rumor transmission" by H. Taylor Buckner. In *Public Opinion Quarterly* 29 (1965): 54–70. Reprinted by permission of the author and *Public Opinion Quarterly*. **P. 56** From the New York *Times*, April 13, 1975. © 1975 by the New York Times Company. Reprinted by permission. **Table 3.3** Alan C. Kerckhoff, Kurt. W. Back, *The June Bug: A Study of Hysterical Contagion*, © 1968, p. 68. Reprinted by permission of Prentice-Hall, Inc. Englewood Cliffs, New Jersey. **Table 3.4** Alan C. Kerckhoff, Kurt W. Back, *The June Bug: A Study of Hysterical Contagion*, © 1968, p. 75. Reprinted by permission of Prentice-Hall, Inc., Englewood Cliffs, New Jersey. **Table 3.5** From "Mystery gas: an analysis of Mass hysteria" by Sidney Stahl and Marty Lebedun. In the *Journal of Health and Social Behavior* 15 (1974): 44–50. Reprinted by permission of the authors and the American Sociological Association. **Figure 3.5** Preprinted from the *Nebraska Symposium on*

For Ban, Julie, Megan,
Paul, Sarah, and Wynn

Preface

P anics, riots, disasters, and social movements are startling departures from conventional social life; and, not surprisingly, these and similar types of events are of compelling interest to many people. Collective behavior is an important part of our lives; it is hard to escape, and it is an exciting academic field. This textbook provides an introduction to the field, including the most recent theoretical developments and research results. It presents substantive information, with a minimum of jargon and pretention.

The book reflects an eclectic approach to the field rather than a single theoretical model. As a consequence, we hope to have gained the advantage of incorporating classic and modern viewpoints as well as competing perspectives. We believe that the field of collective behavior has recently undergone considerable change, and that it no longer is dominated by a single theoretical paradigm.

Realizing this, we attempted to include representative materials from the general disciplines of anthropology, psychology and sociology. All of these fields account for the interdisciplinary character of collective behavior as an academic enterprise. We hope examples of research from each of these disciplines will indicate the broad empirical basis of the field of collective behavior, as well as make its subject matter more concrete for the student.

Throughout the four parts of the book, we emphasize the continuity between everyday activity and the forms of group action typically identified as instances of collective behavior. Part I is a *theoretical overview* of the field, Part II introduces collective behavior as it is revealed in *disaster research*, Part III concerns *crowd violence* in the context of both urban riots and prison riots, and Part IV is an introduction to *social movements* as a form of collective behavior. Although this text is intended as an independent source, it can be used in combination with external references. Whether external references are required reading depends upon each instructor's teaching objectives, students' needs, and the time available for instruction. We hope users of this book will be able to adapt it to their own particular purposes.

Naturally, at this point we would like to express our gratitude to all of those people who have helped in the preparation of this book. Special thanks are due to those individuals who wrote critical reviews of the manuscript at various stages in its development: Shelly Chandler, San Diego State University; Evans Curry, Texas Tech University; J. Eugene Haas, University of Colorado; Thomas C. Hood, University of Tennessee; Jerry M. Lewis, Kent State University; and Edward E. McKenna, Central Michigan University. We also wish to thank our typist Barbara Asmus, and several graduate students for their assistance: Jon Hoelter, Brad Larsen, Dave Neal, Robin Rex, and Pete Widmer. In conclusion, we wish to acknowledge the help, encouragement, and *patience* of our editors at the West Publishing Company.

Contents

LIST OF FIGURES

LIST OF TABLES

*

COLLECTIVE BEHAVIOR

Response to Social Stress

†

PART I *Theoretical Overview*

ollective behavior provides a strategic research setting for identifying the best and worst in people; their reserves of courage and altruism, as well as their potential for weakness and hatred (Milgram and Toch, 1969: 508). Collective behavior can take the form of destructive social conflict just as it can lead to the emergence of new norms and values, the development of new social groups, and even to the creation of new societies. Consequently, the study of collective behavior can contribute to our understanding of both social conflict and social change. But what is collective behavior, and what do we know about it?

The field of collective behavior is one of the oldest specialties in the social sciences and yet it is not a highly refined discipline. It is a field that lacks consensus on even its most basic definitions and it is a field characterized by competing viewpoints and scientific controversy. This is the challenge and excitement of collective behavior as a field of study. It is not a cause for despair.

The next three chapters deal with some theoretical issues in the field. Chapter I concerns the fundamental problem of defining collective behavior. Also considered in this chapter are situational stress, the organizational characteristics of collective behavior, and some of its traditional stereotypes; its alleged emotionality, irrationality, violence and spontaneity.

Chapter II is a critical review of some of the major theoretical perspectives in the field. We have chosen to represent different approaches as perspectives rather than theories because they are not highly formalized systems of thought. Considered here are Gustave LeBon's classical perspective, Herbert Blumer's interactionist perspective, Richard Berk's rational calculus model, and Neil Smelser's value-added model.

Chapter III covers three distinctive forms of social interaction in collective behavior: rumor, social contagion, and deindividuation. They are such prominant topics in collective behavior that we felt they should receive special recognition in a chapter of their own.

1

Ohio National Guardsmen assemble near the burning ROTC building on the Kent State University campus in May 1970.

CHAPTER I

The Definitional Problem

C ollective behavior, like many terms in the social sciences, has no single definition on which there is wide agreement, and which serves to set the limits of the field (Currie and Skolnick 1970:61). Definitions gathered in a recent survey of specialists vary from broad formulas equating the field with virtually all of social science to narrow definitions restricting the field to a limited range of crowd behavior (Quarantelli and Weller 1974:63). One scholar seems to have suggested that we may be unable to define the nature of collective behavior (Klapp 1972:31) and another has claimed that the term itself is useless rubric (Brissett 1968). The problem posed by this lack of consensus is to define collective behavior broadly enough to encompass its principal expressions without including all forms of human action.

Collective Behavior Defined

Collective behavior refers to *relatively unorganized patterns of social interaction in human groups.* It is *collective* because it occurs in *groups,* it is a *process* because it involves social interaction between people, and it is *emergent* because it cannot be fully explained by psychological propositions about individuals acting in isolation from other people (Webster 1973:269). Human groups are something more than simple aggregations of individuals, and what happens in groups cannot be explained solely on the basis of individual personalities.

Roving bands of policemen reportedly attacked "nonprovocative" citizens during the riots of the 1960s and on some occasions the police were allegedly "*the major or even the only* perpetrators of disorder, violence and destruction."

3

(Stark 1972:16). The "rotten apple" theory would explain this kind of police action by blaming the personality defects of a few "bad" officers; yet there is little evidence in its support. On the contrary, there is evidence that the police who lose their self-restraint when confronting members of the public are indistinguishable on the basis of personality characteristics from those who display a high degree of self-control (Stark 1972:12). The problem is people do things in groups which they would not do as individuals. Consequently, police riots and other examples of collective behavior are difficult to understand without an appreciation of the nature of social groups.

The Nature of Social Groups

Donald Campbell (1958) argues that the epistemological status of groups is no different from that of things such as stones and rats. The difficulty is, as he put it, that the "natural knowledge processes with which we are biologically endowed somehow make objects like stones and teacups much more real than social groups or neutrinos" (1958:11). Why is this so? What are the factors which lead people to perceive unit elements as parts of a single entity. How do we know who is in a group and who is not?

Early Gestalt psychologists identified four principles which help us set a boundary around the constituent elements of an entity. Proximity and similarity are important factors since similar elements located close together are more likely to be perceived as parts of the same entity than are widely separated or dissimilar elements. Elements that appear together in successive temporal observations and share a "common fate" because of their contemporaneous movement with each other are also likely to be seen as part of the same entity. And finally, unit elements that form a pattern are more likely to be seen as an entity than are unit elements which do not lead to the recognition of a particular pattern.

Obviously the constituent elements of stones and rocking chairs easily meet this set of criteria, whereas the applicability of the Gestalt principles to social groups may be less apparent. Nevertheless, human groups can be distinguished from their surroundings, including other people, on the basis of three criteria: (1) the *proximity* of group members to each other, (2) the *similarity* of group members to each other, and (3) the pattern of the *relationships* between group members. For example, most Americans would have little difficulty spotting two football teams on a playing field. Each team is a relatively compact cluster of people located on either side of the field; and each team is further differentiated from its surroundings by the uniforms its members wear. But unless we paid close attention to the patterns of interaction occurring on the field, to the nature of the relationships between the team members, we would not be certain that these two clusters of people were actually football teams. Similarity is helpful in recognizing the boundaries of groups, but it is neither a necessary nor a sufficient condition for group recognition. Proximity, on the other hand, is a necessary although not a sufficient condition. A simple cluster of people is transformed into a group by the *social relationships* that exist between its members. Social relationships are evident in groups as regular patterns of social interaction. Take away the relationships between the members of a group and you are left with a simple *aggregate* of people. And in this respect, social groups have been compared to mosaics (Denisoff and Wahrman, 1975: 80). A mosaic of plain stones is a mosaic because of the relationships between the stones; take away the pattern of relationships, and all that is left is a pile of pebbles. The Minnesota Vikings are a football team not just because they wear the same uniform, and not merely because they play in the same stadium, but because of what they *do* together on a football field.

Up to this point it has been suggested that groups are real, recognizable things. Nevertheless, it must be understood that social groups are not "things" in exactly the same sense that cars are things. Social groups are not perfectly analogous to either biological organisms or mechanical structures because social groups possess "physiology without anatomy" (Katz and Kahn 1966). When the football game is over, the uniforms taken off, and the field abandoned, the football team is gone as a recognizable entity until it is reassembled for a new game. There is no comparable magic for cars which have bodies and can be seen in junkyards long after they stop running.

This conception of reality does not mean that only cars are "really" real. Social groups are also real, as we can readily appreciate by observing that countries are not invaded by imaginary armies. It does mean that one must be careful in thinking about the nature of social groups and have a reasonably clear definition of what they are. *A social group is a spatially located cluster of interacting people characterized by size, density, and shape.* Social groups, unlike the car, do not have impermeable physical boundaries. Instead, they may have membership committees to determine who should not be admitted. Social groups can tolerate much more variability of internal activity than either machines or organisms. Individuals can be members of more than one group, or can change groups as their attitudes toward them change; the components of cars, on their own initiative, cannot become parts of other automobiles.

Each of the preceding features of social groups can have important implications for collective behavior. Multiple group memberships, for example, have a significant effect on the way a group of people will react to disasters (Killian 1952). A group of workers with families at home will not respond to the threat of a tornado in exactly the same way as a group of workers without families. People differ in the *number* and *kinds* of groups they join. Groups themselves differ in many ways, one of the most important of which is social organization. The concept of social organization in groups is necessary to an understanding of collective behavior.

Social Organization in Groups

Interaction in human groups is organized on the basis of both *social norms* and *social roles.* For this reason it is essential to define these terms before considering the organizational characteristics of collective behavior.

Social Norms

Social norms are the rules or standards of conduct that tell members of a society or cultural group what they should or should not do. *Prescriptive* norms indicate appropriate behaviors, and *proscriptive* norms indicate inappropriate. In the United States there is a prescriptive norm that tells us we ought to pay our income taxes, and there is a proscriptive norm that tells us we must not drive our automobiles faster than 55 miles per hour. Both of these are also *explicit* because they have been written down in criminal codes, but some important social norms are *implicit* rather than explicit. Implicit social norms are a matter of common understanding. In our country it is generally understood, for example, that we are supposed to tell long-lost friends that they are "looking good" even when they are actually looking "terrible." When someone asks "How are you?", most Americans realize they are expected to say "great," "fine," or at least "OK," in reply. People who give their medical histories in response to simple greetings are often viewed with suspicion and sanctioned for their unusual behavior.

The sanctions attached to social norms are an important aspect of the function of these norms in human groups. Encounters with other people teach social norms through positive and negative reinforcements associated with conformity and deviance from widely accepted standards of conduct. Children quickly discover that deviance from group norms can lead to social disapproval, punishment, and unpopularity. People who deviate from norms are likely to be given the worst jobs to be done in a group, they are less likely to be group leaders, and they are more likely to be asked to leave a group.

Just as the sanctions attached to certain crimes can be onerous, the rewards associated with conformity to social norms can be very gratifying. Social approval, honor, and money are important motivational forces for most people. In short, the reward contingencies operating in a person's environment help to account for the ability of norms to regulate human behavior. Inappropriate behavior is suppressed by negative sanctions and acceptable conduct is encouraged by positive reinforcements.

Social norms regulate a variety of human behaviors. Some social norms are found in virtually all societies, others are limited to relatively few societies, and still other social norms are limited to special groups within a society. *Conventional* norms are widely followed in a society as a whole and are applied to all people on a *universal* basis regardless of their personal differences. The norm prohibiting speed, for example, applies to lawyers and doctors as well as students. Many people consider conventional norms to be a matter of tradition and for this reason they are likely to perceive behavior regulated by conventional norms as *customary* and *normal.*

Unconventional norms, on the other hand, are limited to special groups within a society. In some cases, unconventional norms are so unusual and so rarely experienced outside of special groups that they are not even recognized by most people; in other cases, they are recognized but not accepted as legitimate standards of behavior. Indeed, unconventional norms are frequently limited to special groups or deviant subcultures within a society precisely because they are not generally accepted as legitimate behavioral standards.

Social Roles

When we meet new people we attempt to "size them up"—to fit them into a set of preconceived categories we carry around with us in our heads. We do this because classifying people makes life easier for us in several respects. The categories we use in classifying people are really nothing more than linguistic labels such as "teacher," "student," "policeman," "criminal," and so on. Our assumption is that the people we label in one way will share some important attributes with similar people we have met in the past. The shared attributes can be personal characteristics, such as wealth and status, traits, such as achievement, motivation, and intelligence; or specific kinds of behavior. *Roles* are the *expected behaviors* we learn to associate with particular social categories of people. Unlike social norms, roles are limited in their applicability to special kinds of people in specific social contexts. Only doctors, for example, can invite people into an office and proceed to ask a series of personal questions culminating in a request to remove all clothing. Car salesmen are allegedly a "crafty" lot; but even so, they don't actually get the shirt off your back.

One of the advantages of labeling people and imputing roles to them is that it makes life simpler. People differ in many ways, but roles allow us to assume we can ignore these personal differences. We expect waiters and waitresses to bring our food whether they are short or tall or have a headache. Likewise, a bus driver is expected to stop at prearranged points on his/her route even though he/she is worried about his/her children. If we had to take such extraneous information into account in order to eat in a restaurant or ride on a bus, social interaction would be much more difficult than it is.

How would you label these people? What social roles would you assign to them? Are these labels and roles accurate?

A second advantage of labeling people and imputing roles to them is the increased predictability of their behavior. To get along with other people it helps to know what they are likely to do and how they are likely to respond to our own behavior. Teachers assume their students will come to class, sit in their seats, and take notes. Students come to class expecting their teachers to deliver a lecture, lead a general discussion of some topic, or show a movie. We expect these behaviors to occur and when our predictions go astray we are usually surprised and annoyed. Professors are irritated by rowdy students who spoil the decorum of their classrooms, and most students are disturbed by teachers who don't teach. Because we adjust our own behavior to the anticipated behavior of other people, we tend to feel they are obligated to enact the roles we attribute to them. Consequently, people are linked together by *reciprocal obligations* and feel let down when another person fails to live up to their expectations.

A third advantage of social roles is that they can serve as a mechanism for coordinating the behavior of people in a group. Some groups can achieve an adequate level of interpersonal coordination through a relatively simple *role structure*. Spectator crowds are an example. Baseball fans know they are expected to find their seats, sit in them, stand up for the National Anthem, sit down again, pass beer and peanuts to one another, stand up for the seventh inning stretch, and file out of the stadium when the game is over. If people didn't know how to behave as baseball fans and spectators, they would be much more difficult to manage. Most people have little difficulty in meeting these rather diffuse role requirements and one baseball crowd is basically the same as the next. In contrast, a baseball team uses a more complex role structure to coordinate the behavior of nine players, and the ability of the players to execute their roles properly distinguishes one baseball team from the next.

Actually, baseball teams—even great ones—do not represent an especially complex role structure. The most complex role structures are found in the labyrinth of bureaucracies with which most of us have negotiated an uneasy truce. Bureaucracies are organizations based on a rational plan in which jobs are distributed to group members to maximize efficiency in achieving a limited set of goals. Interaction between people is expected to follow a master "blueprint" or organizational chart that includes job titles (labels), job specifications (roles), lines of communication, and rules and regulations covering such things as wages, work loads, promotion procedures, and vacation time.

The complexity of role structures in bureaucratic organizations is reflected in both an elaborate *division of labor* and a *hierarchy of authority.* The division of labor insures that each job entails a specialized set of tasks which will interface properly with the duties of other jobs. The high degree of *role specificity* associated with each job category also guards against the unnecessary overlapping of functions, insuring every person a clearly defined set of *obligations* to the organization.

All the positions (jobs) in a bureaucratic organization can be ranked from high to low on a vertical dimension; the higher up the "bureaucratic ladder" a position is located, the greater its authority. The hierarchy of authority is a way of distributing decision-making responsibility to the members with the highest qualifications in particular areas of expertise. The greater the authority and decision-making responsibility the greater the rewards (salaries, prestige) given to various positions in the organization.

In bureaucracies people are supposedly hired and promoted on the basis of their qualifications (skills, education, experience) for performing in a particular job. The personality and social background of a job candidate therefore should not make any difference to the organization. As a result, it should be able to function without the services of a special person. Assuming roughly equivalent qualifications, people are interchangeable on an organizational chart and no one is indispensable. At least in theory, even the leaders (management) of a bureaucracy are replaceable.

Anyone involved with bureaucracies must realize that the preceding description is highly idealized. Bureaucracies are not always efficient and their members do not always perform as expected. The leaders of bureaucracies recognize such problems in their attempts to monitor the performance of various tasks in a more or less continuous process of self-regulation. Even so, there are times when organizations break down and the ritualistic shuffling of paper comes to a temporary halt. Despite their deficiencies, bureaucracies embody complex role structures that can serve as a standard of comparison when considering the organizational characteristics of collective behavior.

Social Organization and Collective Behavior

Collective behavior has been portrayed in the past as a polar opposite of organized group activity because of its lack of organizational characteristics (Pfautz 1961:168). But collective behavior is not totally unstructured. Even rumors frequently reflect a pattern of social relationships. Here, for example, is the case history of a rumor about an elephant in New York City (Buckley 1975).

The story concerns a woman from New Jersey who drove her red Volkswagen to Madison Square Garden to buy some tickets for the circus. After making her purchase, she returned to her parked car and discovered that its hood was squashed. Upon subsequent inquiry she learned that one of the circus elephants being taken out for exercise had mistaken her vehicle for a stool. The police were summoned; the circus people admitted their elephant had caused the damage, and they gave the woman a note for her husband. On her way home across the George Washington Bridge, the same woman encountered a serious multicar accident. She was able to squeeze past the debris, but was stopped by the police who thought she had been involved in the accident because her hood was so badly dented. The woman told the police about the elephant in New York City; and only the note saved her from being arrested for drunken driving.

A newspaper columnist established that the whole story was untrue: the police indicated there "hadn't been any elephant molestations reported by a Volkswagen owner or by anyone else"; press representatives for the circus said the incident had never happened and dismissed the story as an amusing slander of circus elephants. Where, then, did the rumor originate?

The newspaper columnist heard the story from a woman named Moses, who heard the story from her sister-in-law, and her sister-in-law said the incident had happened to the cousin of a friend of hers. The friend's cousin said that an elephant had not sat on her car, but that she had heard the story from an acquaintance who taught interior decorating in the hinterlands of New Jersey. The interior decorator, naturally enough, said the story was certainly true and she had heard it from one of her students, and the student said she had heard the story from a neighbor. The neighbor declined further comment, and the investigation was stymied. But if it had continued, the pattern would have remained the same, the people who heard the story were linked together in a social network based primarily on kinship and friendship. In almost all well-documented accounts of rumor transmission there is a discernible structure or pattern.

Other forms of collective behavior appearing to be totally unplanned may also have organizational features. Protest demonstrations and student rallies require some organizational planning: "Where should people meet?" "At what time?" "Who will speak?" "Who will get the parade permit?" "Who will serve as crowd martials?" Even apparently chaotic community reactions to threatening situations frequently reflect a minimal level of organizational capacity. Consider the community reaction to a mysterious prowler who supposedly tormented a small town in rural Illinois during World War II.

"The Phantom Anesthetist of Mattoon" (Johnson 1945) allegedly carried a green tank on his back as he entered private houses to spray a sweet-smelling gas on sleeping occupants. The "gasser's" victims awoke feeling miserable with fevers, vomiting, and even partial paralysis. Most of the victims reported to local health authorities, and news of the gassing attacks quickly spread throughout the state. Thousands wrote local officials to express their sympathy and offer advice on coping with the mad gasser. The local citizens of Mattoon took heed. They requested the aid of the state police and organized themselves into patrol groups. Although they failed to capture the elusive, if not imaginary, gasser their attempt demonstrates that Mattoon's reaction to a *perceived* threat was not as "hysterical" as it is sometimes implied. The Mattoon patrols were ad hoc groups that developed in congruence with *social norms* upholding the right of private citizens to protect themselves from attack.

Collective behavior, more generally speaking, usually has both *normative* and *structural* features. Its norms—explicit and implicit—are either *conventional* or *unconventional* (see Figure 1.1), and its social relationships are structured at either the *simple* or *intermediate* level or organizational complexity. Crowds are usually characterized by relatively simple role structures that tend to be ephemeral rather than permanent. Social movements, on the other hand, are characterized by greater permanence and an intermediate level of organizational complexity. They are a midpoint between loosely organized crowds and fully organized bureaucracies. Social movements generally have an organized core of leaders, but lack many of the organizational features usually attributed to bureaucracies. In effect, they are a transition phase in organizational development. This does not mean that crowds always mature into bureaucratic organizations or that bureaucracies cannot become disorganized and serve as a context for collective behavior. It indicates, however, that collective behavior is part of a *continuum* with bureaucratically organized group action. Nevertheless, collective behavior *can be* a startling departure from the ordinary flow of social life. This aspect of collective behavior is frequently magnified by the *social context* in which it occurs.

FIGURE 1.1: Collective Behavior and Social Organization

		SOCIAL NORMS	
		Conventional	Unconventional
	Simple Structure	I	II
SOCIAL ROLES	Intermediate	III	IV
	Complex Structure	V	VI

TYPE I = Conventional crowds (e.g., spectator groups)
TYPE II = Unconventional crowds (e.g., rioting police groups)
TYPE III = Conventional social movements (e.g., some religious groups)
TYPE IV = Unconventional social movements (e.g., terrorist groups)
TYPE V = Conventional organizations (e.g., business groups)
TYPE VI = Unconventional organizations (e.g., syndicate crime groups)

The Social Context of Collective Behavior

The context of social interaction is unusually important when circumstances place heavy demands on groups. Collective behavior is especially likely to occur under conditions of *situational stress*. In fact, one could call collective behavior a *group level* response to social stress in the sense that its occurrence is frequently contingent upon the existence of problematic circumstances or strains (Lang and Lang 1961, Smelser 1962). For this reason, the concept of situational stress is critical to a further elaboration of the nature of collective behavior.

Collective Behavior and Situational Stress

The social sciences have used the concept of stress in a confusing variety of ways (Haas and Drabek, 1973:250). In general, stress suggests "excess demands on men and animals, demands that produce disturbance of physiological, social and psychological systems" (Lazarus, 1968:338). *Situational stress refers to a natural or social condition that places excess demands on the capacity of groups to achieve collective goals.* As a context for collective behavior, situational stress has its origins in either the social or natural environments shared by groups of people. The concept of stress at a sociological level of analysis is used to characterize the functioning of social *organizations* but at a psychological level, stress is experienced by *individuals* as frustration, deprivation, fear, and anxiety.

Fear and anxiety are both products of situational stress, and yet they are not equivalent terms. And they have different implications for the emergence of collective behavior. Fear is often the result of an obvious environmental threat; anxiety, however, is frequently the result of a much more ambiguous environmental dislocation or problem. People can feel anxious or ill-at-ease without being able to pinpoint what's troubling them; and in this circumstance, they cannot make an effective response. Collective hysteria, for example, is an ineffective response to a sense of anxiety experienced by a number of people in a shared social context. Consider the following case history as an example.

On a Wednesday night in June 1962 word first reached the public of a mysterious illness that had forced the closing of a local clothing plant in a small city in the South. The six o'clock news program had carried the report that at least ten women had been admitted to a local hospital for treatment of severe nausea. The outbreak of the sickness at the plant was blamed on "some kind of bug" that allegedly had come from England with a shipment of cloth. Later that night the eleven o'clock news program explained that the stricken workers had blamed their illness on the biting of a small insect that left a wound similar to that of a gnat. It was also announced that the plant would reopen on Thursday morning even though company officials admitted the cause of the outbreak was still unknown.

On Friday of the same week two experts were summoned from the U.S. Public Health Service Communicable Disease Center in Atlanta, Georgia to help local officials locate the source of the mysterious illness that still plagued the plant. These two experts were accompanied on a tour of the facility by plant officials, representatives of its insurance companies, and two entomologists from the state university. This task force of experts searched the entire textile plant for anything that might have caused the outbreak of illness, but they were especially looking for the small black bug employees had consistently blamed for their sickness. Close inspection and the use of a vacuum cleaner to get specimens resulted in a total catch of a black ant, a housefly, several gnats, a small variety of beetles, and a mite (chigger). None of these (except perhaps the chigger) was famous for a rapacious appetite for human flesh, and none could account for the reaction observed in the plant (Kerckhoff and Back 1968:5). It was concluded at the end of the search that "the cause of illness is still unknown."

Sixty-two people were eventually affected by the epidemic and had to be sent home from work. The array of technical expertise marshalled to resolve the problem allegedly created by the "June Bug" (Kerckhoff and Back 1968) is an indication of how seriously the outbreak of illness was taken by plant and community officials. Nevertheless, an organic cause was never determined for the sickness. The case of the mysterious June Bug is now recognized as one of the most exhaustively studied episodes of collective hysteria on record. And contrary to what might be supposed, the case of the June Bug is not a unique event in social life.

In May 1968, students at a junior high school in Baltimore were victims of "epilepsy-like" attacks which they believed were caused by a smelly gas. Gas masks in place, firemen rushed to the school where they found still more students on the floor gasping for breath. No traces of the gas were ever found (Kramer 1973). In 1972, employees of a computer center at a midwestern university were victims of another mysterious gas which subsequently could not be detected by environmental experts (Stahl and Lebedun 1974). In April 1976, 15 Mississippi pupils were victims of "mysterious fainting spells." During a period of a week, the girls fell to the ground at a public school, writhing and kicking in apparent agony. Before losing consciousness during the attacks, which usually lasted for only ten minutes or so, they frequently shouted such things as "Don't let it get me!" or "Get it off!" Again it was impossible for state officials to identify a physical agent as a cause of the attacks. But the victims of the seizures—as in other cases of collective hysteria—shared a common social context; yet they were unable to make the connection between their experience of situational stress, the onset of disturbing physiological symptoms, and problems confronting them in their social environment.

In the case of the June Bug, 58 of its 62 victims were working together in the dressmaking department of the plant, where the month of June is the rush period for preparing the latest fall fashions. Employees were under pressure to maintain a high level of productivity and many of the stricken women were working overtime shifts that interfered with their family responsibilities. The stricken women blamed their illness on the June Bug because they were unable to see a connection between their experience of situational stress and working conditions in the plant. In a similar manner, the workers affected by the undetectable gas at the university computer center were distinguished from their nonaffected colleagues by their higher levels of job dissatisfaction. The pupils who suffered from fainting spells in Mississippi were involved in a dispute over a boyfriend, although they personally blamed their seizures on voodoo spells cast by one of the girls involved in the argument (Toledo Blade, April 1976). In Chapter III we will consider these cases in more detail as illustrations of the process of social contagion.

Collective hysteria is only one form of collective behavior. But all forms are shaped to some extent by the social context in which they occur. Obvious external threats such as fires and floods are more likely to result in panics than in wildcat strikes, just as long-term social movements are more likely to be associated with chronic social conditions rather than with short-term emergencies. Allen H. Barton (1969) developed an elaborate typology of collective stress situations for which he has supplied numerous examples. His work is the basis for the simplified typology presented below.

A Typology of Stress Situations

Stress situations can be differentiated on the basis of three criteria: (1) the *origin of stress;* (2) its *locus of control;* and (3) its *duration of impact.* A fourth dimension, scope of impact, will be discussed at a later point. For now it should be clear from Figure 1.2 that the origin of stress is determined by whether a problem or threat arises either in the natural or social environment of a group. Famines, tornadoes, power failures and pollution are basically natural conditions whereas invasions, racial discrimination, and job layoffs are social conditions.

Stress situations are sometimes within the potential control of an affected group, while on other occasions they are not. We presume pollution is amena-

FIGURE 1.2: A Typology of Natural and Social Crisis

| | LONG-TERM SITUATIONS | | SHORT-TERM SITUATIONS | |
	External	Internal	External	Internal
NATURAL CRISIS	Epidemics	Air Pollution	Tornadoes	Explosions
	Droughts	Water Pollution	Floods	Blackouts
SOCIAL CRISIS	Colonialism	Discrimination	Propaganda	Police Brutality
	Trade Embargos	Unemployment	Terrorist Attacks	Work Speedups

Adapted from: Barton (1969: 52-5).

ble to human technology since modern manufacturing contributes to the problem; tornadoes, however, are beyond our technological control at the present time. The loss of a foreign market is frequently beyond the effective control of a group, and is thus under external control. In contrast, power failures and job layoffs are at least potentially subject to internal control through modern technology and labor arbitration.

Figure 1.2 considers stress situations on a time dimension, calling fires and earthquakes short-term events and pollution and famines long-term events. Work speedups are classified as short-term stress situations even though it is recognized that some work speedups may be imposed for a relatively long period of time. Another complication illustrated by work speedups is that they repesent stress situations which are likely to occur on a repetitive basis. Business cycles and seasonal fluctuations in the availability of raw materials, for example, may indicate periods when employers are eager to extract maximum productivity from their employees. Some natural crises such as earthquakes and tornadoes also occur repeatedly in certain geographical areas, and this possibility is inadequately reflected in our typology. No typology, however, can hope to be a perfect representation of the world we live in.

A more important problem than that of accuracy or disagreement on the classification of particular events is the problem of determining the scope of stress situations. Barton indicates that *scope of impact* involves collectivities ranging in size from family groups and work groups through large formal organizations and communities to states, regions, and entire nations. The

In 1976 an explosion blew apart this Liberian tanker. This was a natural disaster subject to internal control through technology.

larger the scope of impact, the greater the extent of social disruption, and the more difficult it is to initiate recovery, reestablish an old equilibrium, or establish a new point of social stability. According to Barton, scope of impact is defined by the *size of the group* affected by a problem rather than by geographical distribution.

Up to this point, the nature of collective behavior has been defined by its organizational characteristics and the social context in which it occurs. Collective behavior is not a fundamentally different kind of group activity and should be analyzed within the framework of standard theories and methodological techniques found in the social sciences (Couch 1968, 1970; Johnson 1974). Unfortunately, the field of collective behavior has given rise to a number of traditional stereotypes—misleading stereotypes that have set collective behavior apart from other forms of social action.

Some Stereotypes of Collective Behavior

Until recently it has been traditional to describe collective behavior as highly *emotional*, largely *irrational*, irresponsibly *violent*, and *spontaneous*. Each of these viewpoints is a stereotype in that it represents an exaggerated distortion of collective behavior. Furthermore, each of these stereotypes is fundamentally wrong in certain respects (Couch 1968). The problem is to account for these perceptions of collective behavior by its organizational characteristics and social context.

Emotionality

The traditional stereotype contrasts the self-restraint and orderliness of conventional organizations with the alleged emotionality of certain crowds. Indeed, such commonsense terms as "crowd madness," "loss of control," and "raving beast" reflect the conviction that crowds amount to a pathological form of social action. But the emotional state characteristic of collective behavior is a *variable* attribute. While we would readily agree there is a great difference between the emotional level expressed by the board of directors of a large corporation and the crowd at the Democratic National Convention in 1968, recent research indicates that collective behavior is sometimes characterized by more caution and less emotion than was originally supposed. Collective behavior usually occurs in the context of situational stress and, as a result, may be characterized by a certain degree of emotionality. But even in extreme situations people can respond in groups with great self-control and dispassionate activity. It has been found, for example, that intensive bombing does not necessarily panic those who are bombed. Instead, as will be discussed later, the consequence may be an increase in morale and self-control. Richard Burton has reported the following incident from World War II:

> I remember seeing . . . men dancing in the street when a landmine, a real monster, failed to detonate near London's Euston Station. The street was roped off . . . (and) sitting athwart the tentacular landmine was an emblematically cool cockney. Not exactly the glass of fashion or the mould of form, but knowing that he was the observed of all observers, he struck—with deliberate indifference to danger—a match against the monster mine and, lighting a Woodbine cigarette, puffed on the weed with aplomb. There was tremendous applause from both ends of the street. (Burton 1974:23).

Traditional stereotypes of collective behavior tended to ignore this kind of incident in favor of events which seemed to display unbridled emotionalism. They also tended, as an inverse corollary, to emphasize the irrationality of collective behavior. But the appearance of irrationality in collective behavior is frequently a superficial product of its involvement with unconventional social norms.

Irrationality

When people fail to recognize unconventional norms they are frequently disposed to see their surroundings as haphazard, irrational, and even dangerous. Tourists from the midwest, for example, complain that the drivers in eastern cities such as Baltimore and Boston are lawless lunatics. Drivers in these cities, however, complain that they have little trouble on their roads until the tourist season begins. The difficulty is that the drivers in Boston and Baltimore follow some rather unconventional and implicit social norms with which most other people are unfamiliar. Baltimore natives generally understand that drivers will go through traffic lights for up to five seconds after the light has changed from green to red (Webster 1975:20); and in Boston it is generally understood that drivers will speed up as they approach intersections to establish their right-of-way by arriving first at a crossroad. Failure to recognize these implicit social norms for driving can clearly have disastrous consequences in either city. But, it would be a mistake to conclude that driving in these cities is unregulated by social norms or that the drivers are mentally deficient.

The problem is one of perspective. What appears haphazard or senseless to outside observers may be quite rational from the point of view of participants. For example, Rudé (1959) has argued that rioting crowds in the French Revolution possessed more rationality than is attributed to them by LeBon. Between 1964 and 1968 approximately 60,000 people were arrested for looting in connection with urban riots. Most people, including government officials, generally saw the ransacking and destruction of ghetto stores as a "meaningless" outburst of senseless violence. After all, the rioters were destroying the very neighborhoods in which they lived (Sears and Tomlinson 1968). Subsequent research, however, suggests an alternative interpretation of looting. Looting was a subculturally legitimated pattern of collective behavior in the 1960s. This was expressed in several ways: first, the looters often worked together in family units or small groups; second, the looters were selective in their choice of places to ransack; and third, the looters were acting on the basis of a collective redefinition of property rights (Quarantelli and Dynes 1970, Berk and Aldrich 1972).

Violence

There is some truth in the traditional stereotype of crowd violence. There is no doubt that crowds can be violent. The students at Kent State University in May 1970 did indeed set fire to the campus ROTC building; and they did indeed throw stones at the National Guard troops. The inmates who rioted at Attica prison in September of 1971 did indeed assault correction officers and take hostages for negotiations. But it should be recognized that in both of these incidents and many others the greatest violence was initiated by agencies of social control. In fact, social agencies such as the police and troops of the National Guard are generally far more violent than the crowds they are asked to confront (Couch 1968). Crowds are no more likely to be violent than many fully institutionalized groups. Armies are far more deadly than crowds as "killing machines," and armies are bureaucratic organizations.

Sometimes agencies of social control such as the police aggravate crowds and increase the level of violence as happened at the Democratic National Convention in Chicago in 1968.

Crowds also have the capacity for prosocial behavior. For example, people usually converge on the scene of a disaster, and will often form ad hoc, "search and rescue" teams. As we shall discuss later, impromptu volunteer groups can play an important part in postdisaster recovery periods.

Spontaneity

The issue of spontaneity in collective behavior is somewhat confused by the vagueness of the term itself. If spontaneity refers to the development of new groups with new norms and social roles there can be little argument. New groups do appear as a result of situational stress. Sometimes the groups are transitory and sometimes they become a part of the institutionalized social order. In either case, collective behavior would have a spontaneous aspect.

The issue is more difficult to resolve when the idea of spontaneity is equated with organizational planning. Outside observers attribute planning to some incidents of collective behavior when there is evidence of little planning; on the other hand, they have seen little planning where there was a great deal of preparation.

The prison administration at Attica, for example, was convinced they were confronting a well-organized band of radical inmates (Oswald 1972). They believed that the riot which broke out in the morning of September 9, 1971 was planned months before as part of a revolutionary conspiracy. Available evidence, however, suggests that the prison riot at Attica was completely unplanned (New York State Special Commission on Attica 1972). The murders committed by Charles Manson and his "family," however, present an example of the opposite kind.

The Sharon Tate murders are among the most brutal and shocking episodes in the annals of American crime. They were immediately branded by local newspaper and law enforcement officials as an irrational outburst of homicidal violence, presumably committed by a band of drug-crazed maniacs. But this version of the crime gave way to an even more sinister account. Manson's family was a loosely organized group that had existed for roughly two years before the murders. The murders had been planned by Manson himself, and were carried out by his followers on his request. Contrary to all reasonable expectations, the murders were committed willingly and without the influence of drugs. Furthermore, the murders were seen by the family as a logical step in Manson's revolutionary plan.

Clearly, the extent of organizational planning in collective behavior is a variable attribute, and the inability of outside observers to see a plan does not mean that little planning has taken place. There is probably more planning in collective behavior than is commonly recognized.

Exclusions and Qualifications

Some of the topics usually treated in collective behavior texts have been excluded by our definitional parameters. These are subjects both interesting and important in their own right, but which need not involve social interaction among a group of people. Turner and Killian distinguished two kinds of collectivity, the compact and the diffuse. The diffuse collectivity is a group "whose members are dispersed" while the compact collectivity is a group "whose members are in one another's immediate presence" (Turner and Killian 1957:-

166). Using this terminology the topics excluded from treatment here are those traditionally associated with a diffuse collectivity. The broadest categories excluded are the mass and the public.

There are fundamental differences between the collective behavior of compact social groups and the mass or the public. The compact group is a distinguishable entity which can exist in its "pure form" while the so-called diffuse collectivity cannot (Turner and Killian 1957:166). Widely dispersed individuals who are never in direct contact or interaction with each other do not form a recognizable and discrete collectivity of people. Some of the most distinctive social processes involved in episodes of collective behavior such as rumor, social contagion, perceptual distortion, and the diffusion of social responsibility are not nearly as significant in the mass or the public as they are in collectivities. The mass and the public involve dispersed individuals who respond to the same stimulus or issue more or less independently of each other, whereas social interaction in collective behavior is strongly influenced by the presence of other people.

The mass, according to Herbert Blumer, one of the most influential scholars of collective behavior, has four main characteristics. It is a heterogeneous aggregate with members from many diverse groups. Its membership is anonymous in that any one member knows only a small proportion of the total in any personal way. As the members of a mass are physically separated there is little or no interaction or exchange of experience. There is no leadership and there is no organization.

> The mass has no social organization, no body of custom and tradition, no established set of rules or rituals, no organization group of sentiments, no structure of status roles and no established leadership. It merely consists of an aggregation of individuals who are separated, detached, anonymous and thus homogeneous. The mass does not mill or interact as the crowd does, the members are separated and unknown to each other. It behaves in terms of each individual seeking to answer his own needs. (Blumer 1951:185–6).

The concept of mass has been used to refer to partial social movements, especially when related to a geographic situation such as land rushes (Turner and Killian 1972:136). It has served as an independent variable which, under certain conditions can be associated with the recruitment of population to extreme social movements (Kornhauser 1959). This view of the mass is discussed in Part IV. The mass has also been considered as an audience which responds in a one-to-one fashion to communications from the mass media.

The public is composed of groups which are confronted by some issue. The members of the groups disagree on how the issue is to be resolved, but through discussion an agreement or decision is reached. The agreement is taken to be public opinion. Since there are many issues there are many publics and the same individual may be a member of more than one. While the public is considered elementary, it is viewed as rational in contrast to the more emotional crowd (Blumer 1951:189–91).

Both the mass and the public fall outside the boundaries of our definition of collective behavior in that they are not collectivities of interacting individuals. Instead they tend to be widely dispersed aggregates of persons between whom there are little or no direct social relations. However, the boundaries are not always so sharp as the distinctions made above suggest. There is often overlap and the excluded topics can be associated with collective behavior.

Summary

Collective behavior is not easily defined and, in fact, there is widespread disagreement concerning its critical features. Some definitions are broadly inclusive and others are narrowly exclusive. The conceptualization of the field offered here defines collective behavior as a *relatively unorganized pattern of social interaction in human groups.* It has both *normative* and *structural* characteristics. *Crowds* are groups characterized by relatively *simple role structures* that tend to be *ephemeral* rather than permanent. *Social movements* are groups characterized by greater *permanence* and an intermediate level of *organizational complexity.* They are a midpoint between loosely organized crowds and fully organized bureaucracies.

As a form of group action, collective behavior is not reducible to psychological propositions about individuals acting in isolation from other people. It cannot be properly understood apart from the social context in which it occurs. The social context of collective behavior is especially important because it is likely to occur in periods of situational stress or problematic circumstances.

Collective behavior does not differ from conventional social behavior by the type, but rather by degree. It is not always or even usually characterized by a lack of planning and social organization. Lynch mobs, for example, require more planning and organization than previously supposed, and we cannot assume that riots are completely randomized and untargeted outbursts of collective violence.

Collective behavior is more than a pathological form of group action to be contrasted with the legitimacy and rationality of institutionalized behavior. The *traditional stereotypes* of collective behavior as highly *emotional, irrational, violent, and spontaneous* are true to some extent, but they are often misleading. Collective behavior is not motivated by primitive desires, nor is it a completely unorganized and utterly spontaneous expression of irrationality and excess emotion.

LeBon asserted that intolerance and fanaticism are the necessary accompaniments of religion; thus torture was an acceptable way of dealing with heretics during the Spanish Inquisition.

CHAPTER II

Theoretical Perspectives

T he stereotypes of collective behavior as completely spontaneous, unplanned, and totally unorganized have tended to isolate
the field from general theoretical developments in the social sciences and
create a gap between the fields of collective behavior and general sociology
(Brown and Goldin 1973, Weller and Quarantelli 1973), which has traditionally made a sharp distinction between purposive, goal-oriented behavior and
seemingly irrational conduct (Brissett 1968:71). Collective behavior, in effect,
has been a *residual category* containing a variety of topics that apparently did
not lend themselves to standard treatment in the social sciences.

Today, however, the field of collective behavior is in a state of flux. The
older stereotypes are being sharply questioned and the organizational characteristics of collective behavior are increasingly emphasized. This chapter will
review, in broad outline, a set of five influential theoretical perspectives in
collective behavior: (1) LeBon's "classical" perspective, (2) Blumer's "interactionist" perspective, (3) Turner and Killian's "emergent norm" perspective, (4)
Berk's "rational calculus" model, and (5) Smelser's "value-added" model. This
set of perspectives is generally representative of the state of *theoretical plural-
ism* found in the study of collective behavior today, but it is by no means an
exhaustive survey of the literature.

LeBon's Classical Perspective

Gustav LeBon, 1841–1931, is usually credited with beginning the modern
study of the crowd, and because of his early work, crowd action is considered
the prototype of collective behavior by many contemporary scholars. For
many people, the publication of LeBon's book, *The Crowd*, in 1895 marks the

beginning of the field of collective behavior. Because of the great importance of LeBon's contribution, we will outline his view of the crowd in detail.

LeBon points out that his time in France was a period of rapid social change and, while he recognized that a crowd can be good or evil, cowardly or heroic, he feared that its existence was a threat to the organized social order. He believed that civilizations are created by a small, intellectual aristocracy, never by people acting in crowds. On the contrary, according to LeBon, crowds can only destroy civilizations, and he was deeply concerned by what he saw as the growing power of crowds in nineteenth century France. For him, crowds were pathological, violent, hateful, bizarre, and threatening. He saw their destructive potential as stemming from the *law of the mental unity of the crowd.*

The law of the mental unity of the crowd holds that the sentiments and ideas of the crowd take the same direction, and that the conscious personalities of its members are *leveled and replaced* by a *collective mind:*

> whoever be the individuals that compose it, however like or unlike to be their mode of life, their occupations, their character, or their intelligence, the fact that they have been transformed into a crowd puts them in possession of a sort of collective mind which makes them feel, think, and act in a manner quite different from that in which each individual of them would feel, think and act were he in a state of isolation (LeBon 1960:27).

From LeBon's point of view men and women, good and bad, as well as the stupid and bright, undergo a radical transformation under the influence of the crowd. As we have seen, LeBon believed that this transformation is, in part, a product of what he metaphorically referred to as a "collective mind"; but, according to LeBon, it also has its basis in the racial origins of crowd members. He believed that among the members of a crowd there is an *unconscious substratum* composed of the hereditary elements of a "race of people." Among these hereditary elements are savage and destructive instincts which have been dormant in people since the primitive ages. LeBon felt that this primitive racial substratum, in combination with the leveling of individual personalities and the *psychological unity* of the crowd, could account for its capacity for cruel and shocking acts. In fact, LeBon theorized that crowds have a regressive influence on people:

> Moreover, by the mere fact that he forms part of an organized crowd, a man descends several rungs in the ladder of civilization. Isolated, he may be a cultivated individual, in a crowd, he is a barbarian—that is a creature acting by instinct. He possesses the spontaneity, the violence, the ferocity, and also the enthusiasm and heroism of primitive beings, whom he further tends to resemble by the facility with which he allows himself to be impressed by words and images—which would be entirely without action on each of the isolated individuals composing the crowd

—and to be induced to commit acts contrary to his most obvious interests and his best known habits. An individual in a crowd is a grain of sand amid other grains of sand, which the wind stirs up at will. (1960:32–3).

LeBon associated a number of relatively specific processes with the malevolent influence of the crowd context. According to LeBon, the spontaneous release of primitive and destructive sentiments is accompanied by a *feeling of power*—a sense of invincibility—which arises as a result of being a part of a large collection of people. A large number of people also provides crowd members with a *sense of anonymity* allowing them to *disavow personal responsibility* for any actions of the crowd. Each member of a crowd may come to believe that he or she cannot be held accountable for misdeeds either because "someone else was responsible" or because "everyone else was doing it."

The primitive character of LeBon's collective mind also allowed him to account for what he perceived to be the *heightened suggestibility* of the crowd. Under conditions of heightened suggestibility, the individual is supposedly unaware of his or her own acts and responds easily to suggestion. Critical ability is reduced, and there is a tendency to convert suggestions into acts without conscious consideration of potential consequences. Moreover, LeBon assumed that in a crowd every idea and every act is highly *contagious* and spreads quickly from one person to another. When crowd members experience heightened suggestibility, sentiments and acts are contagious to such a degree that individuals are capable of sacrificing personal self-interests for the advancement of the collective interests of the crowd.

Unfortunately, the collective interests of crowds are often irrational or counterproductive, according to LeBon, because they are *stupid, emotional,* and *impulsive.* Crowds are easily stirred to blood-thirsty ferocity, and they cannot conceive of logical processes nor can they handle complex ideas. Members of crowds do not doubt the ultimate validity of their own opinions and are intolerant of prolonged discussion. Contradictory ideas and alternative visions of the truth are rejected with fanatical vehemence and the moral certainty of complete self-rightousness. LeBon recognized that crowds can show extremely high and lofty morality in their actions, as well as in their sentiments, but he felt that crowds were generally too impulsive to be moral.

When he came to the question of ideas and the imagination of the crowd, LeBon took the view that crowd members are influenced by two kinds of ideas: (1) those which are accidental in passing and come from the situational context of the moment, and (2) those which are fundamental to a people. Fundamental ideas come from the cultural environment of a group, from its racial heredity, and from public opinion. LeBon distinguished between remote factors and immediate factors affecting the ideas of a crowd; but for any idea to be influential, he claimed it must be absolute and uncompromisingly simple in its imagery. This is because crowds do not reason, but instead respond to images and illusions that are easily understood.

LeBon believed that images of the "marvelous and legendary" are particularly effective in crowds because of an individual's prior commitments to traditional cultural myths. Consequently, he believed that appeals to religious convictions are especially infuential. LeBon also believed that the emotional experience of crowd members was similar to religion in its single-minded devotion to a cause, and in its complete submission of will to an overriding principle of action. LeBon asserted that intolerance and fanaticism are the necessary accompaniments of religion, and he argued that the Jacobins of the French "reign of terror" were basically as religious as the Catholics of the Inquisition.

Finally, in LeBon's view, crowds tend to place themselves under despotic leaders of which there are two kinds. The first is energetic but possesses

During the French Revolution, the crowd carries the head of Princess de Lamballe through the streets of Paris.

relatively little strength of will and therefore loses influence in a fairly short period of time. The second is not only energetic but also has enduring strength of will. The leaders themselves are people of action and are not deep thinkers, yet they can arouse the faith of a crowd and wield wide-ranging influence. Crowd leaders, according to LeBon, typically begin with a *simple affirmation* of some idea—an affirmation without reasoning or proof, but which is concise and to the point. *Repetition* is a second technique used by crowd leaders. Whatever is affirmed is repeated again and again until it is imbedded in the unconscious minds of crowd members. LeBon believed that the *prestige of leaders and their ideas* was also an extremely important factor in their effectiveness. The prestige of an idea, in his view, was acquired through the process of repetition, affirmation, and contagion.

LeBon's work has had a tremendous influence on collective behavior as a field of study, but his theory of crowds has been criticized on many grounds. First, his writing style resembles a journalistic flow of observations more than a tightly organized treatise. Second, many of LeBon's concepts are descriptions rather than explanations. Third, his discussions are unduly mentalistic in that he speaks of crowds as if they were individuals who could really think for themselves. A fourth criticism focuses on the debatable accuracy of his facts. It has been observed, for example, that crowds often form without the presence of leadership. A fifth criticism of LeBon's theory is that it does not explain why crowd action stops and why some people do not join crowds (Berk 1974b:24–5). A sixth criticism of LeBon's work is that his empirical referent shifts from mobs and riots to juries and parliaments without distinction. This is a formidable array of criticisms, but many contemporary readers find it easier to forgive LeBon for his analytical weaknesses than for his social prejudices.

The Crowd serves as a vehicle for a patrician attack on nineteenth century events and reflects the elitist biases of LeBon's era. It accommodates the idea of racial inferiority and equates the "stupidity" and "emotionalism" of crowd members with a lower level on the evolutionary scale of human existence. LeBon's implied contrast between the irrationality of the crowd and the rationality of educated individuals is simplistic. Yet despite its faults, *The Crowd* remains a classic. LeBon's fear of the crowd does not overwhelm his genuine insights—insights that with modifications have appeared in almost all general treatments of collective behavior. His influence, still strong today, reaches beyond formal sociology. For example, his theory was recently used in *Time* magazine to analyze the behavior of the crowd gathered to observe Evel Knievel attempt to jump the Snake Canyon (Janos 1974:64, 69).

The Park and Burgess introductory text, *An Introduction to the Science of Sociology* (1921) is an especially significant contribution after LeBon's work because it first defined collective behavior as "the behavior of individuals under the influence of an impulse that is common and collective, an impulse in other words, that is the result of social interaction" (Park and Burgess 1921:865). This work did much to introduce collective behavior to American social science. But perhaps the most influential statement on collective behavior since LeBon's work is that of Herbert Blumer which was first published in 1939. Although it has been revised several times, Blumer's basic view has remained much the same and is commonly identified as the "interactionist" perspective in the field of collective behavior.

Blumer's Interactionist Perspective

Blumer considered conditions of "social unrest" to be the crucible from which collective behavior emerges. Without social unrest, when life goes on smoothly according to conventional social norms and roles, there is little reason to expect the development of collective behavior. Social unrest is a sign of the *breakdown* of the normal social order, and Blumer's discussion of the forms of social interaction that commonly occur during such periods is a classic contribution to the field of collective behavior.

Behavior during periods of social unrest has three general characteristics. First, people move about in an erratic and aimless way as if they are looking for something or, alternatively, as if they are trying to avoid something. Second, behavior during periods of social unrest is generally characterized by excitement associated with exaggerated opinions, distorted perceptions, and rumors. The third general characteristic is increased irritability and suggestibility. Aside from these three general behavioral characteristics, Blumer discerned five distinctive forms of social unrest.

The first type of social unrest is experienced as anxiety, a vague sense that everything is not right, that something is out of gear. The future is indefinite and fraught with "dire possibilities." The second type is characterized by a sense of frustration or protest over an existing mode of life, while the third type of social unrest is marked by a "flight from the existing world." Frustration and protest set the stage for the development of aggressive crowds, whereas the third type of unrest leads to the development of expressive crowds or utopian movements. The fourth general type of social unrest features expansive enthusiasm for doing something, but lacks any sense of what should be done. This kind of unrest can ultimately manifest itself in frivolous group activities or in a headlong pursuit of sensual gratifications. The fifth of Blumer's general types of social unrest is marked by despair and apathy or "expressions of lamentation." All five forms of social unrest are capable of expressing themselves in new patterns of social behavior. And one of the basic mechanisms underlying all forms of social unrest is a process known as *circular reaction.*

Floyd Allport (1924) introduced the idea of circular reaction to explain the spread of mood and conduct throughout a crowd. It describes an interactive process that occurs when one person's behavior serves as a model for another's. When a person sees that his or her behavior is being imitated by others he or she is stimulated to even higher levels of activity and excitement. The imitators correspondingly increase their own levels of activity and simultaneously serve as behavioral models for still more people. According to Blumer's account (1975:26), milling "can be thought of as a pure instance of circular reaction."

Blumer considered milling to be one of three special forms of social interaction that occur during periods of unrest. In milling, individuals move around among each other in an aimless and random fashion analogous to a herd of agitated cattle. As milling continues, individuals become more and more sensitized and responsive to one another. As they become increasingly preoccupied with each other's behavior, their field of attention is increasingly restricted and events which would ordinarily concern them become less significant.

When the milling process is sped up and the imitated behavior reflects an excited state, social interaction enters a stage which Blumer labeled "collective excitement." Collective excitement is distinguishable from milling as a second special form of interaction precisely because it involves the imitation of excited, highly agitated behavior. It is difficult to ignore emotionally aroused behavior which seems to compel close attention in all societies. The imitation of excited behavior promotes a particularly intense form of circular reaction in which mood and conduct "spread like wildfire." Social contagion, Blumer's third special form of interaction, develops from milling and collective excitement.

Social contagion "may be regarded as an intense form of milling and collective excitement" (Blumer 1975:28), but it is distinguishable from these forms of interaction because it involves a loss of "self-consciousness," which is a "means of barricading oneself against the influence of others." This loss causes decreased social resistance and increased group conformity; social contagion can infect bystanders whose involvement is neutral or even disapproving.

A participant in such an incident, which occurred during the Spanish-American War, has described the social unrest associated with the rigors of an army training camp in Florida. It was hot, especially so in wool uniforms, the discipline was hard, home was far away, money was short, and the dangers of combat were ahead. There was little the soldiers could do about these conditions and their hostility began to focus on the sutler, an Armenian, who sold beer, soda pop, and other small articles. The sutler was thought to shortchange his customers, although the writer of the article was not convinced that this was so. When at last a large number of soldiers went to the sutler's shack to "have fun," the writer, who was more or less disapproving or neutral, went along to watch. However, he quickly lost his sense of self-consciousness and joined the crowd.

> In the clearing, under the flickering gasoline torch, hundreds of men were packed about the front of the sutler's shack. The Armenian stood in his doorway, pale but imperturbable, his eyes glaring fiercely, his thick lips curving in a nervous smile. The crowd was keeping its distance, as word had passed back from the front that the sutler had his finger on the trigger of a six-shooter. We were after fun, not shooting, and it was enough to hurl imprecations at him. When Buck and I arrived, the spirit of the crowd was good humored, for the most part, but occasionally one could perceive a note of real hatred. What seemed like a deliberate competition in imprecations got in motion, and the more violent curses gained rapidly over the milder ones. The character of the voices, too, began to change: the original miscellaneous clamor split into two well-defined currents of deep notes and high that would occasionally reinforce each other and make one thrill unaccountably. The crowd was pressing closer. The Armenian still kept his nerve, but the movements of his head were becoming spasmodic. It was still fun with us, but the idea that it was serious was visibly gaining on the Armenian.

> "Poor devil," I thought, "this has been carried about far enough." And then a new baying note rose from the mob, a note I had not supposed to be within the range of the human voice. I shivered, and as I glanced again at the Armenian, darting his eyes from one quarter to another, in suppressed panic, I felt my pity slip from me. I began to exult, like a hunter who has found a wild animal in a trap, to finish at leisure. "Kill the damn thief! Kill the damn dago!" the crowd was yelling. It thrilled!

> There was a lull—something was going on that we in the center could only divine. About the mutterings, subdued for the moment, we heard a sound like the splitting of timber. Word passed from the flanks of the crowd. "They've pried out a plank behind." The Armenian turned to look back into his shack: his jaw dropped; his thin acquisitive profile quivered; the white of his eyes seemed to glaze. A sharp pebble hurled from behind him, struck him just beneath the cheek bone: it clung for a second, like a hideous black growth, then dropped, thrust out by a jet of blood. A mantle of frenzy fell upon the mob. An atrocious roar arose, carrying on its waves all the obscenities and blasphemies known to young America.

> "Kill the damn Jew! Kill the God damn Nigger!" (Johnson 1918:382)

Blumer's contagion process has been criticized on several grounds. It has been suggested that his theory depends too much on extreme and rare cases. The view that crowds require a level of psychological functioning different from organized groups tends to perpetuate the simplistic idea that people are just animals with an easily removed veneer of civilization. It has been pointed out that contagion theory is an extremely difficult subject for empirical verification and offers little basis for predicting shifts in crowd behavior. Furthermore, one scholar argues that classic contagion theory offers nothing to the study of the organization of collective behavior (Turner 1964a:384–7). However, we will take a closer look at contagion theory in Chapter III.

Convergence

Opposed to Blumer's contagion process is convergence theory.

> While contagion theory stresses the transformation of the normal decent individual who is infected by the crowd, convergence theory argues that the crowd consists of a highly unrepresentative grouping of people drawn together because they share the same qualities (Milgram and Toch 1969:-551).

People who make up a crowd are behaving in response to their prior individual predispositions and the opportunity given by the presence of a crowd of like-minded persons. They are not characterized by intense feelings and behaviors at variance with their usual activities. Likeminded individuals converge when some event or object draws their attention. Under such conditions there can be a release of usually repressed "primitive impulses" when some person strikes a blow that all the others want (Allport 1924).

The convergence approach in collective behavior has not been popular in recent years. It has been pointed out that individuals in a crowd may have more than one latent tendency toward the same object, and convergence theory does not predict which will be expressed. Crowd processes are taken for granted by convergence theorists, but it is probable that social interaction in crowds helps establish how a situation is defined (Turner 1964b:128–9).

In contemporary usage in collective behavior, the term "convergence" is more likely to be applied to a phenomenon that occurs after the impact of a disaster. After disaster there is frequently a convergence (discussed in Chapter VI) of people, communication, and materials to an impact area. This type of convergence, however, is composed of many different elements, rather than individuals who necessarily have the same predispositions. In any case, the controversy surrounding the contagion-convergence issue remains unresolved and, to some extent, has been superceded by the "emergent norm" perspective.

Turner and Killian's Emergent Norm Perspective

The theory of emergent norms originally appeared in the first edition of the Turner and Killian text (1957). Since then it has received further elaboration (Turner 1964a, 1964b; Turner and Killian 1972) and is now a well-established position in the interactionist approach to collective behavior. The emergent norm perspective is derived from a series of small groups studies which indicated that people interacting among themselves will, in time, evolve common standards of behavior (Sherif 1936, Asch 1956). New behavioral standards have high priority in ambiguous situations, and once these standards or norms have evolved they exert a constraining influence on individuals. Social pressures in crowds for conformity to group norms are often quite strong and people are usually reluctant to deviate. Most people realize that deviants are frequently sanctioned for noncompliance by ridicule, disapproval, ostracism, and on occasion by overt attacks. The central analytical problem for emergent norm theorists is the explanation of how new behavioral standards are developed in crowds.

The emergent norm perspective rejects the notion that collective behavior develops because social norms and their associated sanctions are inoperative. Collective behavior may begin as a spontaneous response to problematic situations, yet emergent norm theory stresses that normative controls will develop in almost all social settings. (Turner and Killian 1972:80). Emergent norm theory, therefore, emphasizes the continuity between ordinary social behavior and collective behavior. It recognizes there are times when ordinary norms do not apply and that a special norm must be imposed on some situations to justify action or overcome the impact of contradictory norms. Emergent norms appear when neither the established social organization nor primary groups can supply a framework for collective decision making and action (Turner 1964b:132). The emergent norm can make possible behavior not usually acceptable, but it may set limits or serve to restrain crowd activity. Indeed, it seems to be the case that some forms of crowd behavior are begun in the belief that it will remain within certain bounds.

In discussing crowds and emergent norms, Turner (1964b:132) points out that "crowd unanimity" is an illusion. What seems to be a unanimous whole may result from the dramatic actions of a few individuals being attributed to all crowd members. In a crowd some participants may feel a pressure to conform to an emergent norm but not share in its sentiments and nevertheless remain silent. The silence of dissenters in a crowd provides a form of passive support for an emergent norm and thus contributes to the illusion of unanimity. The illusion of unanimity, in turn, discourages open dissent.

To illustrate the importance of miscontruing the homogeneity of crowds, Turner and Killian point to the variability of crowd participants. One type of participant is a person who is ego involved in the crowd situation. These persons are totally committed and define their situation as demanding immediate action. They may or may not have a clear idea of what must be done, but they do feel the situation requires some activity.

Next are those who are concerned, although they do not feel sufficiently committed to take immediate action. Such persons are likely to be highly responsive to emergent norms that define appropriate action. Eventually they may come to feel that an issue must be resolved, and that the solution must be consistent with their own side of an argument. Ordinarily, group loyalties predispose individuals to this sort of attitude. Consequently, some people may feel they should support their group even though they believe it is wrong—a sentiment expressed in statements like "my country right or wrong."

Another kind of participant gains satisfaction from participation regardless of the circumstances. In this category, Turner and Killian include adolescents and the poor. They are attracted by the sense of power they find in a crowd— even if it is small—and by a feeling of moral righteousness. Another type of participant is the spectator—the person who is drawn to a crowd merely by curiosity. Such persons may eventually be absorbed into the crowd as their level of active involvement increases. Finally, the exploiter is the person who is egotistic and looks on the crowd as a means to some end. These individuals may be looters or they may be attempting to precipitate violence in order to advance their own political causes.

Emergent norm theory has been subjected to sustained criticism in recent years. One of its major weaknesses is the tautalogical character of Turner and Killian's implicit definition of collective behavior. They refer to collective behavior as "individuals interacting in such a manner as to create and acknowledge social norms" (1972:5). The circularity of logic inherent in this definition renders the emergent norm perspective unfalsifiable (Tierney 1977:14). Defining collective behavior in terms of the emergence of new norms precludes the possibility of finding negative cases. For example, crowd behavior that did not involve new norms could not constitute a negative case because by definition it is not collective behavior.

Another area of weakness associated with the emergent norm perspective centers on the concept of social norms. Only a short time ago Jack Gibbs (1965) noted the lack of agreement among sociologists, on the definition of "norms." This circumstance is reflected in Turner and Killian's use of the term as a "virtual catchall under which all types of collective ideational phenomena —e.g. cognitions, expectations, beliefs, symbols, definitions-of-the-situation, and ideological systems—are subsumed" (Tierney 1977:16). Lack of conceptual clarity leads to confusions and undermines the testability of the perspective. But a second problem is even more serious.

A major weakness of the emergent norm perspective usually pointed out is its failure to say much about the *content* of the norms which are created during episodes of collective behavior. This deficiency is especially important in an explanation of collective violence. The occurrence of violence suggests that any operative norms reflect an overall, or at least an unchallenged, consensus on an extreme point of view. The difficulty is that the literature from which the emergent norm position is derived indicates that consensus should be reached around a moderate point of view. Specifically, Sherif's pioneering work on the autokinetic effect demonstrated convergence of general opinion around the mean of all individual opinions. Therefore, the original work on norm formation is an insufficient explanation of how members of a group develop norms favoring an extreme course of action.

Berk's Rational Calculus Model

One of the most recent efforts to grapple with the problem of how crowds decide on a course of action is that of Richard Berk (1974b:59–61). Berk discredits the traditional approaches embodied in contagion theory and convergence theory and argues that people in crowds seek information which they hope to employ in making *rational* decisions. Decision theory, Berk suggests, may provide a good foundation for the examination of crowd processes precisely because it emphasizes rational thinking rather than the alleged irrationality of crowds. Furthermore, decision theory may be able to account for some aspects of crowds that are largely inexplicable in the older theoretical approaches. For example, circular reaction and milling cannot account for the real dialogue that often occurs among members of a crowd. According to Berk, the dialogue might go something like this: (1) crowd participants seek information, (2) they use their information to predict probable occurrences, (3) they list all of their behavioral options, (4) they rank order the probable outcomes of alternative actions, and (5) they decide on a course of action which will minimize their costs and maximize their rewards. The more favorable a likely outcome, figured in subjective terms of anticipated rewards minus potential costs, the more likely an action is to be initiated. In addition, the probability of a course of action being initiated is equally dependent upon the belief that other people will support it. When the probability of general support is zero, or very low, no action will be taken even if anticipated payoffs are very favorable.

Here is how Berk's (1974b:67–75) *rational calculus model* could apply to a decision facing the members of a crowd. The choice is simple: the crowd can undertake a particular course of action (Oa), or it can reject a particular course of action (Oā). The anticipated net payoff for acting (Oa) in contrast to not acting (Oā) can be expressed in the simple notation, *Payoff = (Oa − Oā)*, where the payoff is the net difference between the anticipated outcome for acting and the anticipated outcome for not acting. Let us assume that subjective evaluation of the rewards and costs associated with acting and not acting leads to the conclusion that the net payoff for acting is extremely favorable. Even so, a member of the crowd might still choose to reject a particular course of action if that person was certain other members of the crowd would not give their support. In collective behavior the maximization of an individual's payoff is often dependent upon a number of people "acting in unison" (Berk 1974a:363). Thus, Berk's rational calculus model proposes that the probability for the adoption of a particular course of action is a joint function of the difference in outcomes associated with acting and not acting (the payoff) times the probability of support(s) for that course of action:

$$\text{Probability of Act (Oa)} = [(Oa - O\bar{a})\,(S)]$$

As logical as all of this may seem, there are still some difficulties. For example, how can decision theory explain a course of action which risks very high costs, yields moderate rewards, and has a low probability for success? When crowd members confront army tanks with stones and clubs, it must be concluded that their risk is high and that their probability of success is low. Of course, it could be argued that pounding on tanks can be especially gratifying when it releases unconscious hostility; but in such a case, the action of the crowd is no longer purely rational, as implied by decision theory, and is premised on a number of people sharing the same sense of hostility. The problem, then, is to explain how crowds generate sufficient support among individuals to initiate *high risk* actions.

Johnson (1974) and Johnson, Stemler and Hunter (1977) have suggested that some insight into the problem posed by a crowd's risking of high potential costs can be derived from the risky shift literature in small groups research. A study completed over fifteen years ago (Stoner 1961) showed that decisions made by a group after discussion are likely to be more risky than decisions made by the same individuals before discussion. In gambling games, for example, people are more willing to accept long-shot bets for higher payoffs after group discussion than they are before discussion. One reason for a risky shift in group decisions may be that discussion of an issue spreads responsibility among group members and reduces individual fear of failure (Kogan and Wallach 1967). Unfortunately, it is not really clear why diffusion of social responsibility should reduce a person's fear of negative consequences or lead to the acceptance of high risks. It may be that people simply agree that no single individual should be held accountable for the collective actions of a crowd. An even more serious limitation of *diffusion of responsibility* as a conditional factor for the occurrence of a risky shift is that such a shift will sometimes occur without prior group discussion and without an implicit consensus of group members. Still, it is possible that some of the high risk taking of many crowds results directly from a sharing of social responsibility.

Another explanation of the risky shift phenomenon involves values and situational relevance (Brown 1965). Here is how the process might work. First, it is assumed that in some situations risk taking is positively valued. For example, many Americans in the 1960s were convinced that public protests were justified on behalf of ending an "illegal and immoral" war, and that such public protests were, in fact, sanctioned by the Constitution. A second assumption is that when risk taking is an approved value, crowd members are likely to see themselves as willing to take as much risk as anyone else. Those who are not willing may leave the crowd, but as a simple matter of self-esteem, most people do not want to see themselves as less courageous than others. Thus, when crowd members are aware of positions more extreme than their own, they should be disposed to change their opinions in what is being defined as a socially valued, and yet risky, direction.

A third explanation of the risky shift phenomenon focuses attention on the *distribution* of risk-taking dispositions in a group. In this approach it is acknowledged that groups can reach consensus on cautious collective action as well as on high risk activity. Group *polarization* toward high risk is most likely when the *initial dispositions* of crowd members, on average, favor risk taking, and when the *range* of dispositions held by individual crowd members is small. A computer simulation model developed by Johnson and Feinberg (1977) elaborates this approach by including two additional variables: (1) the type of *influence effort* made in a crowd, and (2) the *suggestibility* of a crowd. Consensus is most readily achieved under conditions of heightened suggestibility and when the positions advocated by potential crowd leaders are favorably received.

When people first come into a crowd they may have ambivalent attitudes which are by definition susceptible to change. Such attitudes seem readily influenced by the *keynoting* speeches of crowd leaders (Turner and Killian 1972:89–90). Keynoting speeches, most effective when composed of terse, forcible statements, set the initial direction of collective behavior. The probability that keynoting speeches will express an extreme, polar position is generally high because crowd leaders usually hold their opinions with great intensity or emotional commitment, which are correlated with extreme positions.

It should be noted that the preceding explanations of extreme actions in crowds are not entirely incompatible. Emergent norm theory does not preclude the importance of convergence theory, just as convergence theory is not incompatible with the risky-shift literature. The emergence of group norms can be facilitated by the convergence of like-minded people who are equally disposed to accept the same polar position on some issue. The theoretical perspectives considered up to this point do not provide a broad, systematic framework with which to organize the data of collective behavior. They tend to emphasize processes occurring within a group of people rather than what has happened to the group in the past, or what is being done to it in the present. A theory that does provide a broad framework for the study of collective behavior is Smelser's *value-added model.*

Smelser's Value-Added Model

In 1962 Neil Smelser published his *Theory of Collective Behavior,* a work regarded as one of the most important statements in the field. By some it is considered the most systematic theoretical treatment of collective behavior and the one most closely related to general sociological theory. It is an extension or variant of structural functional theory, especially as developed by Talcott Parsons (1937,1951).

Collective behavior, according to Smelser, is "mobilization on the basis of a belief which redefines social action" (1962:8). The belief, called a "generalized belief," pictures the world in terms of omnipotent forces, conspiracies and extravagant promises, all of which are seen as imminent (Smelser 1964:117). It is a cognitive structuring of an uncertain threat into a definite prediction of disaster (1964:120). In the case of a financial panic, for example, the closing of a bank for whatever reason can support the belief that the monetary system is shaky. It is then a belief that focuses on changing something and develops only when there are no normal institutionalized means of reaching whatever goal is desired. This leads to collective behavior which jumps over or "short circuits" the normal channels through which people attempt to restructure their social environment.

In this theory an incident of collective behavior moves through a series of six stages. As each stage takes place, the number of subsequent alternative actions is reduced. That is, the determinants for each stage go from the general to the specific and each is logically prior to the next, but they do not necessarily occur in any exact order. Furthermore, each stage is necessary, but not sufficient for the occurrence of the next step. However, the process—at least in its early stages—does not have to result in collective action nor does it accurately predict what form the collective action will take. Yet, as each stage occurs, alternative possibilities decrease until some collective action becomes inevitable This scheme, referred to as Smelser's "value-added" approach, is borrowed from the economics of manufacturing. The first step is *structural conduciveness:* the structure of the society must be conducive to a manifestation of collective behavior. Financial panic, an example suggested by Smelser, requires that it be possible to move resources quickly when people wish to do so through such institutional arrangements as stock exchanges and bonds. But if, on the other hand, property is associated with kinship and changes hands only through the holder's death, then structural conduciveness which would permit financial panic does not exist (1964:119).

The second stage of the value-added model is *structural strain* which occurs when various parts of a system are not well articulated with one another. In the contemporary United States, for example, the position of women is characterized by considerable strain reflected in the existence of the women's liberation movement. In the United States of a hundred years ago the position of women was more clear cut, causing little structural strain.

In the third stage the *generalized belief* described above emerges. The generalized belief "explains" the source of structural strain and its consequences for society and includes ideas about a program of action to reduce or eliminate strain. It is an initial attempt to reduce the uncertainty and difficulty posed by structural strain. Generalized beliefs can take various forms which are identified as hysterical, wish fulfillment, hostile, norm-oriented, or value-oriented (1962:33). The presence of a generalized belief does not insure that collective behavior will occur; some beliefs have existed for centuries.

The fourth stage called *precipitating factors* occurs when something acts to confirm the generalized belief. This gives concrete and immediate substance to the generalized belief and direction to collective action. But the precipitating factors must take place in the context of the other determinants for collective behavior to occur.

Fifth comes *mobilization of participants for action.* Crowd action or panic begins, or there is agitation for reform or revolution. At this point the behavior of leaders becomes extremely important.

In the last stage, *the operation of social control,* counter determinants operate to prevent or deflect collective action. Some social controls are applied to structural conduciveness and strain to prevent an occurrence of collective behavior; others are applied only after a collective episode has started.

The value-added scheme has become one of the dominant theories in collective behavior. It has also received sharp criticism on both analytical and ideological grounds. Smelser's approach has been repeatedly criticized for its lack of empirical criteria specifying the connection between the real world and the value-added scheme. There is frequent disagreement on how to classify real events since some incidents of collective behavior do not fit Smelser's paradigm. A study of a riot of university students on High Street in Columbus, Ohio, found only four of the six elements of the value-added model. Two of the most important stages in the value-added process did not appear, (1) a hostile generalized belief, and (2) mobilization for action (Quarantelli and Hundley 1969). However, Lewis' (1972) study of the Kent State University incident of May 4, 1970 found that the event proceeded through the stages of Smelser's value-added process. Furthermore, it is frequently difficult to identify the critical stages of collective behavior; it is not always easy, for example, to isolate a critical precipitating event. Smelser's approach does not adequately specify what conditions are even likely to precipitate collective behavior. Consequently some critics argue that the value-added scheme is not a "true specification of causes."

The stages of collective behavior described by Smelser are really empty categories. For example, the value-added paradigm does not specify the social conditions which constitute structural strain or structural conduciveness. Both strain and conduciveness are inferred after the fact of collective behavior. Post hoc interpretations of collective behavior may generate hypotheses for future research, but they also risk reducing analysis to the realm of tautology. Milgram and Toch (1969:561–2) argue that Smelser's model is more a typological scheme than a theory and fails to lead to hypotheses. They ask why, if collective behavior has the same six determinants, does one form rather than another arise.

Other criticisms of Smelser's paradigm focus attention on the concepts of structural strain and generalized belief. While it is unclear whether structural strain refers to objective social conditions or to people's perceptions of strain, it seems likely that structural strain concerns perceptions and " reflects a poor fit between what people think should happen and what actually does happen" (Berk 1974b:41).

Structural strain generates an ambiguous situation in which people supposedly develop a common generalized belief to explain their experience. But according to Milgram and Toch (1969:561), the Berkeley student movement of 1964 lacked a clear generalized belief. That is, Berkeley students with diverse beliefs participated in the protests. If Smelser is referring to a dominant belief, what is a dominant belief? What percentage of a group has to share a generalized belief? Even if generalized beliefs can be found, are they necessarily exaggerated or naive explanations of events? Smelser implies that they are, but this is not necessarily the case. The perceptions and beliefs of Viet Nam antiwar demonstrators were no less valid than the positions taken by the Johnson and Nixon administrations.

According to Smelser's value-added model, this demonstrator in the Berkeley Free Speech Movement of 1964 should share a common generalized belief with other protesting students.

Currie and Skolnick (1970:37) suggest that Smelser has a political bias favoring an administrative or managerial position which allows him to uncritically accept the old negative view of collective behavior participants. This leads, in Smelser's work, to an overemphasis on the control of incidents of collective behavior. In his answer to this attack, Smelser (1970) argues that

Currie and Skolnick deliberately misinterpreted his position. These questions, then, remain unresolved.

Summary and Conclusions

The traditional stereotypes of collective behavior have tended to isolate its study from theoretical developments in the social sciences. Collective behavior, even though it is one of the oldest sociological specialities, has been residual to mainstream sociology. Perhaps this is because collective behavior was considered *irrational*, and consequently *less predictable*, than institutionalized social action. Recent theoretical work in the field, however, emphasizes the *rationality* of collective behavior as well as its organizational characteristics.

LeBon's approach and Blumer's *interactionist* perspective have a common focus on contagion processes in social groups. Blumer's approach uses the relatively modern idea of *circular reaction* as a mechanism to account for the spread of uniform behaviors, whereas LeBon resorts to the classical use of a metaphor: the *collective mind*. LeBon's major insight was that the appearance of uniform behaviors in a crowd cannot be explained by homogeneous crowd composition. He believed that crowds of people acting in unison can be composed of quite different people—the good and the bad, as well as the educated and uneducated. Convergence theorists, on the other hand, have been largely unsuccessful in arguing that crowds are composed of similar, "like-minded" individuals who come together for a common purpose.

Turner and Killian's *emergent norm perspective* and Berk's *rational calculus model* also focus on social interaction within groups. In the case of emergent norms, they argue that instances of collective behavior are not entirely without structure, but that groups of interacting people develop norms unique to that particular situation. The norms are often associated with prior ones and set limits to the activity that occurs in a given instance. The emergent norm perspective is significant in its emphasis on the continuity between collective behavior and organizational behavior, and in its derivation from research on norm formation that is central to the field of social psychology.

Berk's *rational calculus model* is another example of the convergence of the field of collective behavior with theoretical developments in the general social sciences. The model borrows directly from "decision theory." Johnson's laboratory studies based on the risky shift literature also borrow from the general field of social psychology. This new trend is important since the field of collective behavior is becoming increasingly eclectic in its use of theory. Thus, with the possible exception of Smelser's *value-added model*, there is no clearly dominant theory in the field today.

The value of Smelser's value-added model is its utility in organizing the variety of data relevant to collective behavior. In contrast to the other theoretical perspectives in collective behavior, Smelser's value-added model offers a broad, *macroanalytic* approach. Its focus is not narrowly limited to what happens within a group during periods of collective behavior.

In the May 1970 demonstrations at Kent State University, National Guardsmen used tear gas in an attempt to control the crowds of student protestors. What sort of social interaction may have occurred within these groups? Could any norms have developed within the groups present at the demonstrations?

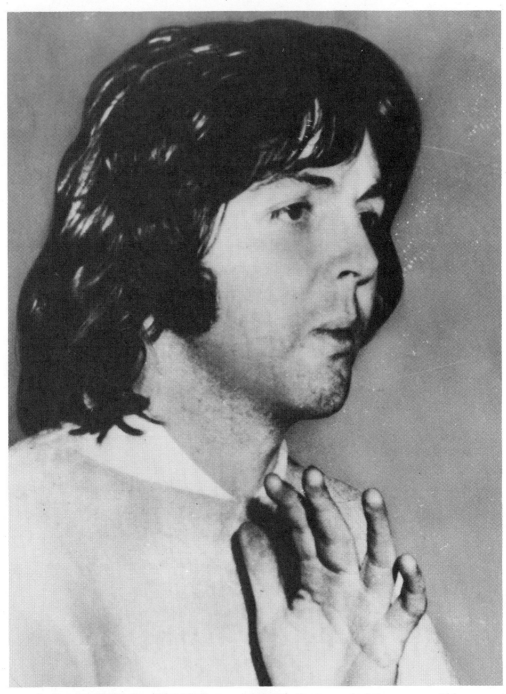

In October 1969 when Paul McCartney of the Beatles learned of the rumors of his death, he protested that they were greatly exaggerated.

CHAPTER III

Rumor Contagion, and Deindividuation

hree basic processes of collective behavior—rumor, social contagion and deindividuation—are considered in this chapter. They are discussed as separate topics as a matter of convenience although they are frequently simultaneous in occurrence. Each of them is prominent in the literature of collective behavior, and all three assume a common social context. First, they are all likely to occur during periods of situational stress; second, they all assume the presence of others; and third, all three processes involve social interaction.

Rumor

The association of situational stress and rumors is not coincidental. Rumors flourish in periods of social crisis (Shibutani 1966:64) because people may agree that a problematic situation exists, yet disagree on what is wrong and how to remedy it. A major concern in disasters is not uncontrolled panic, as is commonly supposed, but lack of coordination in community response. After reviewing the findings of the National Opinion Research Center (NORC) disaster studies, Fritz and Marks (1954) concluded that lack of coordination occurs when individuals are "each acting on somewhat different definitions of [the] situation." The absence of commonly shared opinions, conventional norms, and social roles creates dilemmas for which there are no easily recognized solutions. There is a growing need for relief from mounting tensions, accompanied by an increasing urgency for news and the resolution of "pervasive ambiguity" (Ball-Rokeach 1973).

Muzafer Sherif's classic experiments on norm formation (1936), using the autokinetic effect, established the behavioral principle that people strive to construct new norms in an effort to define ambiguous situations. The autokinetic effect occurs whenever people are exposed to a stationary point of light in a darkened area. For reasons still not adequately understood the light will appear to move, and when the light is turned off and on, it will appear to move again, but not necessarily in the same direction. Sherif exposed each of his subjects to a stationary pinpoint of light and asked them to indicate how far the light moved after he turned it off and on. Using this procedure he discovered that the subjects would establish their own norms. After several trials he found that the subjects' answers to his questions began to stabilize; the range of variation in reported distances began to decrease and become fixed around a set distance. For example, a subject might first report that the light moved 15 inches, then 2, and then 8 inches; eventally the reported distances would be closer together and distributed around a fixed distance.

After demonstrating this result Sherif extended his work to include more than one subject simultaneously viewing the same stationary point of light. In this new situation Sherif found that when two or three subjects are placed together in a darkened room there is a convergence of opinion regarding the distance apparently traveled by the light. A subject who had initially established a norm of 12 inches when paired with a subject with an initial norm of 2 inches would usually change his opinion in the direction of his partner's estimate.

Against the background of Sherif's pioneering effort there is now general agreement on the assumption that *people will construct a social reality whenever they fail to perceive a stable and unambiguous environment.* Festinger (1950) suggests that the emergence of norms in unclear situations comes from an individual's desire to validate his own opinions by comparing them with the beliefs of other people. Furthermore, Festinger's "social comparison" theory makes the assumption *that the greater the situational ambiguity the greater an individual's need for information from other people in defining the meaning of events* (1954). In a context of social crisis and situational ambiguity when the meaning of events is not self-evident, rumor can be understood as an information exchange used in the social construction of a shared "definition of situation" (Turner 1964a).

Rumor Defined

Rumor is defined as an "unconfirmed message passed from one person to another in face-to-face interaction" (Buckner 1965:55). It is both a product (a message) and a process (an exchange of information). Two of its essential features are that the message is (1) unconfirmed and (2) passed directly from one person to another. One difficulty raised by this definition of rumor is its implied exclusion of mass media from the rumor process. In a recent theoretical statement, Rosnow argues that face-to-face communication is an unnecessarily restrictive and unrealistic criterion (1974:28).

There is little doubt that the mass media often play an important part in the development of rumors. Written accounts of "The Seattle Windshield Pitting Epidemic" (Medalia and Larsen 1958), "The Phantom Anesthetist of Mattoon" (Johnson 1945), and Cantril's description of "The Invasion From Mars" (1940) indicate that most people first heard about these events from mass media sources. Seventy-five percent of the Seattle sample (interviewed just after the epidemic in March and April of 1954) said that the windshield pitting problem first came to their attention by way of newspapers, radios, or television (see Table 3.1). Only 19 percent of the Seattle residents interviewed by Medalia and Larsen said they had first heard about the windshield pitting from some other person. But these data do not necessarily reflect the relative impact of mass media communication versus interpersonal communication.

**Table 3.1:   How People Learned About the Seattle
Windshield Pitting Epidemic**

News Source	Percent Naming Source
Newspapers	51
Interpersonal	19
Radio	18
Television	6
Direct experience	6
Total percent	100
	(N=895)

Source: Medalia and Larsen (1958:182).

It is generally assumed that *face-to-face exchange of information is more persuasive and commands greater behavior compliance than any other channel of communication* (Middlebrook 1974:166). Perhaps the apparent discrepancy between frequency and impact can be placed in a more consistent relationship by considering Katz's (1957) *two-step model of communication*. Mass communication may be the first step in the widespread dissemination of a message, followed by a second step in which individuals pass it on to other people within their own social networks. Something of this sort happened in several of the case histories reported in Cantril's, *The Invasion From Mars* (1940). Middlebrook's analysis of the Martian invasion concludes that "one of the recurrent themes found to account for the panic reaction ... was the reaction of other people ... other people's behavior corroborated the broadcast" (1974:235). Here are two examples which illustrate the process:

I was resting when an excited person phoned and told me to listen to the radio, that a big meteor had fallen. I was really worried. (Cantril 1966:-140).

I was getting worried when my friend came in and his face was ghastly white. He said, "We're being invaded," and his conviction impressed me. (Cantril 1966:142).

Basic Law of Rumor

Regardless of their exact form of communication, there is consensus on the conditions that promote rumors. It is generally assumed that *rumors will tend to emerge in ambiguous situations* (Shibutani 1966:66). Turner and Killian have defined rumor as "the building up of a collectively sanctioned version of what has happened in a situation which lacks cognitive clarity" (1957:60). The phrase regarding a lack of cognitive clarity parallels a principle proposed in 1948 by Leon Festinger and his associates. The principle of "cognitive unclarity" asserts that "rumors will tend to arise in situations where cognitive regions especially relevant to immediate behavior are largely unstructured" (Festinger et al. 1948:484). In disasters and riots, news is one of the first things people seek. News, information, and unconfirmed rumors provide a basis for immediate action and future planning.

Aside from situational ambiguity, a second consideration essential to the emergence and diffusion of rumors is the importance of events and rumored information to a person. Following Allport and Postman's classic formulation (1947), it is usually assumed that *rumors will tend to emerge when events and rumored information are important rather than unimportant.* Situational ambiguity and importance are quantitatively related to rumor: $R \sim i \times a$, where "R" represents the frequency and distribution of rumor, "i" represents importance and "a" represents ambiguity. The formula indicates that rumor transmission is an inexact function of a multiplicative rather than additive relationship between importance and ambiguity. If either factor is zero, a rumor should fail to spread.

Of course, even this so-called "basic law" of rumor is not universally true. A number of disturbing factors usually prevail. One is the rumor listener's orientation to what he is hearing. H. Taylor Buckner's theory of rumor transmission suggests that "the individual may find himself in one of three orientations or situations in relation to a rumor" (1965:55). These three orientations were labeled: (1) critical set, (2) uncritical set, and (3) transmission set. If a person takes a critical set toward rumored information it means he or she is capable of using "critical ability" to separate truth from fiction and reject false information. The capacity for critical judgment is determined by an individual's level of general knowledge, personal experience with the subject of a rumor or personal experience with similar situations, and by the ability to size up the reliability of the rumor teller.

In some circumstances people are unable to exercise critical ability. An "uncritical set" is frequently caused by some combination of the following factors: (1) lack of knowledge, (2) lack of experience, and (3) lack of any clear-cut basis for assessing the reliability of the rumor teller. In addition, there is sometimes too little time to ponder new information. If a neighbor yelled "tornado," a person probably would not take time to evaluate the warning since it is better to be foolish than dead.

Another reason for uncritical set toward a rumor is self-interest. Sometimes people want a rumor to be true; they may want something exciting to happen as a relief from boredom. Rumor mongering may also be a form of social exchange in which "precious" information is exchanged for personal attention and status within a social group. After interviewing students at Temple University, Rosnow and Fine (1974) reported that the "Beatles rumor" was retold most frequently by the less popular students. There were no other significant differences between students who repeated the rumor and those who did not. The unpopular students may very well have used their "precious" information regarding the "death" of Paul McCartney as a way of gaining attention. In any case, the Beatles rumor was a hot commodity in the fall of 1969. It was an intriguing mixture of mystery and fantasy.

On October 12, 1969, a Detroit disc jockey, Russ Gibbs, received a telephone call on the air from a young man who described some curious evidence indicating that Paul McCartney of the Beatles was dead:

> In the album "Revolution," [sic, The White Album] if one listens carefully to the voice saying, "Number Nine, Number Nine, Number Nine" being played backwards, the words become: "Turn Me On Dead Man! . . ." At the end of the song, "Strawberry Fields" in the "Magical Mystery Tour" album, . . . there is someone saying: "I buried Paul!" when the background noises are filtered out." (Rosnow and Fine 1974:66).

Two days after this incident Fred LaBour published a review of the album "Abbey Road" for the *Michigan Daily* accompanied by a picture of a bloody, decapitated head. That article declared the "Paul McCartney was killed in an automobile in early November 1966. He had sped off from EMI recording studios, tired, sad, and dejected." LaBour also presented additional evidence from recent Beatles albums suggesting McCartney's death:

> Sgt. Pepper shows the lower part of a grave with yellow flowers shaped as Paul McCartney's bass guitar—or, if one prefers, the initial P. Inside the cover, McCartney wears an arm patch reading O.P.D., for Officially Pronounced Dead. The medal on his chest commemorates heroic death.

On the back cover, everyone is facing forward—except, of course, Paul McCartney!

Abbey Road shows John Lennon garbed in white to resemble an anthropomorphic god (or a minister), Ringo Starr dressed as an undertaker, George Harrison resembling a grave digger and McCartney barefoot to suggest the way corpses are sometimes buried in England. They are leaving a cemetary. The license plate on the Volkswagen parked along the road reads "28IF" the age McCartney would have been if he had lived." (Rosnow and Fine 1974:66)

Paul McCartney was supposedly dead and replaced by a double, he wore a black carnation, he appeared as a walrus (a folk death symbol), and for a time some people believed that the apple insignia on Beatles' albums would turn blood red when placed in water. The tale captured the interest of American youth and quickly spread across the country. The picture and reported automobile crash were, of course, both fictitious. There was no actual evidence that McCartney was dead (Rosnow and Fine 1976, Sheinkopf and Weintz 1973).

The final orientation to rumor described by Buckner is what he called "transmission set" (Buckner 1965:59). Transmission set means that information is simply relayed to other people because a person feels obliged to pass it on. Transmission set is characterized by an absence of critical assessment since the rumor listener isn't really concerned with its accuracy. Public and private bureaucrats may feel obliged to relay unconfirmed information to their organizational superiors even before they are able to critically evaluate its accuracy for themselves.

Unconfirmed information may also be passed on when there is a scarcity of reliable news. When official sources of news are closed, people may spread stories with little regard for their validity. The Detroit castration rumor illustrates how even an exceptionally unlikely story can become a widespread belief when official news is limited.

The Detroit castration rumor circulated in the winter of 1967–68 against a backdrop of urban ruin left behind by violent rioting in the previous June (Rosenthal 1971). Official communication in Detroit was limited by a four-month-old newspaper strike, and the absence of reliable news was compounded by a "cross-fire of printed flyers and articles" written by white, right-wingers, and black militants. The castration rumor eventually made its way to a badly needed Rumor Control Center belatedly established by Mayor Cavanagh. The story, apparently widespread by late February 1968, went like this:

A mother and her young son are shopping at a large department store ... the boy goes to the lavatory. He is a long time returning, and the mother asks a floor supervisor to get him. The man discovers the boy lying unconscious on the floor. He has been castrated. Nearby salesclerks recall that several teenage boys were seen entering the lavatory just before the young boy and leaving shortly before he was discovered (Rosenthal 1971:36).

Depending on who tells the story, the mother and son are either black or white, and the boys entering and leaving the lavatory are the opposite. Clearly, the credibility of such a story owes a great deal to the social context in which it appeared. Suburban whites were afraid of a black invasion, afraid of a poisoned water supply, and afraid that their children would be kidnapped and killed. Detroit was a frightened city, and frightening rumors seemed much more believable than they would today.

If the critical orientation of the rumor listener is important, it should be included in the basic formula. Consider this situation: a violent storm is expected to raise the water level of a major lake endangering adjacent low lying areas; an unidentified although respectable person tells us that the water level has just breached an important set of dikes, but from our past experience we believe this report is unlikely. Even though the facts are unclear and the message is important, we might fail to pass it on if we are sufficiently skeptical and have a high level of confidence in our own judgment. In such a case, critical assessment of rumored information would alter the outcome predicted from the basic formula. Chorus (1953) consequently modified the original rumor equation by adding a fourth term: $R \sim i \times a \times \frac{1}{c}$ where "c" represents a rumor listener's degree of critical ability in evaluating a rumor in a particular set of circumstances. As "c" grows larger, the rumor will become weaker; and as "c" grows smaller, the rumor will become stronger. It is formally assumed that *the spread of rumors is inversely related to levels of critical ability in a social network.*

Despite the superficial elegance of the refined "law" there is little quantitative evidence in its support. Data from one of the best field studies in this area of research, however, do provide some positive evidence (Schachter and Burdick 1955). Under conditions of "widespread cognitive unclarity," Schachter and Burdick found that "there is far more transmission of a planted rumor, and far more speculation involving new rumors when the issue is important rather than unimportant (Schachter and Burdick 1955:371). Without explanation they had removed a girl from each of four classrooms in a private prep school, and knowledge of the incidents spread quickly throughout the student body. The teachers were bombarded with questions from students trying to find out what had happened. But they could not clarify the situation since they had been asked to say they didn't know anything about the matter. The only clue to the nature of the mystery was provided by the experimenters who had planted a rumor two days before the girls were removed from their classrooms.

Two girls from each of the four classrooms from which another student would be removed were interviewed by various teachers about their "academic progress." Each of the individual interviews was concluded by asking a girl whether she knew anything about some missing exams.

Two days later when different girls were mysteriously removed from their classes the connection between the missing exams and the unusual classroom incidents was easy to make. By the end of the day, the whole student body had heard the rumor that the girls had stolen the exams. The importance of the classroom incidents to the students was gauged by whether or not a girl had been removed from a student's own classroom. Schachter and Burdick found that 78 percent of the students in classrooms from which a girl had been removed had initiated one or more retellings of the rumor. This compares to only 40 percent of students who were not classmates of a girl removed from class. Moreover, 70 percent of the classmates reported discussing other rumors compared to only 15 percent of nonclassmates. Regarding these new rumors, Schachter and Burdick reported one finding of particular interest: the rumors spread by classmates were more favorable accounts of what had happened then those spread by students from other classrooms. Classmates, for example, suggested the girl was "a great beauty and has been invited to tea at the principal's house," but other students felt the girl was "being disciplined for going to a wild party last weekend" (1955:369). Systematic differences of this type are not uncommon. The general question of distortion in the spread of rumors has received a great deal of attention.

Social Interaction and Rumor Distortion

It is commonly assumed that rumors become more and more distorted with each telling, and this is sometimes the case. Allport and Postman's original study (1947) suggested that three forms of distortion occur as rumors are transmitted from one person to another: leveling, sharpening, and assimilation. *Leveling* refers to the elimination of details, and *sharpening* to the selective emphasis of other details. There is a reciprocal relationship between leveling and sharpening since the elimination of some details from a story will serve to emphasize others. A study of rumor mongering during the Nigerian Civil War (1967–70) provides an excellent example of leveling and sharpening (Nkpa 1975).

The immediate cause of the Nigerian war was the secession of the Eastern part of the country which later became known as Biafra. In October 1967, a rumor surfaced about the death of General Gowan, the head of the Nigerian Federal Government. The rumored event was important because some people in Biafra believed the war would end as soon as General Gowan died. In the initial version of the story, Gowan had been invited to a meeting in Kaduna by the rulers of Northern Nigeria. The Emirs wanted to know when the war would be over and General Gowan had apparently obliged them by predicting a specific date for the end of the war. When Gowan's date had come and gone, and the war continued to rage, the Emirs invited the General back to Kaduna to explain what had gone wrong. General Gowan produced another date at the second meeting and succeeded in convincing the Emirs that he would not fail again. But just as before, the war was still raging when the new date came and passed. General Gowan was called to Kaduna for a third meeting. The Emirs were in an ugly frame of mind, and worse yet, General Gowan did not have a convincing explanation for why the war had not yet ended. In a fit of anger, the Emirs pulled out their swords, which they had concealed under their garments and, one after another, stabbed the hapless general. After nearly two years of circulation in Biafra this richly detailed story of Gowan's death had been leveled (and sharpened) to the simple statement: "I heard that Gowan has died in Kaduna" (Nkpa 1975).

Assimilation refers to the distortion of rumors to fit social prejudices or other preconceived cultural expectations. Knopf (1975) has drawn attention to the thematic contents of rumors as frequent expressions of community conflicts or of racial and ethnic stereotypes. An example of this kind of rumor occurred in Orleans, France, in the spring of 1969. The anti-Semitic rumor alleged that young women had been lured into the stores of Jewish shopkeepers where they had been drugged, imprisoned and spirited away to foreign centers of prostitution (Morin 1971). There was not a kernel of truth in the allegation; in fact, no women were even missing in Orleans that spring.

The early laboratory studies of rumor distortion were based on the serial transmission of a message from one person to another. But in social life there are actually two different kinds of rumor pattern: chains and interaction networks (Buckner 1965:62). At each point in a serial chain there is an interaction between a person who knows the rumor and a person who does not; in multiple interaction networks many people hear the same rumor from more than one source (see Figure 3.1). Both of these patterns are ideal types and may occur simultaneously as rumors diffuse throughout a group. Multiple interaction networks are common in permanent, formally organized groups; serial chains are probably more common in temporary, less-structured groups which lack both formal communications networks and social cliques.

According to Buckner's reconstruction of the rumor process, the content of a rumor is affected by both the type of social interaction taking place and the critical set of the rumor listener (Table 3.2). The least distortion occurs when a rumor is passed through a multiple interaction network in which the rumor listeners' levels of critical assessment are high. Conversely, the greatest distor-

FIGURE 3.1: Serial Chains and Interaction Networks

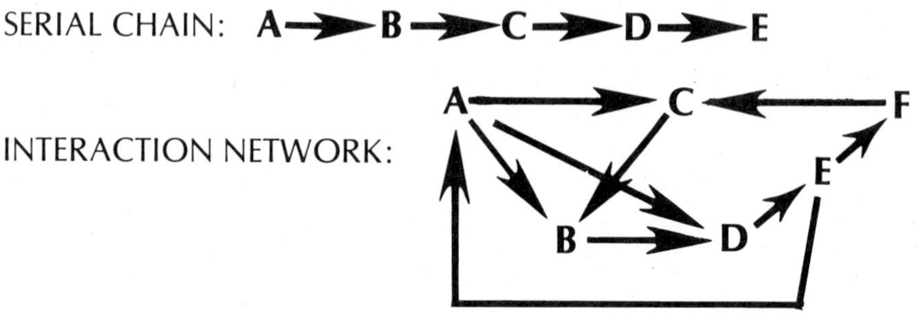

SERIAL CHAIN: A ➤ B ➤ C ➤ D ➤ E

INTERACTION NETWORK:

Source: Buckner (1965: 62).

tion occurs when a rumor is passed through a multiple interaction network characterized by low levels of critical assessment. Distortion in this context is indicated by a decrease in the ratio of true items to false items in a message (a truth/falsity ratio) rather than by the number of items omitted from a message. The greatest number of items omitted from a message occurs when a rumor is passed through a serial chain characterized by a transmission set.

Table 3.2:   Rumor Patterns and Orientations and Their Expected Effects on Transmission of Rumor

Pattern	Critical Set	Uncritical Set	Transmission Set
Serial chain	Slight decline in accuracy through memory flaws. Truth/falsity ratio remains high.*	Slight increase in distortion. Truth/falsity ratio drops at each interaction.	Rapid decline in information. Leveling, sharpening, assimilation.
Multiple-interaction network	Increasing accuracy as rumor moves through net. Truth/falsity ratio rises rapidly.	Great increase of distortion as accurate rumor is lost in false ones. Radical drop in truth/falsity ratio.	(Hypothetical). Very slow decline in information. Rumor stays intact.

*Truth/falsity ratio is arrived at by dividing the number of true items by the number of false items in the message. As such it is useful only when there are true or false items in the message, not, that is to say, in past laboratory experiments, where the items are neither true nor false, since they are unrelated to an external reality.
Source: Buckner (1965:63)

The Death of a Rumor

What happens to a rumor? Does it disappear in short order, or does it fade away slowly? Some rumors fail to catch on, but others persist for months, years, and even centuries. They can become a part of national mythology enshrined in historical tomes. The story of the "Black Hole" of Calcutta is an example. The Black Hole is an atrocity tale of an incident which supposedly took place in 1756 in connection with the British conquest of India (Hartmann 1948). In a period of renewed conflict between the native ruler of Bengal and the British trading community at Calcutta, Fort William was overrun and many of the local British taken prisoner. About 150 British prisoners were reputedly crammed into a cubical dungeon roughly 18 feet square. There were only two windows and no provision for food and water. Many of the prisoners supposedly died standing on their feet because of the tight press of so many people jammed into such a small space.

The essential features of the story were initially contained in a letter written by John Howell after his release from the dungeon. There is no satisfactory contemporary corroboration for Howell's version of what happened, and "he may have taken to the pen in order to clear himself of reflections on conduct not exactly heroic" (Hartmann 1948:22–23). Hartmann's careful analysis of historical records suggests that the episode never really took place, at least not in the way described by Howell. What factors, then, could have accounted for the remarkable persistence of the story?

Hartmann's research on the Black Hole of Calcutta led him to propose a number of factors which he believes apply to rumors in general: (1) the rumor should be vivid enough to impress a person's memory; (2) the rumor should evoke "powerful emotions;" (3) the rumor should fit an established set of cultural expectations; (4) the rumor should be plausible; and (5) the rumor cannot be forcefully refuted by an authoritative source. All of these factors seem reasonable, yet a note of caution is required. Plausibility, for instance, is not a very certain criterion for assessing the vitality of a rumor. Believable rumors are more likely to survive than unbelievable stories, but this is not always the case. The Eastern Airlines ghost story is a recent example of an improbable rumor that has proved difficult to stop.

> According to sources in the industry, several Eastern pilots and stewardesses have refused to fly one or more of the company's Lockheed-1011 Tristar jetliners because the planes were haunted.
>
> It was said that the faces of the pilot and other crew members of an Eastern Tristar that crashed in Florida Everglades on December 30, 1972, have appeared mysteriously in the cockpits of other Tristars, and as a result, some pilots and stewardesses have been scared out of their wits.
>
> The story of the haunted jetliner was circulated extensively among Eastern's employees, and it has been heard and repeated by passengers and flight crews of other airlines.

The owners of the Bellevue-Stratford hotel in Philadelphia claimed that rumors about the mysterious "Legionnaires disease" forced the hotel to close.

"We've heard 10 or 12 versions of the story," an Eastern executive said last week. "We've heard that planes have been grounded and that passengers have seen the ghosts, but we can't find where the story started."

Flight crews have been interviewed, logs have been checked, and other steps have been taken to find the roots of the story. But there has been no documentation whatsoever of any existence of ghosts, the company spokesman insisted. Yet the reports of the ghost are continuing to circulate, he acknowledged.

"It's kind of a 'flying Dutchman,' " the official said referring to the specter of the legendary sailor sentenced to pilot his ship until Judgment Day. "It's amazing what can happen when a rumor starts." (New York *Times*, April 13, 1975)

Even authoritative announcements made by local officials may fail to squelch a vivid rumor once it is well established. The "phantom slasher of Taipei" makes the point (Jacobs 1965). On May 4, 1956, Taipei newspapers reported that a number of allegedly authenticated slashings had occurred on the city streets. The victims, children between the ages of six months and eight years, appeared to have been cut by razor blades or similar weapons. One account "described a youngster being cut on the left arm while he was being carried, Chinese style, on the back of his mother" (Jacobs 1965:319). The Taipei City Police Bureau, and later the Criminal Investigation Division of the Provincial Department of Police, actively investigated the slashings. On May 7 these officials reported that an "alleged cutting on May 3 had been disproved as a result of an on-the-spot investigation." The public was urged to ignore the rumors circulating throughout the city. Nevertheless, on May 11 a "woman in red" was accused of cutting a baby girl:

It seems that a mother and a baby in arms were on the street. Suddenly the baby cried. Looking about, the mother noticed that a girl in a red jacket was immediately behind her. The mother cried out, whereupon the strange girl fled and the mother chased after her (Jacobs 1965:325).

Social Contagion

Social contagion "refers to the relatively rapid, unwitting, and nonrational dissemination of a mood, impulse, or form of conduct . . ." (Blumer 1975:27). Aside from rumor, social contagion is one of the most startling and frequently discussed processes associated with collective behavior. Social contagion often involves the spread of unusual and even bizarre conduct throughout a group under mysterious circumstances. Descriptive material is rich and colorful, while analytic treatments are sparse and generally unsophisticated, as discussed in Chapter II. Nevertheless, social contagion is one of the principal concepts used to account for both uniformity of mood within a crowd and heightened emotionality.

Considering the popularity of the contagion concept, it is surprising that contagion theory "continues to be troublesome" (Turner 1964b:129). Too many questions are left unanswered. Under what conditions is social contagion most likely to occur, or why does the observation of another person's behavior have such a strong influence on our own mood? The mechanics of social contagion are left unexplained, as if they were automatic. What seems to be missing is a broader theory of emotional arousal capable of subsuming the process of social contagion. Schachter's cognitive theory of emotional experience provides such a framework.

Cognitive Theory of Emotional Arousal

Schachter's theory of emotional arousal emphasizes the importance of cognitive cues in determining emotional experience. Unlike more traditional theories of emotional reaction, Schachter's theory does not assume a simple one-to-one relationship between specific physiological reactions and discrete emotional experiences such as anger and euphoria. On the contrary, his formulation assumes that the relationship between physiological arousal and emotional reaction is nonspecific. No matter what emotion is aroused the underlying physiological reactions are the same. Physiological arousal in itself, then, is not very informative since the physical reactions associated with discrete emotional states are similar or identical. If the physiological symptoms are the same, the only distinctive aspect of an emotion can be the situation in which it occurs. Whether we interpret our feelings as love, hate, or joy should depend on situational factors, such as what we are doing, what others say to us, and what they are doing. The labels we attach to physiological arousal—a feeling of being stirred up—depend upon our interpretation of situational cues. But to say the label given to a particular experience depends on the situation does not mean a conscious process is involved. We do not operate as abstract intellects tediously pondering the meaning of situational cues. In everyday life our experience of a physiological reaction and situation are inextricably intertwined and we are not aware of the interpretive process.

Based on this general scheme, Schachter and Singer (1962) designed an ingenious experiment which induced a general state of physiological arousal in subjects who were then placed in different situations. The experimental subjects were injected with a stimulant, epinephrine, then divided into three groups. One-third of the subjects had been correctly informed about the effects of the drug which caused an increased heart rate, a flushed feeling, tremors, and sweaty hands. Another one-third of the subjects had been told the drug was being tested as a vitamin supplement and were unaware of its likely effects. The last one-third of the subjects had been deliberately misinformed about the drug's side effects. They were told to expect mild tingling sensations in the bottoms of their feet. Schachter and Singer reasoned that all of the subjects would be experiencing roughly the same physical symptoms, but that only the uninformed and misinformed subjects would be particularly sensitive to environmental cues which could be used in interpreting their experiences. After the drug had been administered to all of the subjects, they were sent individually to a waiting room, supposedly in preparation for some tests on visual perception. There was always one other person, a confederate of the experimenters, in the waiting room. His activity while waiting with the subjects provided them with a behavioral model. The confederate behaved in a manner consistent with either of two emotional states: euphoria or anger. In the euphoric condition the confederate appeared to be frivolous and silly; he threw wads of paper into a wastepaper basket, flew paper airplanes, built a paper tower, and played with a hula hoop. In the angry condition the confederate appeared to be hostile and abusive; he reacted angrily to a request to fill out a questionnaire, he complained about personal items on the questionnaire, pounded his fist on the top of his desk, and finally he tore up his questionnaire in a fit of rage and stalked out of the waiting room.

The results of the experiment supported Schachter and Singer's prediction; the uninformed and misinformed subjects were affected much more by the behavioral model than the subjects who had been correctly informed of the drugs effects. When the confederate behaved angrily the uninformed and misinformed subjects also began to behave badly; when the confederate behaved frivolously they began to laugh and join in the fun. The deliberately misinformed subjects were most susceptible to the euphoric behavioral model. These subjects, who believed they had been injected with a vitamin supplement, were most confused by their aroused state and were apparently most willing to accept the behavorial model's activity as a basis for interpreting their own feelings.

Schachter and Singer's basic design has been replicated and extended by a number of subsequent studies. Stuart Valins (1966) used Schachter's approach to explain various aspects of sexual arousal and Schachter and Nisbett (1966) used the same theory as a basis for altering subjects' perceptions of pain. Schachter's cognitive theory of emotional experience has even contributed to our understanding of why fat people eat too much, but the implications of this line of research have only been hinted at in the literature on social contagion (Kerckhoff and Back 1968:34).

Social Stress and Contagion

One hypothesis easily inferred from this perspective is that *social contagion is associated with situational stress.* When people experience situational stress, psychological tension is sometimes manifest in physical reactions such as increased heart rate, sweating, flushing, muscle tension, and fainting spells (Engel 1962:383–384). These reactions would be susceptible to a wide range of cognitive interpretations when they occur in the absence of an easily recognized, objective cause. In this circumstance behavioral models can strongly influence people, facilitating social contagion. Evidence confirming the linkage of social contagion and situational stress is substantial.

The so-called dancing manias of the Middle Ages were closely associated with the occurrence of social crises in Europe (Rosen 1968:195–225). Although the dancing manias are usually presented as examples of mass hysteria rather than social contagion, Rosen's exhaustive analysis makes it clear they were not spontaneous, mass phenomena. Neither characterization is accurate; they were neither spontaneous nor mass phenomena. The dancing manias were not mass phenomena in two important senses of the term: (1) they were confined to small, compact collectivities; and (2) they involved significant social interaction between participants. To imply that the dancing manias are mass phenomena involving large numbers of "atomized" individuals spread out over wide geographic areas is misleading. Moreover, the dancing episodes were "clearly linked with religious ritual and institutions" of the time (Rosen 1968:199). Dancing to a state of euphoric frenzy was an anticipated, if not fully organized, religious activity during the Middle Ages. Rosen's interpretation (1968) of the so-called medieval "dancing manias" is emphatic on these points.

One of the most commonly mentioned episodes occurred around July 15, 1374, at Aachen. Rosen's description of the event, synthesized from information available in contemporary chronicles and an eye-witness account of a local monk, provides a remarkable portrait of the Aachen episode:

> The dancers are described as setting wreaths on their heads, being bound around with cloths and towels, and carrying statues. Moreover, various chronicles describe them as half-naked or stark naked, except possibly for a loin cloth. Not only did they hold hands, but sometimes they clapped their hands above their heads. When the dancers achieved a state of ecstasy, they exhibited a variety of other motor phenomena. Some suddenly threw themselves on the ground and began to move around on their backs; others lost consciousness and fell down foaming at the mouth; still others described ecstatic visions in which the heavens opened to reveal the enthroned Savior with the Holy Mother at his side. Most characteristic of all, perhaps were the paroxysmal convulsive movements and twitchings (Rosen 1968:197).

Who were these people, how many were involved, and how did the dancing episodes get their start? Rosen's work provides at least part of the answer to these questions. The people who danced at Aachen were comprised of a "large number" of Hungarian pilgrims. Hungarian pilgrimages to the Rhineland and Westphalia occurred annually between 1221 and 1769, except for some religious shrines which were visited every seventh year. For example, the shrine of the Magi at Koln was visited every seventh year by pilgrims who came to offer "thanks by dancing to musical accompaniment" (Rosen 1968:199). Rosen continues, "this fact may be coupled with the observations that many danced in churches, churchyards, monasteries, and other holy places." The dancing episodes reflect both a chronology and geographic distribution consistent with the notion of a religious pilgrimage. In earlier years the German tribes had moved eastward and southward into Hungary following the development of mining. These German immigrants apparently retained fond recollections, and frequently returned "home" to pray at the shrines of their father-land.

Although the accounts are vague about the number of people involved in separate incidents, it seems clear that it was not large. In no case was a whole community involved and the actual number of participants might have been no larger than 500 to 1,100 (Rosen 1968:197–8). Bystanders were sometimes beaten when they refused to join the dancers and the magistrates of Maastricht had to issue an edict "prohibiting anyone suffering from the dance frenzy from dancing in churches or streets" (Rosen 1968:199).

The dancing incident at Aachen in 1374 was not an isolated historical event. Similar episodes have been described in other years. In 1188 a Welsh churchman and historian Gerald de Barri (Giraldus Cambrensis) associates dance with religious rites at St. Almedha in Brecknockshire. Pilgrims came to the shrine to be cured of illness and absolved for their sins. To satisfy these needs, "song and dance were employed to achieve a state of ritual trance . . . to reduce emotional tensions and to achieve some degree of relief" (Rosen 1968:201).

In 1588 the dancing mania reappeared in Strassbourg. It began eight days before the feast of Mary Magdalene and, over the course of the next month, it spread to "more than four hundred" people. The dancers had to be restricted to guild halls and were eventually sent to St. Vitus' Chapel at Hohlenstein. This episode is significant because it clearly occurred in a period crisis:

> Various chroniclers point out that this was a period of ruined harvests, severe famine, general want, and widespread disease. This was the time of the early reformation and thus of religious unrest (Rosen 1968:201–2).

The dancing at Strassbourg is only part of a larger pattern (see Rosen 1968:172–225) indicating the importance of social stress. Life was marked by famine, pestilence, and strife. Tension, despair, social alienation, and frustrated aspirations were probably more common than rare. According to Rosen, the dancing manias allowed people to transform their psychological tension into a pleasurable experience. The euphoric frenzy of the dancing mania may have been one of the few payoffs for living in an otherwise odious period of history. From this perspective it is not surprising that peasants, servants, unmarried women, beggars, and idlers were disproportionately represented among the dancers (Rosen 1968:197).

The connection between situational stress and social contagion is even more clearly delineated in Kerckhoff and Back's analysis of *The June Bug* (1968). One of the underlying assumptions of their study was that (hysterical) contagion is "a form of response to stress and that it tends to occur in situations in which nervous tension is high" (Kerckhoff and Back 1968:65). The incident took place in a newly constructed clothing factory in the South and involved 62 women who were supposedly "affected" by the bite of vicious bugs (see Chapter I). Most of the women had fainted or complained of severe pain and nausea; all had reported to medical authorities. Yet the mysterious bugs could not be located after an exhaustive search of the factory. Kerckhoff and Back investigated three general sources of situational stress: (1) work conditions, (2) work and management relations, and (3) work and family finances. As shown in Table 3.3, most of the indices are consistent with the tendency for women affected by the epidemic (the "victims," $N = 56$) to be under more stressful conditions than a comparable set of women not experiencing any of the bugbite symptoms (the controls, $N = 71$). Four of the comparisons between the victims and the controls show particularly large differences. The affected women worked overtime at least two or three times a week (66.1% vs. 40.8%), were less likely to take a complaint to their job supervisor (44.6% vs. 25.4%), worked in sections where output varied (41.1% vs. 25.4%), and provided half or more of their family income (43.4% vs. 22.4%). There were also some curious anomalies in the data that were inconsistent with expectations. For example, the victims were more likely to work overtime than the controls, yet they were less likely to say that overtime work interfered with something (50.0% vs. 59.2%). This apparent discrepancy is accounted for by Kerckhoff and Back's finding that the June Bug's victims were more likely than controls to deny any problem. Presumably this was a coping mechanism developed by women working under stress (1968:84).

One question usually raised in this type of analysis is whether or not these various indices of stress are cumulative. Table 3.4 shows clearly that the differences discussed above individually between affecteds and controls are increased by accumulatively combining the four measures. When these four sources of stress were combined only 4.2 percent of the controls compared to

Table 3.3: Situational Stress and "Victims" of the June Bug

Situational Stress Indicators	Percent VICTIMS (N=56)	Percent CONTROLS (N=71)
Work Conditions		
Work section varies in output	41.1	25.4
Work overtime at least 2–3 times a week	66.1	40.8
Work overtime with a child at home under 6 years of age	33.9	14.1
Work and Management Relations		
Would *not* take complaints to supervisor -	44.6	25.4
Would take complaints to union steward	28.6	15.5
Work and Family Finances		
Are sole family breadwinners	21.4	9.9
Provide half or more of family income	43.4	22.4

Adapted from: Kerckhoff and Back (1968:68).

32.2 percent of the affected women experienced two or more stress conditions. Thus it seems reasonable to tentatively conclude, making allowance for some irregularity in the data, that situational stress and psychological tension are a prerequisite of social contagion. But this prerequisite condition does not, in itself, account for the spread of symptomatic behavior in a group. Interaction with appropriate behavioral models is the second necessary condition.

Table 3.4: The Cumulative Impact of Situational Stress in the Case of the June Bug Victims

Number of Indicators Experienced*	Percent VICTIMS (N=56)	Percent CONTROLS (N=71)
Zero or one	35.7	74.6
Two	32.1	21.1
Three or more	32.2	4.2
TOTAL	100%	99.9%

*The four measures of strain are as follows: worked overtime at least two or three times a week, do not mention supervisor as one to go to with a complaint, the section varies in output, and provides half or more of family income.

Adapted from: Kerckhoff and Back (1968:75).

Social Interaction and Contagion

One of the most important findings reported in *The June Bug* is that the pattern of *social interaction* found in the southern clothing factory determined the bug's biting victims. The nonexistent bug first bit social isolates, the women without many friends. Apparently these women were less restrained by group pressure and had less status to lose by behaving in a socially suspect manner. Next, the behavior of the social isolates spread to their few friends who subsequently experienced the same symptoms. From then on, the bug biting epidemic spread rapidly through the friendship network of the original nucleus of women. Kerckhoff and Back found that the June Bug's victims, the affected women, were "twice as likely to be chosen (as friends) solely by other affecteds" and that the unaffected controls were "twice as likely to be chosen solely by other controls" (Kerckhoff et al. 1965:9). Assuming the presence of situational stress and psychological tension, the basic hypothesis is that if an "appropriate" symptomatology is to spread through a group, it must be learned from an available behavioral model. Recent investigation of still another unknown substance, a "mystery gas," confirms this expectation.

In March of 1972 a strange case of gas poisoning occurred at a university data processing center (Stahl and Lebedun 1974). Roughly 35 women were exposed to a gas "from an unknown source" which caused fainting, nausea, and dizziness so severe that 10 of the workers were taken to the University Medical Center. The data processing center was evacuated for the day and a group of "environmental specialists" was brought in to examine the building. An additional precaution was taken: "extensive blood and urine tests of affected workers were conducted in order to locate traces of the noxious 'gas' " (Stahl and Lebedun 1974:44). Since samples of air from the building met health standards it was reopened for business the following morning. Nevertheless, several more women became ill and the Data Center was shut down for a second time and even more "environmental and physiological tests" were conducted. Even so, no physical reason for the episode was ever found.

The data shown in Table 3.5 indicate a clear relationship between levels of job satisfaction and severity of symptomatology. Job satisfaction can be reasonably interpreted as an index of social stress; the greater the level of job dissatisfaction, "the more readily the individual used the now 'legitimated' route of illness to adapt to this dissatisfaction" (Stahl and Lebedun 1974:47). But the investigators' findings with regard to friendship patterns are more germane at this point.

Based on the premise that symptomatic behavior is spread by behavioral models, Stahl and Lebedun tried to discern a relationship between seating arrangements and the severity of symptomatology. The task proved fruitless; there was no spatial grouping evident. They found instead that "similarities in symptomatology were better defined by interpersonal networks of friendship patterns" (1974:48). Moreover, they extended Kerckhoff and Back's results by

Table 3.5: Level of Job Satisfaction, Severity of Symptomatology, and Mean Severity Score

	Severity		
Satisfaction	Low	High	Total
Low	2	5	7
Medium	7	2	9
High	2	2	4
Total	11	9	20
$\overline{X}$ Satisfaction	2.0	1.7	..

γ-.380.

Source: Stahl and Lebedun (1974:47).

showing that even the level of severity of symptomatology is influenced by friendship patterns:

> The eight workers reporting the highest severity (severity scores of 3 and 2) selected friends in a sociogram who reported a mean severity score of 2.06 while the remaining ten workers reporting low severity scores (1 and 0) selected friends who reported a mean symptomatology score of 1.61 (Stahl and Lebedun 1974:48).

Deindividuation

One of the major problems of social contagion theory is its failure to identify all of the circumstances which promote the rapid spread of behavior from one person to another. Something more than the simple imitation of behavioral models by people under stress is needed to account for the diffusion of normally restrained actions (Wheeler 1966). Selfish, greedy, lustful, and destructive acts are common features of social contagion. Social contagion can also involve the spread of more positive behaviors such as intense happiness and open love for others. A compelling aspect of social contagion is that it allows for the spread of behaviors which are either nonnormative and strongly sanctioned, or socially approved and yet ordinarily restrained in public gatherings. Consequently, it seems likely that the occurrence of social contagion is dependent upon conditions which combine to "lower thresholds of normally restrained behavior" (Zimbardo 1969). The term *deindividuation* refers to a process in which both social and psychological conditions promote a loss of self-consciousness and self-restraint. Deindividuation is complex and little research has been done since an early study by Festinger, Pepitone, and Newcomb (1952). Zimbardo's paper presented at the Nebraska Symposium on Motivation breaks the process into three stages: (1) social inputs, (2) subjective states, and (3) behavioral outputs. The scheme shown in Figure 3.2 is a useful framework for discussion.

The burning cross symbolizes the Klu Klux Klan and the racist attitudes of its members.

Social Inputs

LeBon's (1960) early attempt to account for the spread of unrestrained brutal behavior in the crowd proposed that individuals, submerged in a mob, are

---
FIGURE 3.2: Social Interaction and Deindividuation

SOCIAL INPUTS	SUBJECTIVE STATES	BEHAVIOR OUTPUTS
Crowds:	**Experience:**	**Action:**
(1) Social Density	(1) Anonymity	(1) Self-Reinforcing Behavior
(2) Behavioral Models	(2) Invulnerability	
(3) Noise and Excitement	(3) Low Self-Consciousness	(2) Amplification of Behavior
(4) Drugs	(4) Low Social Responsibility	

Adapted from: Zimbardo (1969: 253).

influenced by the emergence of a primitive "collective mind." Contemporary theorists, however, largely reject LeBon's early speculation as an example of an antidemocratic bias. Conditions associated with the existence of a spontaneously assembled collectivity are more important than anything as vague and as unlikely as a primitive "collective mind." What are some of these conditions?

From an individual's point of view, crowds provide collections of other people of a given *size* and *density.* Nonperiodic assemblies are often *noisy* and *excited* gatherings of people. In addition, crowds provide engaging *behavioral models* and in some circumstances sanction the use of *consciousness-altering drugs.* Each of these conditions affects the subjective states of crowd participants. Noise and excitement can result in physiological arousal; drugs can alter a person's sense of self-consciousness and self-restraint. The belligerent drunk is a part of our national folklore. Of all the conditions associated with a spontaneous assembly, size has undergone the greatest research effort to determine its effects on subjective states.

Subjective States

The basic premise underlying research on crowd size is that people will be less restrained and more aggressive in their actions when social conditions reduce the saliency of probable punishment for misdeeds. Group size promotes a sense of *anonymity* among crowd participants. Punishment seems less likely when people feel that they cannot be personally identified. Furthermore, the presence of other anonymous individuals *reduces a person's sense of distinctive-*

ness. Some investigators have even speculated that submergence in a crowd may also give a person a sense of *invulnerability,* a sense of protection from social sanctions. It's important to remember that the question of whether individuals in a crowd are really anonymous and vulnerable is distinct from how they feel. People may feel anonymous even though they can be identified in photographs and films. In any case, anonymity, loss of distinctiveness, and a sense of invulnerability are overlapping aspects of a *general loss of self-consciousness* in a crowd. It is the loss of self-consciousness which presumably frees ordinarily restrained behavior. The *anonymity-aggression hypothesis,* for example, predicts that aggression is more likely to occur when circumstances make people feel anonymous rather than accentuate their individuality and distinctiveness.

The anonymity-aggression hypothesis has been tested in a number of laboratory studies. Making students feel anonymous significantly increased their aggressiveness in one experiment: the total duration of electric shocks given to a "victim" by girls made to feel anonymous was greater than that given by girls whose individuality had been emphasized (Zimbardo 1969). This result has been successfully replicated (Baron 1970) and is consistent with earlier indications that anonymous individuals are less reluctant to use obscene language and less restrained in their criticism of parents.

The anonymity-aggression hypothesis has received additional, but more indirect support from several recent field studies. One three-year study of crime rates in New York City public housing is revealing. The study found higher crime rates in high-rise buildings (over 13 floors) than in three-floor walk-ups. The difference between the two types of public housing is accounted for by large differences in the incidence of crime in the interior public areas of the buildings. People seem to feel more anonymous and inconspicuous in the public areas of a high-rise than in the more limited public areas of a three-story walk-up. Zimbardo's study of automobile vandalism shows the same tendency (1969). An abandoned car was quickly destroyed in the anonymity of New City City, but a car left in a smaller community was untouched.

Another study found that people made to feel anonymous were able to express pleasant feelings ordinarily restrained among strangers. College males and females interacting in a dark room were more likely to purposively touch each other than students left together in a lighted room. Half of the persons in the darkened room hugged another person; none did in the lighted room. The subjects in the darkened room showed little concern for identifying each other even though they had become friends and were sexually excited (Gergen and Gergen 1971). An individual may wish to retain anonymity if his gains outweigh his short-term losses. Furthermore, when the social environment offers the possibility of punishment, embarrassment, or humiliation for an act, an individual prefers anonymity to public recognition.

A second hypothesis relating group size and changes in the subjective state of crowd members concerns an individual's sense of *social responsibility*. The greater the size of the crowd the less likely an individual will feel personally responsible for what happens around him (Darley and Latane 1968). When a person is being attacked, the probability of helpful intervention appears to decrease as the size of an onlooking crowd increases. The list of assaults witnessed by crowds of bystanders who fail to aid helpless victims continues to grow. The rape-murder of Ann Jiminez in San Francisco is a brutal example cited in Zimbardo's study:

> One cannot help but be horrified by the brutal rape-murder of young Ann Jiminez in San Francisco witnessed by perhaps 25 other teenagers, who watched or participated in her being abused, sexually violated, kicked, and left to die in an alley with obscenities scrawled on her body with lipstick. The reason? She allegedly stole a friend's pair of motorcyle boots (1969:242).

Why do people watch a vicious attack without doing anything? How is it possible for a mugging victim to bleed to death on a subway in view of his fellow travelers? And more important, why do bystanders join the attack? Part of the answer is that people simply don't feel personally responsible. But why are they so reluctant to assume personal responsibility?

Four factors seem to be important in understanding why people refuse personal responsibility. Sometimes they don't feel *competent*. "I couldn't do anything about it," and "I didn't know what to do," are common refrains when crowds of bystanders are asked to explain their collective inaction. As the size of a crowd increases, it is easier to believe that someone else is more competent and ought to be doing something. A second variable is *embarrassment*. People won't intervene if there is any chance of being publically embarrassed. The larger the crowd, the greater the embarrassment when you bungle the situation. A stronger reason for not intervening on behalf of a victim is a high *risk of physical harm*. If intervention demands confrontation with a gang of youthful thugs, it is not likely to occur. The fourth variable seems to be *fear of involvement*. People avoid involvement for a variety of reasons: fear of retaliation, fear of police, or fear of notoriety.

Why unrestrained aggression can spread through a group is only partly explained by the diffusion of social responsibility. Certainly lack of personal responsibility is one factor. If someone else is made responsible, or if someone else can be blamed for an action it is easier to "join in the fun." Moreover, when everyone else appears to be "in the same boat," a person feels a sense

This propaganda poster from World War I was employed to dehumanize the German people.

of shared responsibility. After three civil rights workers were killed in Missis-sippi in 1964, Klansmen passed the murder weapon from hand to hand so all shared equally in the responsibility for the slayings (Huie 1965). Even so, the deindividuation process supposes that a reduction in subjective guilt is also an essential ingredient in accounting for the spread of antisocial behavior.

The presence of other people, all involved in the same act, may tend to legitimatize behavior. From an individual's point of view, if everyone else is doing it, it must be all right. Others present may also reduce personal guilt if they believe their actions are morally required. The dogma of the Ku Klux Klan plays an important role in legitimating the collective violence of the association. Another mechanism for reducing guilt is "dehumanization" of the victim, such as calling the North Vietnamese "dumb gooks."

Another way of reducing responsibility is suggested by the "just world hypothesis." Individuals can sometimes reduce their sense of guilt by feeling a victim deserves his or her punishment: the victim is basically a bad person, therefore punishment is justified. Such an assumption is consistent with a generalized belief that the world is a fair place. Many people are apparently uncomfortable with the idea that the world is unfair. When punishment is considered fair or necessary, people will frequently derogate a person whom they have just injured. For example, in one study students paid to humiliate other students convinced themselves that the humiliated students were, in fact, inferior and deserving of ridicule (Davis and Jones 1960).

Behavioral Outputs

Deindividuated behavior is characteristic of social contagion and is usually described by emotionality and spontaneity. But more important, deindividuated behavior is frequently self-reinforcing. Once initiated it is difficult to terminate because it provides strong reinforcement for continuing. The act itself is sometimes so pleasurable that a person can become totally involved in what he or she is doing. As physical involvement in the act intensifies, other situational factors seem to recede in importance. Zimbardo's description of the total destruction of an abandoned car at Stanford University is an instructive case. The students were initially reluctant to attack the car and began to participate only after Zimbardo and two of his assistants personally attacked the abandoned vehicle. Prior to that point the car had escaped injury, but once behavioral models were present the attack began:

> First of all, there is considerable reluctance to take the first blow, to smash through the windshields and initiate the destruction of a form. But it feels so good after the first smack that the next one comes more easily, with more force, and feels even better. Although everyone knew the sequence was being filmed, the students got carried away temporarily. Once a person had begun to wield the sledge hammer, it was difficult to get him to stop and pass it on to the next pair of eager hands. Finally they

all attacked simultaneously. One student jumped on the roof and began stomping it in, two were pulling the door from its hinges, another hammered away at the hood and motor, while the last one broke all the glass he could find. They later reported that feeling the metal or glass give way under the influence of their blows was stimulating and pleasurable. Observers of this action, who were shouting out to hit it harder and smash it, finally joined in and turned the car completely over on its back whacking at the underside. (Zimbardo 1969:290–2)

The self-reinforcing nature of the automobile demolition is a salient feature of Zimbardo's description. Pounding the machine was fun, and each blow added to the pleasure of the participants. Self-reinforcement of deindividuated behavior may account for the amplification of activity so often observed in social contagion. The dancers of the Middle Ages danced to a state of euphoric frenzy and exhaustion just as Zimbardo's car smashers continued until they had reduced their ojbect to rubble.

Summary and Conclusion

Rumor is an unconfirmed message passed from one person to another in face-to-face interaction. Rumors tend to emerge in ambiguous situations and are commonly interpreted as a form of information exchange used in the *social construction of a shared definition of situation.* The demand for information expressed in the spread of rumors is a multiplicative function of the ambiguity of a stress situation and the importance of the events to those involved. The spread of rumors is also inversely related to the levels of critical ability in a social network. Sometimes circumstances or personal interests will reduce a rumor listener's level of critical assessment. Rumor mongering, for example, may be a form of social exchange in which scarce information is traded for status or recognition within a group.

Allport and Postman's original study of rumor (1947) indicated three basic types of distortion: *leveling, sharpening,* and *assimilation.* But these forms of distortion are probably characteristic of complex messages passed through serial chains. There are two kinds of rumor patterns: *serial chains* and *multiple interaction networks.* The least distortion occurs when a rumor is transmitted through a multiple interaction network and the rumor listeners' levels of critical assessment are high.

Social contagion refers to the relatively rapid, unwitting, and nonrational dissemination of a mood, impulse, or form of conduct. One of its most compelling features is that it frequently involves the spread of overt antisocial behavior. The connection between social stress and social contagion is clearly delineated in Kerckhoff and Back's account of *The June Bug* (1968). One of their most important findings is that the pattern of social interaction found in the southern clothing factory determined the bugbite victims. *Assuming the presence of social stress and psychological tension, the basic hypothesis is that if an "appropriate" symptomatology is to spread through a group, it must be learned from an available behavioral model.*

One of the major problems of social contagion theory is its failure to identify all of the circumstances which promote the rapid spread of behavior from one person to another. It seems likely that deindividuation is an essential condition for the occurrence of social contagion. *Deindividuation refers to a complex process in which both social and psychological factors promote a loss of self-consciousness and a loss of self-restraint.* Deindividuation is analyzed in three stages: (1) social inputs, (2) subjective states, and (3) behavioral outputs. Deindividuated behavior is frequently impulsive and emotional, but its most important aspect is self-reinforcement. *Once initiated, it is difficult to terminate.* The *anonymity-aggression hypothesis* has been tested in laboratory studies which corroborate the results of several field studies. People made to feel anonymous are more aggressive than people whose individuality has been emphasized. People may *feel anonymous* in a crowd even though their behavior is being photographed and filmed.

*

PART II *Disaster Research*

S ome years ago it was observed that there are hundreds of disasters every year (Lemons 1957). There is no reason to suppose that there are fewer today than when Lemons' review was published. Certainly it is difficult to read a newspaper, watch television, or listen to the radio without hearing of a disaster somewhere in the world. In addition to the fact that there are many disasters, people find them intensely interesting. The tornado, the earthquake, the industrial explosion, the bombing raid, and the impact of famine all generate curiosity and interest.

The study of disasters is important on both practical and theoretical grounds. Since disasters alter the usual patterns of social interaction they provide realistic opportunities to examine reactions to extreme situational stress. Such study aids the development of plans for effective warning of approaching disasters, controlling them, and recovering from their impact. But what do disasters have to do with collective behavior?

In Chapter I, collective behavior was defined as "relatively unorganized patterns of social interaction in human groups." It was stated that collective behavior is frequently associated with conditions of situational stress which were described as "excessive demands on men and animals, demands that produce disturbance of physiological, social and psychological systems." (Lazarus 1968:338). Disasters create situational stress as a social context in which collective behavior is likely to emerge.

Part II, "Disaster research," is divided into three chapters. Chapter IV begins with the question of *what is or is not disaster* and how many stereotypes of behavior in such situations have been overthrown by contemporary research. Most of Chapter IV is devoted to the *preconditions* of disaster—the *period of threat and warning* prior to impact. Different responses to long-term and short-term periods of warning are discussed, as well as the question of how different kinds of communications from authorities affect reactions to disaster.

Chapter V considers the *impact* of disaster, focusing on matters such as group behavior during the actual impact of a disaster. What differences are there between reactions to a short-term local impact, such as a tornado, and a long-term widespread impact, such as famine. Chapter VI treats problems related to *recovery* from disaster: the kind of work which goes on after the impact, the emergence of informal ad hoc work groups, whether or not there is lasting social change, and the consequences of disaster for individuals.

Disasters can be conceptualized on a time continuum as shown below moving from left to right:

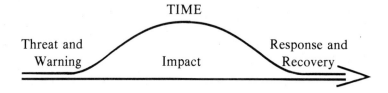

The division of Part II into three chapters based on the time periods shown above is a matter of convenience. In actual disasters the boundaries between warning, impact, and recovery are not so clear cut or simple.

In the top photo, a winter gale in December 1977 causes washout of beach and destruction of the seawall that protects properties at Ocean City, N.J. Below, sand has been dumped in an on-street parking area as a makeshift barrier to protect the street and nearby houses.

Citizens of a flood-threatened community cooperate in building a dike of sandbags.

CHAPTER IV

Preconditions

S ince the term "disaster" is used to refer to such things as the death of an individual, the impact of a hurricane, or the invasion of one nation by another, the definition of disaster is not a simple problem. The events we choose to call disasters differ in their (1) origin, (2) predictability, (3) frequency of occurrence, (4) speed of onset, (5) scope of impact, (6) destructiveness, (7) controllability, and (8) other variables. Some disasters are the result of naturally occurring environmental forces, others are largely the result of man-made causes, and still others may be both natural and man-made in origin. Disasters vary in their frequency of occurrence. There are differences in the speed of on set of disasters; some are instantaneous and offer little or no warning, while others are progressive in their development and provide a longer period of warning and preparation. The scope of impact varies: some disasters may involve whole societies, as in the case of nuclear attack or famine, while others may affect relatively few people. The destructive effects of disaster on people, physical objects, and the natural environment may differ enormously. It is possible to exercise much more control over some disasters than others; some can even be prevented (consider flood control using dams and levees). The diversity possible with disasters illustrates the difficulty of formulating a precise definition.

Disaster Defined

The term "disaster" has been described as a "sponge" concept. It can refer to the *event itself*, an earthquake or explosion; it can refer to *physical damage* which is variously defined by individuals and communities; or it can refer to the *social disruption* associated with the event (Quarantelli and Dynes 1970:-

328). Barton (1969) suggests viewing disaster as a particular type of collective stress situation; situations of collective stress are those in which "many members of a social system fail to receive expected conditions of life from the system" (Barton 1969:38). A social system, to complete Barton's set of definitions, is a "collectivity of human beings whose interaction maintains itself in identifiable patterns over a relatively long period of time" (Barton 1969:38).

Usually not considered disasters are the countless events such as death, auto accidents, and house fires, which—while tragic and stressful to the individuals suffering them—are not usually disruptive to the larger social order. Smelser (1962:85) called this kind of situation "structured ambiguity" and considered it a part of the social system involving those aspects of life in which it is expected that there will be irregularity, ambiguity, and unpredictability. The business world, for example, includes formal and informal rules which exist alongside irregularity and unpredictability. A general awareness of "structured ambiguity" is expressed in such common clichés as "those are the breaks of the game," "that's the way the cookie crumbles," and "that's life." "Structured ambiguity" may at times become extreme, yet continue to be accepted as part of the daily routine. For example, the response to regular bombing raids during World War II became more or less institutionalized. The raids, while very stressful, were seldom so disruptive as to lead to extreme social disorganization among target populations.

It is possible to see not only how much continuous stress and structured ambiguity there is, but also the structural means of dealing with it: the mass media report the daily activities of such organizations as police departments, fire departments, and hospitals. Whether it is through the control of traffic, the sirens of rescue vehicles, or the flow of information on such matters as traffic patterns, weather conditions, and pollution levels, everyone is brought into daily contact with the tasks assigned to these highly organized groups. While these events are often tragic, disorganizing, and stressful to those involved, they do not involve the total society. Instead the thousands, perhaps even millions, of such daily events are randomly distributed over the whole society. They are not highly focused and centered, and people are familiar with them and handle them through the well-established organizations mentioned above. Fire departments, for example, can either quench or control most of the fires that come to their attention. When there is an unusually large fire the help of other fire departments may be requested, involving many more people. It is only when the fire cannot be contained and controlled or places a very heavy demand requiring considerable outside help that the situation is likely to be viewed as a disaster.

Disasters introduce severe stress upon whole societies or significant parts of them. While the system is prepared to cope with daily "structured ambiguity," the disaster—a case of "unstructured ambiguity" (Smelser 1962:86)—is an irregular, abnormal event requiring considerable response and adjustment. It may be so severe that the existing social order is greatly altered or destroyed. Nevertheless, it is expected that the formal organizations which deal with the everyday stresses will also deal with disasters. Special agencies, such as the Civil Defense Organization, have at times been designed and established to cope with particular kinds of disaster. Such organizations often have little or no part in dealing with problems of everyday stress. Instead they concentrate on planning and training for the purpose of dealing with anticipated disasters. This planning is often based on the assumption that behavior patterns will be much like those typical of everyday stress, only more acute, although recent publications such as the newsletters *Natural Hazards Observer* and *Unscheduled Events* suggest the development of more realistic planning in recent years. It is also often assumed by planners that persons victimized by disasters will respond according to widely held stereotypes.

Stereotypes of Behavior in Disasters

The popular image of disaster has often centered on the theme of personal and social chaos. Such a view is frequently documented by isolated anecdotes used to prove the universality of such behavior; mass media focus on these kinds of incidents which suggest that individuals panic and lose their concern for others in their immediate social environment. They act irrationally in their own self interest or become hostile and take aggressive action toward others. Another facet of the image suggests that victims develop a "disaster syndrome," a docile childlike condition, and as a result must be "cared for" by some protective organization, acting in a parental way. The victims become psychologically disturbed by their traumatic experience, some temporarily, but others permanently. At the level of the community, the image of a "social jungle" prevails. People, hysterical and helpless, gradually shed the veneer of civilization and exploit others. It is said that looting is common, and outside authority is perhaps necessary to inhibit these resurgent primitive urges. It is assumed that many will flee from the disaster area in mass panic, leaving the community stripped of its human and natural resources (Wenger, et. al. 1975).

Recent research has cast doubt upon and even overthrown many of these notions about disaster. It has been found, for example, that panic is rare, and that greater problems develop from the convergence of people to the scene of disaster than from those fleeing it. Frequently the victims help themselves. They do most of the immediate rescue and relief work rather than wait in stunned passivity for outside help.

Threat and Warning of Approaching Disaster

A disaster can be totally unexpected and occur without any threat or warning at all, but many are preceded by a period of threat and warning. The indications of approaching disaster may be natural signs of various kinds, such as storm clouds and hail which indicate the approach of severe weather conditions. Natural signs of approaching danger are referred to as threats. Warnings may be considered "a system involving the origin, coding, and transmission of information about the existence of possible or probable danger, together with responses to, and feedback from responses to this information" (Williams 1964:79). The very presence of threats and warnings can be stressful to the potential victims. Moreover, the signs of approaching disaster are sometimes ambiguous, fragmentary, and subject to varied interpretation.

Threats and warnings can refer to a disaster whose impact, or its possibility, is *remote*. The potential victims find it difficult to assess the reality of the threats and warnings. There is, in fact, a large body of "doomsday" literature on the energy crisis, pollution, destruction of the ozone layer, nuclear war and proliferation of nuclear weapons, famine, and many others. Another topic of potential disaster is overpopulation: it is argued that population growth, if not controlled, will eventuate in famine, war, disease, epidemics, and general social disorganization. The situation has been compared to "a long, thin powder fuse that burns slowly and haltingly until it finally reaches the charge and then explodes" (Davis 1945:1). Concern with this potential disaster is certainly not new, as modern interest in the problem dates at least from the publication in 1798 of Thomas Malthus' *An Essay on the Principle of Population as it Affects the Future Improvement of Society, with Remarks on the Speculations of Mr. Godwin, M. Condorcet, and Other Writers.* As the title of the work shows, the threat of overpopulation was ambiguous even then since it is clear that others had different views of the problem. The most detailed and accurate signs of threat and warning of the dangers of overpopulation are primarily contained in census data and the interpretations made of them by demographers. These materials are not noted for their popular appeal to the reading public, and until very recently they have received little general attention. From the point of view of the general public there are few signs to suggest that continued population growth will end in disaster. While the view that uncontrolled population growth will lead to disaster is still controversial, concerned groups are attempting to deal with the threat using birth control clinics and social movement organizations like Zero Population Growth (ZPG). However, the general worldwide response today shows little concern with the possibility that population growth will lead to disaster, although overpopulation has commanded more attention in recent years.

The energy crisis provides another example of how difficult it is to assess and evaluate threatening signs and warnings of remote disasters. Superficially the shortage of petroleum seemed to develop with astonishing rapidity in the early 1970s. Warnings were, however, present many years before the appearance of the actual shortages (if they were indeed shortages). They were to be found in textbooks and reports on world and natural resources and even in more popular works such as Stuart Chase's *The Tragedy of Waste* (1925:247–52) published over 50 years ago.

These literary sources repeatedly sounded the warning that petroleum reserves are finite and exhaustible. Yet these assertions, like those of the demographers, were controversial and lacked wide reader appeal. The lack of personal experience in this country with the problems of overpopulation, famine, and energy shortages made it difficult for people to appreciate the reality of literary warnings. It is easy for people to dismiss warnings of remote events, especially when their acceptance is, in itself, stressful.

Threats and warnings of remote disaster can become a permanent part of life. Nuclear weapons have created an ever-present threat to human survival (Mills 1958). The invention of these weapons provided the potential for disaster far beyond any that has occurred in the world before. Shortly after the U.S. developed and used nuclear weapons, other countries began to manufacture them and continue to do so. One reaction on the part of authorities in the United States was to attempt to prepare for the consequences of nuclear attack. These preparations, which will be described in more detail later in the chapter, included the construction and marking of shelters, stockpiling of food and other supplies, marking of evacuation routes from cities, practice alerts, and drills. During the early 1960s, these activities reached their greatest height; and during the Cuban missile crisis of October 1962, warnings of a possible nuclear attack reached their highest intensity. Since then there have been other periods of heightened stress involving the possibility of nuclear attack but none so severe as the Cuban crisis. Now such threats and warnings have decreased to the point that the possibility is seldom mentioned, and it is a matter which commands little public attention. However, there is growing official concern over the possibility of terrorist organizations using nuclear weapons and the continuing proliferation of nuclear weapons in various countries. It is possible that the next few years will produce new warnings of possible disaster involving nuclear weapons. In becoming permanent, warnings of this kind of remote disaster become a part of the normal state of affairs for most people. As such they receive little more general attention than any other part of the daily round of life and may even be considered a dead issue (Lowther 1973).

In contrast to these long-range possibilities, threats and warnings frequently precede much more *immediate* disasters. However, the distinction between remote and short-term threats and warnings is not always clear cut, and there can be important technical developments over time which make possible longer periods of warning. For example, it has long been known along the Atlantic seaboard and the Gulf Coast that there was a hurricane season, and that during this time there was a high probability that a hurricane would strike somewhere. But it was not possible to be very precise about the time and place. The threat and warning times for hurricanes were quite short and involved such measures as drops in barometric pressure readings, heavy storm clouds, rising tides, and increasing wind velocity. With the development of aircraft, radar, and satellite observation of storms, it is now possible to be much more precise and give a much longer period of of warning. Awareness of a hurricane, which may lead to an offical warning, begins today with the observation of the storm forming in the South Atlantic Ocean. It is then followed throughout its development and movement across the Atlantic toward the American hemisphere until it is possible to tell potential victims that it will return to the open sea or strike within a very narrowly defined area. Although prediction of the path of a hurricane is not yet perfect, since the storm can take yet another direction just before its impact, today's techniques are vastly improved. In contrast to a situation only a few years ago in which there were only a few hours of warning, the present system usually permits several weeks of warning and preparation.

Similar changes have occurred in monitoring tornadoes and floods. A few years ago there was an acknowledged "tornado season" and "tornado alley"— the general area in which tornadoes were expected. But knowledge of an approaching tornado depended primarily upon the observation of natural signs associated with the event itself. Today, while there is much to be done before the establishment of a completely adequate warning service, it is possible to be much more precise in predicting severe storms such as tornadoes. The National Weather Service releases two kinds of messages: the watch and the warning. The watch is usually issued some hours before the storm has matured and covers an area of some 60,000 square kilometers. The warning refers to a storm that has actually been detected and confirmed, usually visually. (Severe Storms 1977:54–55)

Several weaknesses in the present system have been identified. One is that the severe storm watch covers too large an area and many people are alerted who do not need to be. The warning message often comes many hours after the watch and may provide inadequate time for reaction. Some storms may be so extensive that they require multiple watches and warnings which can lead to confusion and misunderstanding on the part of the public. Another inadequacy is that vital information as to specific towns along the most probable path of the storm and its expected time of arrival is not given. (Severe Storms 1977:55)

It has been suggested that an intermediate message, the "alert" be added.

The alert would be released one or two hours before the anticipated arrival of the storm after its speed, path, and magnitude are well understood. Such a system might be understood in a way analogous to "ready, set, go;" that is "watch, alert, warning." (Severe Storms 1977:56) An example of the manner in which this procedure might be defined geographically is "(a) Watch: within 50 miles of the affected area boundary for 90 percent of the events, (b) Alert: within 20 miles of the affected area boundary for 90 percent of the events, (c) Warning: within 5 miles of the affected area boundary for 90 percent of the events." (Severe Storms 1977:42)

Earthquakes provide another example of immediate disasters. In recent years there have been remarkable strides in knowledge of earthquakes. While they are still imperfectly understood, earthquakes were almost a complete mystery at the beginning of this century. Now it is possible to make rough predictive statements about them, to build resistant structures, to avoid especially dangerous building sites, and to specify how to behave during and after them (Yanev 1974). This kind of information is being used to prepare for expected earthquakes in the United States, especially in California (Turner 1976). As a part of this preparation there has been some research on the consequences of an earthquake prediction itself. Should a severe earthquake occur more or less as predicted, there would be a very substantial reduction in casualties and damage. But, the prediction, if the lead time was a year or more, would have disruptive consequences for the concerned area. Property values would decline and with them property tax revenues. It would become more and more difficult to obtain earthquake insurance and mortgages, and there would be a decline in the availability of investment capital. Along with this there would be a decline in employment opportunities and general business activity. These would lead to outward population movement, some permanent and some temporary. There would also be a reduction in public services since communities would no longer have the revenue to support them as in the past (Haas and Mileti 1976).

Even with improved monitoring, communications of threats and warnings often present varying degrees of ambiguity and uncertainty to potential victims. Authorities who transmit warnings have been urged to make their messages clear to avoid confusion. For example, in a city about to be flooded, the driver of a sound truck said, "An all-time record flood is going to inundate the city. You must evacuate immediately. (Pause) The . . . Theater is presenting two exciting features tonight. Be sure to see these pictures at the . . . Theater tonight" (Williams 1964:92). This is, to be sure, an extreme case. However, while messages of threat and warning can be relatively clear and unambiguous themselves, they (or their context) are likely to be ambiguous to some of the receivers in every case (Williams, 1964:91–93). In the population receiving warnings, there are different levels of education and perceptual sets which can lead to inappropriate responses.

A striking example of misunderstanding is provided by the warnings, and the actions taken in response to them, of the approach of Hurricane Audrey which caused extensive damage and killed over 400 people in lower Cameron Parish, Louisiana, in 1957. There were at least two important sources of misunderstanding in this case. Radio announcements from a local station in Lake Charles, Louisiana, told listeners on an evening program that there was no reason to worry that night. Persons in the area where the hurricane struck did not understand that the announcements were meant to apply to the Lake Charles area, some 60 miles away, and consequently they did not evacuate. Another source of confusion was the instruction from authorities for persons in low places to go to high ground. This was done by many persons in the area, and from their point of view they were following instructions. However, the impact area was very low (in some places actually below sea level), and "high ground" to the people who lived in the area consisted of ridges 6 to 12 feet above sea level. Unfortunately this was not high enough to provide much protection against the rising water (Williams 1964:80–1, 92–4).

Warning From Authorities and Informal Sources

It has been suggested that warnings may be best understood from a systems point of view. These systems included evaluation, dissemination, and response. The evaluation system involves the detection, measurement and collation of the available information about a potential disaster. This system can and often does include several social units within and external to the threatened place. Dissemination refers to the actual issuing of some kind of warning and includes decisions about who should be warned and about what dangers and in what way. Response refers to behavior which takes place as a result of a warning. Figure 4–1 shows how this set of systems might operate in an actual situation. As Figure 4–1 illustrates the two interrelated evaluation and dissemination subsystems activitate the response system. There is likely to be feedback between and among the systems and some parts may be bypassed. (Mileti, Drabek, and Haas 1975:35–39)

Evaluation

Warnings of impending disasters can come from *formal authorities* and/or from *informal communication networks*. It is part of the job of authorities,

FIGURE 4.1: Systems Model of a Warning System

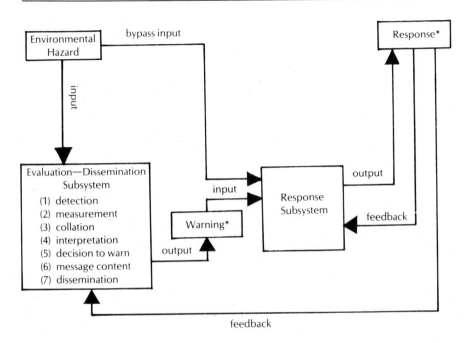

*Major dependent variables in the system.

Source: Mileti, Drabek, and Haas (1975: 37).

such as persons working in weather bureaus and police departments, to issue warnings and instructions to potential victims of impending disaster providing an opportunity for them to take protective action against its impact. The formulation of a warning depends on several factors: the number of persons and groups involved in the detection of the threat; the interpretation of the threat; and the transmission of information about it including instructions that can be used to prevent, avoid, or reduce the consequences of the approaching disaster.

Agencies or formal organizations which issue warnings of impending disasters face a number of problems while making a decision about the advisability of doing so. Questions they may consider include whether the threatened disaster will actually occur, and the possibility that the threatening signs are not really as ominous as they appear. Warning of an event which fails to materialize can reflect badly upon the issuing agency. Potential victims who receive warnings of approaching disasters which fail to materialize may come to disbelieve and distrust the issuing organization. There are problems too as to when and where the potential disaster will strike, and how much warning time people need to protect themselves. Agencies must consider the consequences if a disaster strikes without warning; how much good will it do to warn the threatened population if there is little time before impact? With this list of practical problems, it is not surprising that agencies with the responsibility to issue warnings are sometimes slow to do so. (Fritz 1961:664–665)

In organizations with a strongly centralized decision-making structure, there may be a delay in response before impact. Such agencies may not take action, such as issuing a warning, until officially ordered to do by the centralized authority. In cases characterized by ambiguity in inter-organizational communication, there may be delay in issuing warnings. The degree of clarity and completness of information sent between the organizations involved is directly related to the probability of issuing warnings as well as the speed of inter-organizational communication. In cases where organization officials have had prior experience in issuing warnings they may have a false sense of security which serves to lessen their sense of urgency. Organizations, such as police departments, which have high communication capabilities are more likely than others to emerge as key centers of warning and information. They are often reluctant, however, to share their information with other agencies. (Mileti, Drabek, and Haas 1975:39–42)

Dissemination

Once a decision has been made to warn a threatened population there is still the problem of transmitting the message. In a society such as the United States which has many channels of communication under the control of different organizations, the potential for confusion is enormous (Anderson 1969a). An example of communication difficulty in a situation with the potential of becoming a disaster rather than the extremely stressful family tragedy it was occurred in the Los Angeles area:

> One day, a fire was reported in the two-year-old home of John Broadbents. The operator mistakenly put the call through to the Orange County Fire Department. The department decided the call was outside its jurisdiction and passed it along to the police department of nearby Buena Park for action. The Buena Park Police desk made some quick checks and turned the call back to Orange County Fire Department. Eventually, the call got to where it was supposed to go in the first place: the Los Angeles Fire Department. The LAFD had a station only two blocks from

the Broadbent residence, but the house was wholly engulfed in flames by the time its engines arrived (Gordon 1963:335–6).

The content of the message may be such that it results in an emotional response more of apathy or terror than effective adaptation. The most effective message seems to be one which combines: (1) enough threatening information to generate optimal anxiety without causing defensive repression, and (2) assurance that preventive action will be effective (Chapman 1962:11). Clearly, the preparation of such a warning is no simple task.

Another complication is that there may be little feedback from the recipients of the message to the warning source(s) which could be used to gauge the effectiveness of the warning. Without such feedback it is difficult for the issuing agencies to gauge the effect of their warnings and make appropriate modifications. Even though there has been much improvement in recent years, much still needs to be done to improve disaster warning systems.

In addition to messages coming from formal agencies, there may emerge an informal system of warning communication; the content of their messages may or may not be similar. People may have more confidence in statements issued by some agencies than others, or they may feel there is more truth value in messages carried over informal communications systems. Often recipients will try, through informal means, to check the validity of official warnings.

Examples of the processes discussed above may be found in the description of the Worcester, Massachusetts tornado (Wallace 1956). At 5:08 p.m. on June 9, 1953, a tornado, which had formed some minutes earlier at Petersham, Massachusetts, crossed part of the city of Worcester. Its speed was about 25 miles an hour and it travelled some 3.5 miles through the northeastern corner of the town in eight minutes.

It was an unusually severe tornado with a diameter of about one-half mile. Within the impact area there were 804 reported casualties, including 66 killed, 327 major injuries, and 411 minor injuries. There were probably others who had minor injuries which were untreated or treated privately. It was estimated that the total casualty rate may have been as high as 25 percent of the population in the impact area. There were about 2,500 dwelling units in the impact area; 250 were completely destroyed, approximately 1,200 seriously damaged, and about 1,000 slightly damaged. In Worcester alone the cost of physical damage was estimated to be at least $32 million.

From the beginning of the tornado until it struck Worcester there was a period of almost an hour during which warnings could have been transmitted to local communities, even though its exact course could not have been precisely predicted. Instead, there was confusion and a lack of coordination in agencies which might have issued such warnings, and most people in Worcester had little or no advance notice of the approaching tornado. The telephone company offices in Worcester, which received warnings of a tornado in the vicinity before 3:45 p.m., alerted its linemen. At the *Worcester Telegram*, word was somehow received of this, and the paper's city editor went to the telephone company for verification. He was told of the alert of the linemen, but the telephone company would not tell him where they had received their information about the approaching tornado. The city editor then called the Associated Press in Boston and asked them to check with the local weather bureau. It acknowledged reports of severe storms but nothing more serious. However, people at the Boston Weather Bureau had discussed the possibility of a tornado early in the morning. The policy at the time was to refrain from the use of the word "tornado" for fear of inducing panic among potential victims. Furthermore, they were concerned with the consequences to them should the warning prove inaccurate (Williams, 1964:88–9). Weather reconnaisance aircraft from the nearby Air Force base apparently observed the tornado early in the afternoon. Protective actions were taken at the base, but warnings were not widely transmitted to other agencies. Also, there was a radio broadcast from an unidentified station which warned of a tornado close to Pittsfield, Massachusetts, southwest of Worcester. Shortly after the impact there was warning over a police radio system. So the warning of the community at large was short term and primarily provided by the tornado itself.

Many persons in Worcester observed and were impressed by the large hailstones, which are sometimes associated with tornadoes, that fell before the tornado's impact. Unfortunately, their significance was not generally known, and lacking prior experience the people did not interpret them as a sign of danger. Some did observe the cone of the approaching tornado, and many who recognized it did something to protect themselves; many used the short period of time before impact to warn others. Most of those who had warning received it through correct interpretation of visual signs of the approaching tornado, or through an informal communication system. The majority in the impact area, neither saw the tornado nor received informal warning. They did not realize that it was more than a hard summer storm until moments before impact when they could hear the noise of the tornado and see the air full of debris.

In short, an effective warning system:

> must be capable of detecting an impending disaster, determining its scope, deciding on the type of warning to be issued, and disseminating the warning. On its part, the community thus warned must be prepared to take appropriate action. All these components must function properly and quickly if lives and property are to be saved. The response time from detection to public action must be made short. While the weather service

does not have the responsibility for public response, it shares responsibility with other agencies for final delivery to the public, and it does have the responsibility of assessing how successful to the whole is its part of the effort (*Severe Storms* 1977:41)

Response

A successful warning also depends upon the reaction of those who are supposed to receive it. This involves variables such as the recipients' past experience and their current social and physical situation in relation to the communications they are getting about the danger situation. In this connection it has been pointed out that: "(1) even though people may be *listening* to the same warning, everybody *hears* different things; (2) people respond on the basis of how what they hear *stimulates* them to behave; and (3) people are stimulated *differently* depending on who they are with, or who or what they see." (Mileti, Drabek, and Haas 1975:43). Thus the response to disasters can be a bewildering array of possible behaviors. Three primary responses have, however, been identified: (1) denial of the threats and warnings; (2) effective adaptation to the threats and warnings; and (3) extreme emotion which may include terror, panic, and hysteria. These response have also been termed underreaction, effective preparatory behavior, and emotional sensitization (Janis 1962:55).

In denial the potential victims seize on any vagueness, ambiguity, or incompatibility in the warning message enabling them to interpret the situation optimistically. They search for more information that will confirm, deny, or clarify the warning message, and often they continue to interpret signs of danger as signs of familiar, normal events until it is too late to take effective precautions (Fritz 1961:665). A number of suggestions have been offered to explain denial. One is a lack of past experience with disaster. Another is a sense of personal invulnerability and immunity which leads to disbelief of the threats and warnings. Sometimes, potential victims are unable to adopt the new frame of reference required by the threatening signs. There may also be an overdependence on protecting authorities. Some potential victims are skeptical about the sources of warnings (Fritz 1961:665–6, Wolfenstein 1957:17–29). Persons can admit the painful prospect on a verbal level while denying it mentally. That is, denial may not be total, but the potential disaster may be given little thought, especially if the threat seems remote.

There are, of course, persons who do concern themselves with remote threat. Wolfenstein (1957:7–8) suggests their concern is an expression of some other emotional difficulty, while those with less inner strain are not as likely to worry about remote threat; the usual response to remote threat is denial.

Grinspoon (1964) employed this approach to explain why people in the United States did not build private fallout shelters when urged to do so by the federal government. He argued that it was not because the facts of the situation were unavailable, but because people could not accept the threatening implications of the world situation at that time.

In disasters characterized by a short period of threat and warning, denial, effective adaptation, and extremely emotional response also appear. In contrast to the more remote situation, if the threat is clearly defined and the warning issued shortly before impact, most people respond in an adaptive fashion if they know how. Denial and expression of extreme emotion involve a smaller number of people in the disaster with a short period of threat and warning (Fritz 1961:671; Wolfenstein 1957:8). It has also been found that as warnings increase in number, accuracy and/or information about choices for survival the probability of effective adaptation increases. The perceived time before impact is inversely related to the probability of adaptative response and those closet to the expected point of impact have a greater chance of making an effective response (Mileti, Drabek, and Haas 1975:48–50).

An example of effective adaptation to the threat of an impending disaster is provided by a study of the response to Hurricane Carla which struck the coast of Texas on September 11, 1961 (Moore et al. 1963). Hurricane Carla caused an estimated 45 deaths and property damage of more than $400 million. The death toll was much lower than expected, due to the long period of warning and the detailed evacuation plans which had been prepared after Hurricane Audrey in 1957. Approximately one-half million people left the impact area in one of the largest planned evacuations in the history of the country. In one county, 96 percent of the population was evacuated. Although there were "monumental" traffic jams, it was considered to be a calm and orderly operation overall.

The decision-making process leading to departure from the threatened area involved two sets of contradictory factors. One included the protection of family property, local responsibilities, pride, the ability to "take it," and a desire to see the storm. The other had to do with fear for physical safety, strong damage warnings from authorities along with official insistance or orders that people evacuate, and the observed departure of friends and neighbors.

Family deliberations were more important in the process of decision making than were the offical warnings which served as a basis for discussion. That is, word-of-mouth communication was probably the most important factor in evaluating the formal warnings. As there was local community discussion of the danger, groups of neighbors tended to travel and find shelter together. Members of larger and more authoritarian organizations were more likely to seek and accept official advice and warning than nonmembers. There was little role conflict among those holding positions of conflicting obligations in the decision to leave. Role conflict that was present tended to decrease or disappear after a decision was made. When the authorities were clear in their orders and advice, discussion tended to give way to action. Elderly persons were less likely both to want to leave and to do so, while women were more anxious to evacuate than men. High and low income families were more apt to remain in the home community than were middle income families. More people with previous disaster experience evacuated than those without such experience.

A more recent pair of studies (Drabek 1968, Drabek and Boggs 1968) of the June 16, 1965 Denver flood, a disaster of much smaller scope than Hurricane Carla, revealed findings similar to those described above. The flood was caused by heavy rains in the mountains. There was little or no rain in Denver nor was there much experience with or expectation of flooding. However, some 3,700 families were evacuated before the flood and there were no deaths.

The warning process involved a number of sources and authorities, and there was considerable confusion. One source of warning was authorities, primarily the police (local, county, and state) and a few fire units. The content of their messages, communicated through public address systems, was varied, but they emphasized the immediacy of the threat and the necessity to evacuate quickly. An informal system of warning communication emerged with 26 percent learning of the approaching flood from friends, neighbors, and relatives. Nearly 50 percent received their warning information from radio and T.V.

Regardless of the source, the initial reaction was one of skepticism (less if the first warning came from an official source). Many families interpreted the first information in a way which permitted them to believe the approaching event was nonthreatening. Most (61%) made some effort to confirm the initial warning: 9 percent attempted direct contact with the authorities to get more information, more than 50 percent used indirect means including radio and T.V., and a large proportion—43 percent—appealed to their peers who had either no information, less information, or contradictory information. Some attempted to confirm their initial information through looking at the river and/or watching the neighbors and police. There was also confirmation by observing police roadblocks or receiving calls from relatives.

Evacuation took place in several ways. In some cases it was by default; those who left to look at the river could not return due to roadblocks. Some 42 percent of the evacuated families stayed with their relatives, many of whom had extended invitations, while only 3.5 percent went to an organized shelter. The lower the social class of the family the more likely they were to go to their relatives' homes, older and younger families were more likely to go their relatives than middle-aged families, and Spanish-American families tended to evacuate to homes of relatives more frequently than Anglos.

The evacuees tended to leave as family units rather than as individuals. One basis for deciding to leave was to reach a general family decision; another was compromise. In cases where a family member had strong doubts about the reality of the threat, he or she would agree to leave to pacify the other(s).

Research such as that described above has led to a number of generalizations about response to warnings (Mileti, Drabek, and Haas 1975). Among them is the finding that people attempt to obtain additional information and seek confirmation through different sources. A warning is more likely to be believed if it comes from some official and recognized source. For example, people are more likely to believe an earthquake prediction issued by a scientist than by an astrologer or psychic (Haas and Mileti 1976:5). Belief increases also as the content of messages is accurate and consistent over several warnings and as the number of warnings increases. Their creditability increases too as the physical environment changes correspondly and as others behave as if they believed the warnings. Older individuals are less likely to believe warnings (Friedsam 1961, 1962). Urbanites are more accepting of warnings than small town people or urban dwellers with small town backgrounds. Women are thought to respond more emotionally than men and to be more willing to evacuate, if that is what is required.

Organizational Response to Threat and Warning of Approaching Disaster

The activities of most formal organizations are a part of the normal on-going state of affairs, some are involved in problems of disaster also, and the activities of a few are almost entirely limited to disasters. That is, established formal organizations, such as the U.S. National Guard often take an active part in disasters, and are expected to do so. The threatened impact of a disaster may also result in the formation of a new organization like the Civil Defense organization. Organizational involvement varies in complex ways differing in scope, intensity, preparation, social ideologies, time stages of disaster, and others.

Occasionally authorities do try to plan for disasters in which the threat is remote, either by establishing new formal organizations, or by expanding existing organizations to take on planning activity. Such programs compete with ordinary activities (Fritz 1960:662). For example, the Civil Defense program in the United States was unable to involve more than a small proportion of the total population in preparatory activity until possession of nuclear weapons was no longer exclusive to the United States. Then a civil defense program was established to set up a system of warnings and preparations to reduce the consequences of an attack involving nuclear weapons. In the late 1950s and early 1960s interest in the Civil Defense program was stimulated by tense and threatening international situations such as the Berlin crisis of 1961 and the Cuban missile crisis of October 1962. Civil defense became a topic of public discussion; it received a great deal of attention in the mass media, and the Federal Government was very interested in developing the program.

The Civil Defense program was very active and offices of the organization became a part of the government structure in nearly every community in the United States. There was much cooperation from social scientists, both in conducting research on natural disasters under the belief that knowledge gained would provide principles that could be applied to nuclear attack, and in helping with various aspects of the planning (e.g., Fritz 1960, Altman et al. 1960). In fact, this interest had much to do with the development of contemporary disaster research.

Elaborate evacuation plans were developed for large cities and then abandoned, as the manned bomber was made obsolete by the missile. After 1961 the administration enlarged its shelter program, with the objectives of providing a space for every person by 1967 and persuading people to accept the idea of using shelters. This was done by stocking the available shelters with food, water, medical supplies, and other goods; constructing shelters in existing Federal buildings; marking all shelters with signs; and campaigning nationally to persuade private individuals to construct fallout shelters at their own expense. Warning systems were developed; special radio frequencies, Conelrad 640 and Conelrad 1240, were set aside for warning use only, and for a time they were printed on the dials of all radios sold in the U.S. Warning tones were developed and often tested over radio and T.V. programs were envisioned for training people to deal with the many tasks anticipated as a result of nuclear attack, including fire fighting and detection of radioactivity levels. Associated with this was the publication of an extensive literature designed to help the potential victims. However, the effort to actively involve the population of the United States in the Civil Defense program was not very successful. For example, in spite of intense pressure from the Federal Government, less than one-half of one percent of the population had built private fallout shelters in 1961, and less than five percent had plans to do so (Withey 1962:25). Since then, Civil Defense has become active in a wider range of disaster recovery called "normalization of threat." The emergent pattern is an amalgamation of the known and familiar with the unknown and unfamiliar through processes of assimilation and accommodation (Anderson 1968:299).

The consequences of many disasters can be reduced, controlled, or avoided through adequate warning and preparation. Prior planning for disasters can serve to reduce organizational stress and make it possible to issue more effective warnings (Haas and Drabek 1973:266). There are some groups of people who experience more or less repeated disasters such as floods, hurricanes, typhoons, coal mine disasters, and during World War II, repeated bombing raids. When the repetition of disasters reduces the danger and loss felt, people develop a fatalistic attitude. In situations like these, the response to threat and warning and the preparation for disaster take on an institutional character and include such devices as informal mutual aid codes. There emerges among the people involved a set of realistic expectations of disaster and its consequences which has been termed the "disaster culture" (Moore et al. 1963:195–213). In all situations, as pointed out above, potential victims will have different levels of knowledge. There are people, for example, who rely almost entirely on others rather than the mass media, and some who lack motivation to seek any information (Spitzer and Denzin 1965).

A number of findings show that in organizations with a strongly centralized decision-making structure there may be a delay in response before impact. Such agencies may not take action, as issuing warnings, until officially instructed to do so. Where there is ambiguity in inter-organizational communication, there is delay in issuing warnings. The degree of clarity and completeness of information sent between organizations involved is directly related to the probability of issuing warnings as is the speed of interorganizational communication (Mileti, Drabek, and Haas 1975).

Summary and Conclusions

Ordinarily there are thousands of individual and small group stressful events which place no serious strain upon the total system or community. They are scattered and not focused in one area, and there are well established institutional means for dealing with them. But a disaster is extremely stressful and can place a system or community under severe strain. Sometimes, but not always, the impact of a disaster is preceded by a period of threat and/or warning. It can be very short or it can be so long that it becomes a permanent part of the society. The threats and warnings of approaching disaster can be clear and distinct or ambiguous to those who receive them. This can be the case both when the source is natural signs and when some official authority transmits the information. The reactions to threat and warning fall into three broad classes: (1) *denial* (2) *effective adaptation*, and (3) *extreme emotion*. Denial is believed to be the most common response to the threat of remote disaster and effective adaptation the most common response to threats and warnings of short-term disasters. Formal organizations also respond to threat and warning of disaster. Some are created or have as a part of their regular acitivity the purpose of dealing with disasters including the transmission of warnings. Potential victims respond to threat and warning of disasters using the cultural definitions prevailing in their own cultures. That is, the response to threat and warning of approaching disaster, as well as the behavior during the impact and recovery periods, takes place in a specific social situation. The characteristics of the specific social situation play a part in the determination of reactions. Reactions to threatened disaster are not random, unordered, and wholly immediate, but follow from the principal cognitive, affective, and evaluative schemes.

A Coast Guard lifeboat on a rescue mission battles the surf off the coast of the state of Washington.

The aftermath of a midwestern tornado. Notice that even the trees have been stripped bare.

CHAPTER V

Impact

The periods of threat and warnings, impact, and recovery in a disaster may be clearly definable, or they may be difficult to distinguish. A famine may develop over a number of years as food shortages increase, and recovery may begin very slowly as yields gradually improve. In contrast, a tornado approaches and impacts in a short period of time and the recovery period usually begins immediately afterward. Like tornadoes, some other disasters are nearly instantaneous, while some have impacts that may last for hours, days, or even years. Still others have impacts that are repetitive. The amount of warning time, the extent of preparation, and the organization and initiation of recovery efforts are all tied to the nature of a disaster's impact and the extent of damage.

When the impact of a disaster is instantaneous, it may have occurred without any warning at all. The completely unexpected industrial explosion may be taken as a prototype of this kind of event. One of the earliest well documented cases is Prince's (1920) study of the explosion of a munitions ship after it collided with another ship at Halifax, Nova Scotia in December 1917. It exploded with devastating consequences, killing and wounding thousands of the unsuspecting population of Halifax. There was no warning, impact was instantaneous, and recovery was halting and required a very long period of time. This situation may be contrasted with disasters in which impacts are either repetitive or long lasting.

There are places which have annual or nearly annual floods, frequent mine disasters, or repeated bombing raids in time of war. In repetitive disasters the victimized populations adjust to the stress and develop institutional patterns to meet the demands of the disaster. But this is not to say that the impact of a disaster can always be accommodated without extensive change or even destruction of the impacted social order.

101

There are also long-term disasters whose impact may last for years, such as epidemics, and military invasions and occupations. The long-term disaster has attracted much more attention from historians than sociologists, although there are significant exceptions such as the work of Sorokin (1942) and Barton (1969:11–21). It has been suggested that when the impact of a disaster is of very long duration it may lead to intense pressure from its victims for radical changes in existing social arrangements.

Extent of Damage

Just as the impact of a disaster may last for varying periods of time, so also may the damage vary considerably. It may be so slight that it is hardly more than an accident, or it may be so vast as to destroy virtually all life. An industrial explosion may be confined to a small area with little loss of life and physical property, while an epidemic disease may take more than one-third of a population as is estimated to have happened in a short period of time in fourteenth century Europe (Petersen 1975:422). The disaster impact does not necessarily cause both high loss of life and high loss of property. An epidemic may leave intact practically all physical property while a typhoon may cause no deaths but leave extensive physical damage.

At times it is difficult to clearly assess the extent of damage since the consequences of a disaster often appear different to persons in an impact area and those outside it. The tendency to exaggerate damage and loss of life, especially in media reports, increases with distance from the disaster. Furthermore, there are some disasters which have not happened, a melt down in a nuclear plant, for example, but which have some potential of occurrence. In such cases, damage prediction is very difficult and may be impeded by political interests and controversy.

Behavior During Impact

The above discussion of the complexities associated with the impact of disasters reveals some of the difficulties of understanding what happens during this period. Much of the research has concentrated on disasters whose impact was short and resulted in little damage.

Among the short-term disasters whose impacts have been extensively studied are tornadoes. There are some 700 to 1200 tornadoes in the United States every year. The majority of them are small, last only a few minutes, and cause very little damage. Most destruction from tornadoes results from the infrequent large ones which can travel over 100 miles and have a width of over a mile (Severe Storms 1977:35).

The impact of a tornado generally lasts about 60 seconds. There are three major phases of impact: (1) a period of extremely high wind, (2) a period of low air pressure, and (3) a return period of extremely high wind. A tornado's front wall of wind breaks windows, plasters everything with mud, and drives debris into people and structures. It knocks down trees, bends flag poles, and rolls over cars, buildings, and people. Anything still standing after a tornado's first wind has been weakened by this initial onslaught.

This is followed by low pressure which occurs after the front wall has passed by. In the center of a tornado the air pressure is several pounds lower than the pressure outside. In places with no means of equalization such as open windows, chimneys, and doors the drop in surrounding air pressure means the sudden application of a great internal force which causes structures to explode outward. Persons caught in this situation may have an impression that things are floating away. Such was the experience of a child who was with her mother and father in the kitchen when a tornado struck Worcester, Massachusetts in 1953.

> The mother and daughter were cooking supper, and disregarded the first high wind as being only a bad thunder storm. They had just put the potatoes for baking in the oven when the pressure differential came. A strange thing happened: 'the potatoes came out of the oven and went over and hit my daddy on the head' (Wallace 1956:44–5).

The third stage begins when the high wind of the back wall of a tornado hits. It finishes the destructive process begun by the first two phases. During this period already weakened structures are further demolished.

The tornado which struck in White County, Arkansas, on March 21, 1952, was one of a series which passed across six states on the same day. It was extensively studied. The tornado killed 46 persons, destroyed nearly 350 houses, and damaged about 600. It came late in the afternoon, around 5:30 p.m., and of the 1500 people living in small towns and farms in its path, about one-third had more than a minute's warning (usually two to three minutes), one-third had less than a minute's warning, and one-third had no warning (Barton 1969:3).

How did people behave during impact? The respondents in the impact area were asked to report their own reactions. As Table 5.1 shows only a small proportion behaved in some "uncontrolled" manner. Instead, 70 percent were "controlled," although 51 percent of these were either highly or mildly "agitated." Male respondents reported themselves as being in better control than female, although the differences are generally small. None of the male respondents acknowledged an "uncontrolled" response while only 4 percent of the females did. To ascertain whether this might reflect a desire to avoid admitting deviation from socially approved behavior—remaining in control during severe stress situations—the respondents were asked to report on the behavior of those with them during impact. Table 5.2 shows a close correspondence between the self-reported reactions and the respondents' reports of the reactions of others during the impact. For example, 25 percent of the male respondents said that they were in a "highly agitated state but behavior controlled" and females with males during impact reported 28 percent of males were in that condition. But female respondents said that 3 percent of the males they were with were in a "highly agitated state involving uncontrolled behavior," while no males admitted being in such a condition. It is important to point out that there were no reports of panic behavior and the percentage of uncontrolled behavior is very small in both tables.

Table 5.1: Percent of Respondents Who Report Certain Affective Reactions of Their Own During Impact

Affective Reaction Reported	Percent of all Respondents	Percent of Female Respondents	Percent of Male Respondents
Highly agitated state but behavior controlled	32	39	25
Mildly agitated state but behavior controlled	19	18	21
Highly agitated state— degree of control unstated	6	10	3
Mildly agitated state— degree of control unstated	6	6	6
Highly agitated state— involving uncontrolled behavior	1	3	—
Mildly agitated state— involving uncontrolled behavior	1	1	—
Confusion, uncertainty, bewilderment	7	6	8
Shocked, stunned, dazed	6	9	3
Shocked, stunned, dazed— due to physical concussion	1	1	—
Unconscious	1	3	—
Miscellaneous—anger, resignation, hostility	4	4	4
Calm, unexcited, self-controlled	19	12	26
Number of Interviews	N=139	N=67	N=72

Source: Fritz and Marks (1954:44).

**Table 5.2:   Percent of Respondents Reporting Certain Affective
Reactions of Adults of Opposite Sex Present with Them During Impact**

Reaction Reported	Percent of Male Respondents—Reports on Adult Females	Percent of Female Respondents—Reports on Adult Males
Highly agitated state but behavior controlled	32	28
Highly agitated state involving uncontrolled behavior	11	3
Shocked, stunned, dazed	1	3
Calm, cool, unexcited	3	4
Number of Interviews	N=72	N=67

Source: Fritz and Marks (1954:32).

Other research on behavior during sudden disasters suggests that disaster victims have a feeling of centrality; they feel the disaster has happened only to them and that its impact is limited to their own immediate environment (Fritz 1961:674–5, Kinston and Rosser 1974:422).

Typhoons (the term "hurricane" is used for the same kind of storm in the Atlantic) are a well known and repetitive threat on Yap in the Western Caroline Islands of the Pacific Ocean. Schneider (1957) studied reactions to four typhoons which struck Yap on November 2 and 10 and December 3, 1947, and January 13, 1948. Since Yap is a high island and not subject to overall flooding, there are usually no deaths or injuries during a typhoon. There were no deaths during Schneider's stay, but there was extensive property damage and considerable danger from flying objects such as coconuts and branches. As the storm approached the island and after preparations had been made (mostly religious rituals and the protection of canoes), the Yap victims took refuge in their houses. The houses provided good protection and when they did collapse, it occurred slowly enough for people to get out and seek shelter in another place.

Schneider observed that inside the houses during impact there was an atmosphere of tension which lacked concrete or specific manifestations. Even though there was little to fear, no one enjoyed the experience. There was no hilarity, joking, singing, or other kind of jollity. The Yaps described their feelings as those of confinement, boredom, and strained inactivity. This feeling and atmosphere carried over to the period after impact. There were no signs of the apathy and daze reactions, discussed in Chapter VI, which have been observed in the United States after impact.

Disasters of extremely long impact have undergone little research. A notable exception is Sorokin's *Man and Society in Calamity* (1942) which is the primary source of the following discussion. There are, in Sorokin's view, four major calamities or disasters: (1) war, (2) revolution, (3) pestilence, and (4) famine. These events are likely to have lengthy impacts and may well occur together.

During such events Sorokin argues that victims' thoughts become focused on the calamity and the things associated with it. They become insensitive to extraneous things and are totally concerned with the calamity. There is a weakening or elimination of all contrary desires and wishes. If the calamity is a famine, for example, persons talk and think primarily of food. There is a tendency for the unity of the self to disintegrate along with a growth of mental disorderliness and disorganization.

As the impact continues, there may be a breakdown of the most powerful values. In famines, persons may do anything for food, even engage in cannibalism in societies in which it is usually viewed with horror. But, as Table 5.3 shows, Sorokin believed the proportion of people who violate the strongest and most deeply held values is very small even under the greatest stress. Instead, many choose to die of starvation. For values which are strongly negative, but not as strong as the prohibition against cannibalism in the United States, there is, according to Table 5.3, a much greater relaxation of old standards. The data in Table 5.3 should be treated with caution since they are primarily based on speculation. They do provide a bench mark against which future research may be compared.

While most people hold to their values, Sorokin also sees calamity as a primary source of social change. Calamity provides a favorable situation for rapid transformation of social institutions and the emergence of radically different social forms.

The impact of such extreme disasters often leads to a sharp increase in the death rate and to depopulation as persons attempt to escape the afflicted area. This may lead to increased government control, especially in those places where there is the greatest emergency. In revolutions the increase in the death rate and depopulation may facilitate the destruction of the previous system of social stratification and can lead to an extensive reallocation of wealth.

The effects of these events are seldom spread evenly over the victimized population, and the responses are also varied. Anyone who has watched contemporary TV films of famine in Africa has noticed that often among the starving are soldiers not suffering from any lack of nourishment. While some persons might use their weapons to take what food there is, others are "ennobled" (Sorokin 1942:159) by their response to the stress of the impact.

Indeed Sorokin emphasizes both "positive" and "negative" responses to calamity. During such crises there are likely to appear social movements of both a religious and utilitarian character. He says:

Table 5.3: How Famine Influences Our Behavior

Activities Induced by Starvation	Percent of Population Succumbing to Pressure of Starvation	Percentage of Population Resisting Such Pressure
Cannibalism (in non-cannibalistic societies)	Less than one third of 1 percent	More than 99 percent
Murder of members of the family and friends	Less than 1 percent	More than 99 percent
Murder of other members of one's group	Not more than 1 percent	Not less than 99 percent
Murder of strangers who are not females	Not more than 2 to 5 percent	Not less than 95 percent
Infliction of various bodily and other injuries on members of one's social group	Not more than 5 to 10 percent	Not less than 90 percent
Theft, larceny, robbery, forgery, and other crimes against property which have a clear-cut criminal character	Hardly more than 7 to 10 percent	Hardly less than 90 to 93 percent
Violation of various rules of strict honesty and fairness in pursuit of food, such as misuse of rationing cards, hoarding, and taking advantage of others	From 20 to 99 percent depending upon the nature of the violation	From 1 to 80 percent
Violation of fundamental religious and moral principles	Hardly more than 10 to 20 percent	From 80 to 90 percent
Violation of less important religious, moral, juridical, conventional and similar norms	From 50 to 99 percent	From 1 to 50 percent
Surrender or weakening of most of the aesthetic activities irreconcilable with food-seeking activities	From 50 to 99 percent	From 1 to 50 percent
Weakening of sex activities especially coitus	From 70 to 90 percent during prolonged and intense starvation	From 1 to 30 percent
Prostitution and other highly dishonorable sex activities	Hardly more than 10 percent	Hardly less than 90 percent

Source: Sorokin (1942:81).

"... the principle steps in the progress of mankind toward a spiritual religion and a noble code of ethics have been taken primarily under the impact of great catastrophes. The periods of comparative stability, order, and material well-being, and hence of complacency, have scarcely ever given birth to a truly great religion or a truly lofty moral ideal (Sorokin 1942:226).

The discussion above makes clear that there is still much to learn about behavior during the impact of disasters. Differences are to be expected in length and force of impact, and certainly there are significant cross-cultural variances. Much of what is known now is tentative and even speculative. Sorokin, for example, provides an important benchmark against which future research might be compared with the data presented in Table 5.3, but he does not indicate a source for the material. However tentative and speculative, Sorokin's table suggests little "uncontrolled" and panicky behavior just as do the data from the White County Arkansas tornado study. Yet panic does occur and presents a special problem.

The Problem of Panic

There is a widespread popular stereotype that the impact of a disaster will be accompanied by panic (Mileti, Drabek, and Haas, 1975:58). It holds that a response to the extreme stress of a disaster impact is highly irrational flight characterized by wild terror-stricken behavior. This view pervades much official thinking, has been reinforced by many journalistic accounts, and, to some extent, is also a part of the sociological literature. Recent research has revealed, however, that panic is rare during and after the impact of a disaster. (Fritz and Marks 1954; Fritz 1961:671; Drabek 1968:3) Before considering what conditions cause panic, we must first consider several ways in which panic has been conceptualized.

What is panic? The term is used to refer to events as diverse as the response to severe business and economic difficulties, lynch mobs, mass hysteria, military retreats, and theater and night club crowds fleeing a fire (Quarantelli 1954:267–8). Some years ago it was suggested that panic originates in a crisis, an unusual event considered by the participants to be a source of danger. It was considered to be behavior characterized by a lack of "regimental leadership" (LaPiere 1938:437–40). It has an irrational aspect in that "as a collective 'solution' to a crisis problem panic behavior is never expedient either in terms of the individual members or in terms of the group." (LaPiere 1938:441)

Quarantelli (1957:189–93) identified several aspects of panic behavior. The panicky person defines the threatening situation as one which directly and clearly jeopardizes his or her physical survival even though there may not be a real danger. Panic participants are concerned with future, not past dangers. Their interest is in the possibility of escape routes becoming blocked and potential entrapment, and thus feel that they must act quickly. They are highly self-conscious. Their fear is unchecked and uncontrolled and they feel they cannot handle the threat except through flight. Panicky people are aware enough of their activities to be able to direct themselves away from the threat. They may flee toward a danger, as flames before an exit, in order to escape worse threat or because they perceive it to be the only alternative. Their flight does not continue till exhaustion, but stops when safety has been attained. Since the panicky person's entire thoughts are focused on escape, his or her behavior is nonrational rather than rational or irrational. Panic, though considered nonrational, might be the most appropriate response both for the individual and the collectivity. Finally, panic is nonsocial; participants are so self-centered that the usual forms of social behavior are dropped in favor of highly individual responses.

In a more recent major work, panic was conceptualized as "a collective retreat from group goals into a state of extreme privatization" (Lang and Lang 1961:83). The Langs consider panic or the collective retreat to occur in a series of stages.

The first of these begins with the impact of danger. Some groups may be *panic-prone* and a group may panic even though it has resisted similar dangers before. Panic-proneness refers to predisposing conditions and the orientation of potential victims to the danger. These are conditions that weaken the members' ability to resist, Including fatigue, undernourishment, exposure, and the loss of friends and leadership (see also Strauss 1944:317). The victims' orientation to the danger—that is, whether they believe it manageable or not—is extremely important. When the danger is thought to be unmanageable, its mere expectation may lead to panic.

The second stage, *privatization and regression*, is characterized by the undermining of group bonds. Among causative agents at this stage are darkness, which prevents people from knowing what has happened, and noise, which interferes with communication.

The third stage is characterized by a *disruption of group norms*. When primary group norms are well articulated with those of a larger group, resistance to panic is high, especially if the norms of the larger group emphasize traits such as loyalty, selfless devotion, and patriotism. Disruption of these normative standards helps create a situation in which people think only of themselves.

Finally, in the fourth stage, *contagion and mutual facilitation appear*. Persons who display signs of extreme fear communicate their feelings to others with consequences that can be quite unnerving and lead to panic (Lang and Lang 1961:98–108).

Another view of panic was developed by Smelser (1962:131–69), whose approach follows the *value-added process*. Panic is "a collective flight based on a hysterical belief. Having accepted a belief about some generalized threat, people flee from established patterns of social interaction in order to preserve life, property, or power from that threat." (Smelser 1962:131)

The beginning of the process is *structural conduciveness*. To ascertain the presence of structural conduciveness, questions should be asked about avenues of communication, escape routes, and the way things are customarily done. Conduciveness is followed by *strain* resulting from a threat perceived as immediate and ambiguous, and whose exact dimensions are unknown. The threat can be considered uncontrollable. Indeed many natural forces are beyond control. The response to structural conduciveness and strain, however, is not necessarily panic. Instead it can be hostility or resignation.

Added to strain, in the next step, is *anxiety:* "the generalized element of a hysterical belief" (Smelser 1962:146). It is most apparent in situations of immediate physical danger and is reflected in tenseness. Again it should be noted that the response to anxiety will not necessarily be panic. A precipitating factor is needed to change anxiety to fear. It must "confirm" anxiety and provide evidence for the existence of a serious threat. Thus, the function of the precipitating event is to create a definite belief in an imminent danger. This "hysterical belief" becomes a shared belief through being communicated among those in a situation.

The last condition necessary for panic is *mobilization for flight*. Often a kind of leadership, which provides a model, appears at this stage. Someone, for example, may start to run and others follow. Throughout his discussion of the value-added process leading to panic, Smelser emphasizes that other responses than panic may occur even up to the point of mobilization for flight. An important physical aspect of structural conduciveness is whether or not a feeling of approaching entrapment develops among the potential victims. If escape routes are completely open there will be no panic, although there may be terror and infantile regression. Nor can there be panic if there is no way for information, opinions, and emotional states to be communicated from one to another possible participant.

Another approach holds that panic is not helter-skelter flight but movement away from some specific danger. There is no attempt to deal directly with the danger itself, but to avoid it. It is more nonsocial than antisocial as ordinary social relationships are disregarded. There can be social interaction during panic, but it is elementary and is considered the opposite of organized group behavior. It is oriented toward the future and does not include the consideration of alternatives. It is not rational, but from the point of view of the participants it is. There are three general conditions which can, but do not necessarily, lead to panic behavior. The first is when persons see an immediate and severe danger to themselves; second, the potential victims must believe that escape routes are limited and about to be blocked; and third, the potential victims must receive contradictory information about the possibility of open escape routes (Chapman 1962:13). Finally, during panic itself there may be a communication failure from front to rear. That is, people at the rear exert strong pressure on the front which causes the people closest to the exits to be crushed and smothered (Turner and Killian 1972:83–4). Mintz (1951:151) has described the process as follows:

> If a few individuals begin to push, the others are apt to recognize that their interests are threatened; they can expect to win through to their individual rewards only by pressing their personal advantages at the groups expense. Many of them react accordingly, a vicious circle is set up, and the disturbance spreads . . . As the behavior of the group becomes increasingly disorderly, the amount of noise is apt to increase and communication may then become so difficult that no plan for restoring order can emerge.

Orson Welles at the radio microphone in 1938.

Panic, even though rare, clearly does occur. Some of the best examples come from the accounts of what happened when rapidly spreading fires, or imagined fires, took place in confined places. A well-known example is the Iroquois Theater fire which occurred in December 1903, killing about 600 persons. During the performance the stage suddenly became engulfed with flames as the curtains caught fire. Someone shouted "fire," and people pressed toward the exits. Some doors had rusted shut and others were locked or poorly marked resulting in hundreds of deaths as people packed themselves together at the closed exits. The fire itself was quickly extinguished (Turner and Killian 1957:-96–7). Another extremely well-known example is that of the Coconut Grove Night Club fire in Boston on November 28, 1942. The fire began when a bus boy lit a match to replace a light bulb removed by a patron. The match ignited an artificial palm tree, and from it the fire spread rapidly. Because of the resulting panic, 488 people died in the overcrowded night club (Veltford and Lee 1943). The May 28, 1977 fire in the Beverly Hills Supper Club seems to present a parallel case. The fire, presumably resulting from faulty wiring and highly flammable material, caused 164 deaths. The club was overcrowded and there was panic as the patrons blocked the exits.

One situation which has received considerable attention is the panic provoked by a radio dramatization of H. G. Wells' *The War of the Worlds*. It was an hour-long program in which a series of "news bulletins" broke into a "regular" program of dance music. The story, broadcast on October 30, 1938, proceeded from believable events to more and more improbable occurrences. It wasn't difficult to accept "atmospheric disturbance" as a real event, nor was it immediately possible to discredit a reported seismographic shock of earthquake intensity, or the news that a huge meteorite had splintered trees in its fall. As the radio program unfolded and events became more incredible, "on-the-spot reporters" bolstered their credibility by indicating that they too had difficulty in believing their eyes. When the top of the "meteorite" unscrewed, the listeners were encouraged to experience the announcer's own astonishment. He gradually became more hysterical as he described what was evidently a "Martian war cylinder" 38 yards in diameter, armed with a "flame ray" which instantly killed 40 onlookers and 6 state troopers. An army of 7,000 men eventually battled the single Martian machine at Grovers Mill; the announcer said in a choked voice that there were only 120 survivors, and finally stated that "as incredible as it may seem" scientific observations and his own eyesight lead "to the inescapable assumption that those strange beings ... are the vanguard of an invading army from Mars" (Cantril 1940:74). An official from Washington, as part of the broadcast, encouraged the nation to remain calm, and explained that everything possible to safeguard the country was being done. But the panic had begun.

Though the program had been conceived as a Halloween stunt, it caused a panic of "national proportions." In spite of four announcements indicating the fictitious nature of the incident, the events reported in the broadcast were taken as real by many people, and their reaction was totally unanticipated. Over a million people reportedly panicked as a result of a "tidal wave of terror that swept the nation." In Philadelphia, women and children ran screaming from their homes, and in New Jersey families fled to their basements to avoid poison gas. Others cried, hospitals were "swamped" with people—some in shock—and highways were supposedly jammed with fleeing motorists throughout the Northeast. The Federal Communications Commission later said the program was "regrettable." Of those taken in by the hoax, many were ashamed of their gullibility, some were bitter, and others were amused by the entire episode.

Many people may wonder if such a thing is still possible; could people be similarly fooled today? In 1971 a localized version of the *War of the Worlds* was broadcast by radio station WKBW in Buffalo. Despite much advanced publicity, the station was deluged with telephone calls from nervous listeners, and the police station received more than 100 messages (John 1973). However, it has been suggested recently that panic under such conditions is unlikely and that reports of mass panic in response to the *War of the World's* broadcast may have been greatly exaggerated (Rosengren et al. 1975).

Cause of the *War of the Worlds* panic were believed to lie in the general social conditions of the time, including the economic depression and rising international tensions. The radio broadcast itself was extremely realistic. The use of "news bulletins" inserted into an ongoing program was a common practice of the time. The radio play also featured persons of authority, that is, actors pretending to be astronomers, generals, and so on, which added an air of reality.

Persons who did not become frightened or disturbed or panicked were said to have a greater degree of "critical ability" than those who did not resist. Critical ability refers to a "capacity to evaluate the stimulus in such a way that they were able to understand its [the program's] inherent characteristics so they could judge and act appropriately" (Cantril 1940:111-2).

A similar event recently occurred in Sweden when, on November 13, 1973, the Swedish radio company presented a program about a fictitious future breakdown of a nuclear power plant at Barseback in the south of Sweden. The presentation of the "accident," said to happen in 1982, was designed to stimulate public interest in problems associated with the use of nuclear energy as a source of power. The description was realistic and included ambulance sirens, authentic-sounding signals, and well-known radio personalities. The accident itself was said to be the consequence of a breakdown in the plant's cooling system which led to the spread, by wind, of radioactive material towards the south including Copenhagen in Denmark. Both before and after broadcast, it was announced that the program was fiction.

Within an hour after the program, the media reported general panic in the South of Sweden. The following day, the morning and afternoon papers published prominent headlines on the panic. There was also debate about the program in the media, among the public, and in Parliament. These discussions examined the fictitious media presentation, rather than the real possibility of nuclear accident.

But a study revealed a situation sharply at variance with the media presentation of mass panic. The results showed that:

> Some 20 percent of the adult population had listened to the programme. About every second listener misunderstood the programme (every fifth till the end of the programme). About 70 percent of those who misunderstood were frightened listeners who also reacted behaviorally in one way or another. That is, some 10 percent of the adult population in the area misunderstood the programme, 7–8 percent were frightened and about 1 percent reacted behaviorally to the programme (Rosengren et al. 1974: 306).

Most fear reactions were slight and of short duration, although in a few cases the effects continued for some hours. Behavioral reactions included activities such as contacting family members, relatives, and neighbors with the telephone or face to face, closing windows, and thinking about what to take in case of an evacuation.

What is the explanation for such a difference between the research results and the mass media reports in the Swedish case? Rosengren and his colleagues pointed to conditions characteristic of the media and the authorities (which might also have given an inflated picture of the War of the Worlds panic). One of these is the telephone calls to police and mass media by alarmed and curious persons seeking more information. Several hundred such calls at once may be enough to clog local telephone exchanges and give the impression of a mass panic and vast concern, while actually representing only a very small proportion of the population. If, as happened in the Swedish case, the reporters get their information from mass media and police sources, they may also gain the impression of a mass panic which they then broadcast on radio and TV or publish in a newspaper. They may not check other sources for verification and, as in the Barseback incident, may be faced with deadlines which do not allow time for careful verification. Thus the reality of panic and the reporting of panic may be quite different.

As the above discussion suggests, panic, especially while it is in progress, does not lend itself to careful and leisurely study. However, a number of studies have been made on an experimental basis to observe in a more careful and systematic fashion the conditions of panic. Such studies may not approach real life situations, yet they are valuable for providing some basis for drawing conclusions and propositions.

Even though panic is rare, the idea that it is a usual consequence of disaster impact persists, perhaps because it adds drama to journalism and fiction. Indeed the myth may be so strong in literature that panic has become expected behavior—an expectation which is seldom questioned. Perhaps everyone harbors an element of self distrust which leads them to believe they will lose control and panic in danger (Chapman 1962:14).

There has been great interest in the control of panic. Indeed this interest in prevention and control may have slowed the understanding of panic (Foreman 1953:302). Although panic may occur under the conditions described above, such conditions are not always accompanied by panic. Instead, there may be (and often is) an orderly withdrawal from the impact, or some other non-panicky way of dealing with these conditions. Orderly withdrawal must be, in some cases, a consequence of prior concern with panic through panic training, previous experience, or indirect norms.

Anti-Panic Training

Existing panic training tends to focus upon possible disaster impacts that are well known. Much of the training of military forces is designed to reduce the possibility of panic even under very severe stress. Ship crews drill frequently to be prepared to deal with such possibilities as fire and collisions. In the United States the most widespread and general source of formal training is that received by school children who have relatively frequent fire drills. Probably they are the persons best prepared to respond without panic to a fire in a building.

A number of training principles for panic have been developed. Strauss (1944:320), for instance, suggests that discipline should be created in groups, that persons be informed of what is happening, that variables which weaken resistance should be avoided or minimized, and that ways to distract the attention of the group should be found, if possible. Smelser (1962:158–9) emphasizes some of the same variables and points out that facilities themselves, such as fireproof buildings, can have an important influence on whether or not there will be panic. But all of these principles presume known forms of disaster impact. Many disasters are unknown in the sense that victims lack previous experience with them. Their panic training may, however, carry over into the new situation and may be either adaptive or maladaptive.

Perhaps the overriding indirect or informal norm affecting response to panic is that one should resist the impulse to yield in the midst of disaster impact. In the case of the White County, Arkansas tornado described above, it was suggested that "uncontrolled" behavior might be so unacceptable that respondents would not acknowledge having engaged in it. Another indirect norm is that, in extreme situations, women and children are to receive first consideration (LaPiere 1938:444).

Communication During Impact

When the impact of a disaster is very short there will be little or no communication among the victims. In those of longer duration, communications may become very difficult, adding to the turmoil of the situation.

The long-term impact may put considerable strain on the communication system as more and more attention is given to the problems generated by the impact. At the same time, other situations normally handled through the communication process may receive less attention than before. Often the impact of a disaster destroys or partially destroys the institutional channels of communication.

During the impact, informal channels of communication and rumor may develop. Larsen argued that rumors are to be expected in disaster situations where there can be a high degree of ambiguity: "in the stepped up social contact of a disaster situation, rumors inevitably develop out of disturbances experienced by individuals as they attempt to cope with unverified and changing events" (Larsen 1954:116). He reached this conclusion from his study of a forest fire which destroyed some 15,000 acres on the Olympic Peninsula in September, 1951. He discovered four communication networks coexisting during the impact of the fire. One involved the local men engaged in fighting the fire; another included the volunteer fire fighters from outside the area and reporters and officials from nearby communities and the state capitol; a third was outside the fire area and involved some 900 evacuees including women, children, and aged men; the last included the general public in nearby communities. Each of the groups had to be contacted in different places. Among these groups and networks there was a high need for various kinds of information. But distortion was great, increasing with distance from the fire, especially among the evacuees.

In such situations there is considerable opportunity for rumor to develop. It can even happen that both institutional and informal channels may carry rumors and misinformation. The misinformation and rumors may be acted upon as readily as accurate communications. For example, the city of Port Jervis, New York, was flooded on August 9, 1955. During the night a rumor that a dam above the city had burst began to circulate. Within an hour about a quarter of the population evacuated.

> The main source of this false report was a message from out-of-town transmitted over the radios on the fire trucks which were pumping out cellars and homes in various parts of the city. The message was quickly picked up and passed on by one or more fire trucks, individual firemen, and by neighbors and friends warning each other by word of mouth and by phone. Some people in cars rode through the streets shouting that everyone must get out (Danzig et al. 1958:11).

After considerable checking of sources, the truth—that the dam was sound— was discovered. But by that time the rumor, spread in part by official and institutional sources, had been acted upon, and many persons had needlessly evacuated.

Conclusion

The impact of disasters varies greatly. Some are instantaneous or nearly so, such as industrial explosions or tornadoes; other, including hurricanes or forest fires, last for hours or days, and the impact period of others, such as famines, may last for years. Disasters vary, too, in extent of damage. The damage may be slight, not much more than an "ordinary" accident, or the destruction can almost totally destroy human cultures as we know them today.

Very little is known about the behavior which takes place during the impact period. The research from the Western World, based mainly on studies of the response to small-scale disasters, suggests that most victims maintain reasonably good control of themselves during the most intense part of the disaster. Where there are repeated impacts there is a tendency for the response to become institutionalized. Disasters whose impact is large scale and of long-time duration can place severe strain on the social structure and lead to significant social change. The case of response to typhoons on Yap was presented to show that response to the impact of a disaster is likely to be different in different cultures.

Panic, often thought to be most characteristic of victims during impact, is actually rather rare. When there is panic, it is thought to be a response to a dangerous situation in which the escape routes are believed to be closing rapidly. Even under these conditions persons do not always panic, but often make an orderly retreat.

If impact is instantaneous there is likely to be little communication. In longer lasting impacts, communication facilities are likely to focus on problems created by the impact at the expense of normal activities. There may be rumors during disasters, carried through both formal and informal channels, and their content may be acted upon whether or not the information is accurate.

Beachfront houses after three-day gale hit Ocean City, N.J. in 1962.

Extra!
Storm Edition

Printed and Published in America's Greatest Family Resort

Extra!
Storm Edition

OCEAN CITY Sentinel-Ledger

81ST YEAR — No. 52

Telephone 399-5411

OCEAN CITY, NEW JERSEY, THURSDAY, MARCH 8, 1962

Sentinel-Ledger Building, 8th St. and Haven Ave.

Publication Office

PRICE 10c

City Mops Up After Violent Storm
South End Of Resort Is Devastated
Damage Runs In Many Millions

RELOCATED BY A FEROCIOUS NATURE. These two cottages are located directly in the center of Central av. between 40th and 41st sts. The structures were lifted virtually intact from their pilings on the beach at left and deposited in the center of the street, almost against the utility poles on the west side of the highway.—Grainger Studio

Ocean And Bay Meet As Three-Day Gales Rake Jersey Coastline

by Edward S. Gore

A stunned and terribly battered Ocean City is cleaning up after one of the most disastrous storms in the city's history.

Striking almost without warning early Tuesday, full gale winds and tides five feet above normal lashed the city almost without let up until late Wednesday.

Below 34th st. in the city's south end devastation was overwhelming. Houses were toppled over; others were unroofed, and few buildings, if any, escaped without some mark of the intensity of the wind and waves.

Yesterday it was estimated that of the 800 houses in the area, 600 had suffered major damage. As many as 300 were so badly broken that early estimates indicated they may have to be demolished.

All persons living in the stricken section have been evacuated. National Guard units are standing by to keep out sightseers and possible looters.

In the central part of the city the boardwalk north of 4th st. and most of it south of 12th st. was either utterly destroyed or in need of complete reconstruction.

Ocean City's two beach-front fishing piers were casualties of the storm. The pier at 14th st. was broken in two on Tuesday, and eventually the remaining rickety sections tumbled into the sea. The pier at 59th st. met virtually the same fate. It too, withstood the first onslaught of the storm but when the tide abated and the wind died down late Wednesday

Editorial
Effects Of The Storm

All of the Southern New Jersey coast has suffered a major disaster. There is no blinking at that.

It will be many years before all the scars left by last week's devastating storm are completely eradicated. Ocean City suffered severe damage, but by the great good fortune no lives were lost here, nor were any serious injuries reported.

The section hardest hit locally was the area south of 34th st. to the end of the island at 59th st. Literally hundreds of homes were so badly damaged that they must be demolished.

Most of our famous boardwalk is gone, and that what remains must be repaired. Our ocean fishing piers are damaged. The central business district was flooded and stores escaped damage to property and stocks.

One would have to be a famous Pollyanna to contend that all this and a great deal more means anything but a serious economic blow to the city. We have no notion of trotting out spurious rays of sunshine to light the picture.

On the other hand, there are some indications that this coming summer this city will be on its feet. Much of our physical plant is completely undamaged. The federal Small Business Administration is setting up to advance long term credit to business men who need help.

There will be many cases of economic hardship brought about by this great natural catastrophe.

Still, it can be truthfully said that, if Ocean City's future was good before the storm struck, it is still good. Not in almost two decades has such a violent storm battered this area. They are extremely rare.

The effects of disasters have a way of disappearing very fast when a community works together.

Teamwork in the immediate future that will relieve the situation in Ocean City and throughout the entire area where the storm left damage.

Gas Co. Crews Search For Break; No Relief Seen For Householders

by heating and cooking in Ocean City ...

We're Late! We're Skimpy! But We're Out!

For the first time in the long and rich history of the Sentinel-Ledger this newspaper missed its Thursday deadline. We are out—we are late and we waste time nor space here explaining why.

This newspaper is about ashamed that the size of our number ...

We're lost but our readers wanted to know all they could about the storm that literally sacked Ocean City from the rest of the world for two days. We gathered all the details—piecing along with a wide selection of photographs to tell the story.

We're late ... we'll be sorry. But we're out.

U. S. Loans Available To Home Owners And Small Business H

CHAPTER VI

Recovery From Disaster

The impact of a disaster may severely alter the usual social structure or leave it in shambles. Ordinary formal organizations may not be available or may be unable to function effectively after an impact. But even though a disaster has destroyed the way everyday needs are met, it has also created new ones. As with warning and impact periods, there are many variations in recovery periods that are determined by the size of an impact, the length of warning time, and the state of preparation. One example, which clearly shows how complex recovery may be, can be seen through examination of Figure 6:1 below. It shows how the city of Rapid City, South Dakota recovered after the flood of June 9, 1972. The flood was highly destructive to the city of 44,000. There were 238 dead and missing, 1600 buildings damaged or destroyed, and property damage of over 80 million dollars (Haas, Kates, and Bowden 1977:7).

The Emergency Social System

After impact an "emergency social system" or "disaster system" emerges to deal with problems generated by the disaster (Barton 1969, Form and Nosow 1958, Form and Loomis 1956). The activities of the emergency social system have been termed the "mass assault," and Barton (1969: 132) says

> disaster studies have repeatedly shown the importance of the 'informal mass assault' in providing disaster services quickly and on a large scale. This mass assault consists of the aggregate of primary group activities to help their own members and community-oriented behavior of individuals and small groups. . . .

119

FIGURE 6.1: Rapid City, South Dakota: Recovery Activity Time
Flood of June 9, 1972

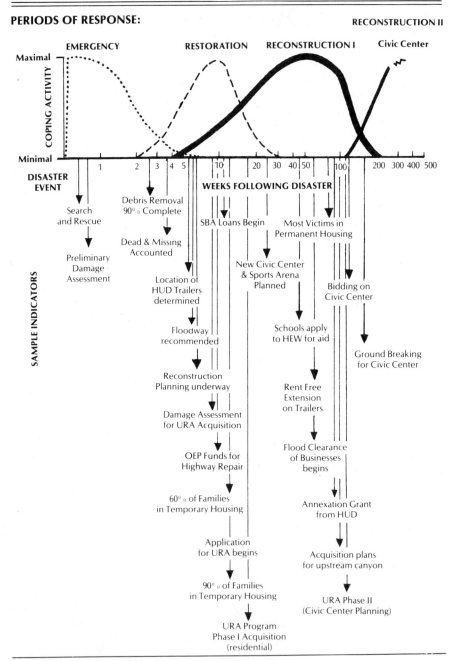

Source: Haas, Kates, and Bowden (1977: 8).

Aid to the victims comes from a number of sources including kin, friends, persons acting spontaneously, and formally organized agencies. (Erikson et al. 1976)

Immediately after impact the informal response is relatively unorganized especially in the case of short disasters, but emerging groups and individuals rapidly become goal oriented and purposeful in their activities. Lightly injured or uninjured survivors soon begin rescue operations and to look for their friends and relatives. The majority of these activities, beginning almost immediately after the impact, are carried out by survivors in the impact area. Most of this work is completed by the time members of official agencies arrive. Many informal leaders, often persons ordinarily considered to lack leadership qualities, and work groups emerge in this situation; under normal conditions, these positions would be filled through formal structures. At times, official but incompetent leaders may be ignored or deserted. Some nondisaster behaviors may be destructive rather than constructive if carried over to the immediate post-disaster situation. In hospitals, for example, physicians with combat experience are often best able to deal with incoming victims, as they are used to moving quickly in such situations.

Stock taking begins with the efforts of the survivors to understand what has happened. They quickly realize the extent of the destruction and may have a strong feeling of loss and abandonment. As they discover others in the same situation, they often feel a strong sense of relief and gratitude at being alive along with a feeling of concern and warmth for others. The impact often eliminates the stratification system, as everyone in the area is indiscriminately affected. The danger, loss, and other difficulties are public rather than private, and all suffer together. Associated with the destruction of status is a strong sense of community, with everyone working together for the common good. Very often, long after the recovery is over there remains nostalgia for the emotional warmth and equality of the immediate post-impact period. A disaster can have unifying and even therapeutic features. It comes from outside the system with causes that are usually easy to understand, and for a time it frees people from their usual cares and worries (Chapman 1962, Fritz 1961:683–4).

As part of the "emergency social system" and stock taking, a consensus on priorities develops. Highest among these is the preservation of life, followed closely by the provision of basic necessities of life: food, clothing, and shelter. Then comes the restoration of essential services with public sectors given favor over private ones. Finally comes the maintenance and preservation of public order and community morale. The usual production, distribution, and consumption patterns are greatly altered and for a time receive much less than the usual attention. Socialization activities such as school are reduced to a minimum, and many of the usual social activities are suspended. Normal social control procedures are often relaxed, while routine burglary may be treated as looting by the police and receive an especially severe response (Yutzy 1970:-344–53).

The Problem of Conflicting Role Demands

During the usual nondisaster situations, people play a number of roles which seldom place severely conflicting demands upon them. In the well-defined social role people know with whom they interact and what to do and for what point or end (Barton 1969:67). In disasters, however, an individual's roles may very well be in conflict, especially when one of them involves service to the community. A study of four disaster-stricken Southwestern communities showed that there were conflicting group loyalties and contradictory roles as a consequence of persons holding multiple group memberships. When disaster strikes, the latent conflict between ordinarily nonconflicting group loyalties may become apparent. Many persons are then faced with the problem of making a choice between conflicting group loyalties (Killian 1952). A police officer, for example, is likely to be expected to work in rescue, traffic control, or other disaster-related activities while he may, at the same time, feel a powerful urge to find out how his family has survived the situation and to look after them if they need help.

It is Killian's view (1952:311) that the majority of such conflicts are resolved in favor of the family rather than the organization. Such decision can intensify the effects of the disaster if those who decide in favor of their families abandon activities which require immediate attention.

A contrary view holds that persons who are faced with conflicting role requirements under conditions of extreme stress are not in a situation which permits a rational consideration of alternatives. First the survivor experiences a retroactive fear of death in which he or she realizes it can come in a random and capricious fashion. This is followed by doubt over the ability to survive either through one's own efforts or through the efforts of the community. This leads to a strong motivation to restore faith by taking some effective action against the disaster. Then survivors realize that they might have been victims and are happy to have survived. The survivors also feel guilty about feeling glad to have lived through the impact. They then sacrifice and work to compensate for this feeling. Under these circumstances the individual may be expected to begin work at the first opportunity which provides a certain solution, that is, one in which the problem is clearly defined and there is something the individual can do. So what is done is whatever opportunity comes first, and the individual puts aside thoughts of other obligations and duties. Also important is the structure of the positions involved. Persons occupying positions which are highly structured and routinized and which involve close social relationships are more likely to play their organizational roles than persons in less tightly organized positions (Barton 1969:114–21).

The Disaster Syndrome

As pointed out in Chapter V, the available data show that most persons maintain reasonably good control of themselves during the impact period. Table 6.1 based on data from the study of the White County, Arkansas study shows that only a small proportion of about 20 percent were either highly agitated or in a state of dazed shock after the impact. Persons in this state are said to be suffering from the "disaster syndrome." It has been described as a condition in which the victims are "dazed," "stunned," or "bewildered" and show an absence of emotion, an inhibition of activity, docility, indecisiveness, a lack of responsiveness together with the physiological manifestations of autonomic arousal (Kinston and Rosser 1974:442–3, Wolfenstein 1957:77–84). The disaster syndrome is explained in various ways: as a psychic closing off from any more stimuli, as energy being drained off for intense internal work, as a response to fantasies as "if I don't react then nothing has happened," of feelings of helplessness and impossibility of undoing all the damage (Kinston and Rosser 1974:442). There is not much data on the length of time the disaster syndrome persists, however, it is believed "that in most cases it is temporary and that most people recover soon," although some contrary evidence has recently appeared (Erikson 1976). It may be followed by euphoria marked by thankfulness at survival and high public spirits and concern for public welfare (Wallace 1957:23–4).

Table 6.1: Percent of Respondents Reporting Certain Affective States Immediately After Impact

Affective Reaction Reported	Percent Of All Respondents	Percent Of Female Respondents	Percent Of Male Respondents
Agitated state but no uncontrolled behavior	45	46	45
Highly agitated state involving uncontrolled behavior	6	10	1
Shocked state (i.e., "stunned," "dazed," "shocked")	14	22	5
Other affective states not specified above	1	3	—
Calm and unexcited	8	4	11
Number of Interviews	N=139	N=67	N=72

Source: Fritz and Marks (1954:33).

Altruism

A part of the emergency social system is *altruism* toward and among those who shared the experience. At the same time there is reduced tolerance of outsiders. Altruism among the survivors and others, as pointed out in the following discussion of convergence, can be very deep and extensive. Private persons may share their houses and goods with victims, and organizations may readily give goods and services that they ordinarily sell. Preexisting values and norms may be considered irrelevant after impact. For example, there develops a feeling that private property has become community property; if a generator or some other item is necessary, one is taken from a place that has one. This redefinition of private property has general support where it is believed that everything can and should be used for the purpose of helping the community. Such behavior might be interpreted as looting by outsiders, but it is not so considered by the people working in the impact area (Dynes and Quarrantelli 1968b).

There are, however, limits to altruism. Many are much more willing to send clothing and food to the disaster-stricken community a hundred miles away than they are for victims of a typhoon in Bangladesh. Altruism is thought to be highest close to the impact area, when the victims are believed blameless, and when there is a sympathetic identification with them, usually based on shared characteristics (Barton 1969:203–79). It is possible, too, that continuous exposure to disaster through mass media such as TV, as in the case of the Viet Nam War, may reduce altruism and instead help create dehumanization and brutalization among those who might otherwise be sympathetic (Bernard et al. 1971).

Other limits to altruism may be set by ideological, financial, and political considerations. Barton (1969:11–21) suggests that though it would have been physically easy to provide aid to Ireland during the 1845–49 famine, laissez-faire doctrine played an important part in the low-level British response. In the recent famine in the Sahel, political and financial factors may have been of more importance than technical and altruistic ones. It is possible, in disasters like these, that altruism may be less evident than profit making and efforts to extend power, both by international bodies and local elites who use the situation to their advantage (Wiseberg 1976).

Organizational Response

Formal organizations, including those which deal with the stressful aspects of everyday life, have routine ways of solving their problems. Those concerned with ordinary stressful events in the community also expect, and are expected, to take part in disasters. They also, in varying degrees, plan for them (Dynes 1970). Police departments are among the most active of the formal organizations dealing with disasters. They often take part in the warning and evacuation process, if there is one, and they are among the first of the organized groups in the impact area to help with traffic control, protection of life and property, and search and rescue operations. Their first priority is to preserve life, then to aid in the restoration and maintenance of essential services, and finally to restore and preserve public order (Kennedy 1970).

However, as a study of 48 emergencies and disasters showed, other groups in addition to formal organizations handling stressful aspects of everyday life are involved in disasters. Four types of organizations active in the aftermath of a disaster have been identified. Since the activities of these groups both formal and emergent are intermixed, they provide an opportunity to use organizational and collective behavior approaches in analyzing the recovery period (Dynes and Quarantelli 1968a, Dynes 1970).

The Type I groups are those expected to take an *immediate and active part* in dealing with the consequences of the disaster. They are involved in every community emergency. This category includes such agencies as the police and fire departments, and the utility companies. They shift their resources to the immediate tasks presented by the disaster. This new allocation creates changes in the use of personnel and the neglect of many of their traditional activities. In many cases they work with other organizations for the first time. However, these groups try to adhere to their regular activities as much as possible and when they must go beyond, they attempt to return to their early state as quickly as possible. This helps the organizations prevent disaster demands from outstripping their ability to cope with them (Warheit 1970).

The kind of shift in activities made by Type I groups was recently demonstrated in a simulation experiment in a metropolitan police department. The subjects, police officers handling communications, were not aware of being part of an experiment. The "disaster" was an "air crash" in a residential district of the city. As the stress—induced by calls coming into the communications center—increased, the police officers performance rate also increased, and they began to limit themselves to activities connected with the "disaster." The frequency with which they initiated contact with other organizations increased, but they knew little about how to coordinate their activities with other organizations (Drabek and Haas 1969).

How a Type I group may be adapted to disaster is illustrated by a recent study of a "department of public works" (Brouillete 1970). It was a highly bureaucratic organization with maintenance and engineering personnel who served in both normal and emergency operations. They responded to nearly all disasters and operated with four distinct levels of demands upon their

Newspaper headlines chronicle the recovery efforts of the residents of Ocean City, N.J. after the storm of 1962.

A U.S. Coast Guard helicopter rescue crew searches for victims of hurricane "Camille" in Gulfport, Miss. in 1969.

services. First was the normal state of affairs. Second were the anticipated and planned-for seasonal or periodic emergencies. Third were those unanticipated emergencies in which the department continued to carry out preemergency responsibilities. Last were the major unanticipated situations in which the department had to engage in entirely new tasks. This department was also important as a communication and coordination center in disasters.

Although Americans believe that their military forces should be subordinate to civil authorities in domestic matters, they generally expect the armed services to be involved in disaster recovery operations whenever necessary. Military forces can be supportive in relief and rescue or can take a leadership and coordinating role, depending on the degree of organization in the stricken community. In more centralized societies the military tends to assume leadership, while in decentralized societies it is more likely to serve a supportive role.

Firemen remove an "injured" girl from an overturned bus during a rescue drill.

Such forces must reconcile sometimes inconsistent expectations by adapting to emergent roles of the disaster and not outwardly breaking established norms. The military is generally expected to participate shortly after impact, but it is also expected to disengage after the immediate emergency is over. Even though, in the United States, the military is expected to operate under civilian control, it often emerges as the primary authority in the aftermath of a disaster (Anderson 1969b, 1970).

Type II groups have a *latent emergency function* as they are expected to take part in disaster activities, although their day-to-day concerns are not usually disaster oriented. After disaster these groups put aside their usual activities, and begin their latent emergency functions. They are likely to mobilize more slowly than Type I groups and to expand in size through the use of prior groups or plans, as in the case of Civil Defense, which allow for the incorporation of other groups. Two very well-known Type II groups are the Red Cross and Salvation Army.

The Red Cross is a permanent organization which plays an active role in disasters through such activities as giving emergency care to victims, rehabilitation, and evacuation both before and after impact (Adams 1970). Similar is the Salvation Army which has a social welfare and an evangelical function. It is able to mobilize rapidly, is experienced and adaptable, and enjoys a positive image (Ross 1970).

A problem facing Type II organizations is that of efficient bureaucratic organization in the aftermath of a disaster. The administrators of such organizations are likely to think efficiency to be desirable, while the disaster victims may not have the same feeling. A comparison made between the Red Cross, a bureaucratic organization, and the Salvation Army, much less bureaucratic, revealed important differences between the two. The quality and quantity of the goods and services received was not as important to the victims for a positive rating as was the quality of the relationship between the giver and the receiver. The Salvation Army gave less material support and more empathy and emotional support than did the Red Cross and thus received a higher positive ranking (Stoddard 1969, see also Moore 1958:176–81).

Type III groups are composed of *organizations in existence before the impact without any disaster functions or activities*. They extend their activities to new disaster-related tasks. Some are contractual groups such as a department store which lends or offers its trucks and drivers to work in the disaster. Others are volunteer or service groups such as the Boy Scouts, who may become active. They may even come from such places as nearby university social work schools (Siporin 1966). Some Type III groups are involved soon after the disaster, but usually their participation emerges later, especially as there are no institutionalized expectations for their participation.

There are tasks imposed by the disaster which are outside the area of the first three group types, and the fourth type, Group IV, emerges to handle them. This period when many community organizations and individuals, ordinarily unrelated, come together to deal with disaster requirements has been referred to as the time of "ephemeral governments" (Taylor, Zurcher, and Key 1970:-129). This *emergent system* tends to disappear after the most important short-term needs are met.

The material reviewed above shows how important the coordination of the groups, both formal and informal, is. Ordinarily there is not much concern with this problem prior to a disaster. Barton (1969:195–201) has identified several variables which may negatively influence the response of formal organizations and ways in which these problems may be controlled. The problem of role conflict may be so severe that the disaster leaves the organization without leadership. One way to deal with this is to emphasize through training the importance of the job over the family. Another is to increase the visibility of organization members so that others can pressure them to stay on the job. Important, too, is the development of a degree of primary loyalty to the organization and its members.

It has also been suggested that poor leadership and/or poor or no plans for dealing with disasters may make organizational response ineffective. This was shown in striking contrast in the Rio Grande flood of 1954 which hit two cities directly across the river, Piedras Negras, a Mexican city, and Eagle Pass in the United States. The Mexican mayor, who occupied his position on the basis of ascription, took little heed of the warnings and paid little attention to the problems of the refugees. His position eventually fell under the direction of the state governor and military command. In Eagle Pass, on the other hand, where officials held office more by virtue of achievement, the warnings received prompt attention, and evacuation and relief activities were effective (Barton 1969:90–1). The demands of the disaster aftermath may be so severe that even competent leaders become overloaded and fatigued, making it impossible for them to function well. Victims tend to look to their formal leadership, but if it is inadequate or nonexistent, then informal leadership will emerge and the official but incompetent leadership may be ignored.

Another variable is that organizations which could play an active part may not see the situation as one requiring their participation. Predisaster patterns of limits of authority and activity, such as those defined by municipal boundaries, may carry over after impact.

In the case of individuals, too, there are conditions which may have a negative influence upon their performance after impact. (Barton 1969:67–89). Individuals may react in a nonadaptive way as a result of having inadequate or conflicting roles. Many may be left without the aid of primary group relations. That is, entire groups may be incapacitated and left isolated. Some impacts may require special skills which are not within the abilities of the victims.

Difficulties may also develop between the activities of individuals and organized groups. The uncoordinated action of individuals and small emergent groups may overload the facilities available in the community, or they may actually interfere with each other. It is also possible that formal organizations may need public support in supplies or personnel in situations where there are no expectations or channels for them.

In spite of the difficulties reviewed above, most studies suggest that the rate of nonadaptive behavior is low. In any community, members possess disaster-related skills which can be transferred and applied to the problem at hand. They also feel a sense of responsibility to the community, little conflict (at least at first) and altruism.

Attention has been given to the problem of *conflict* in disaster-stricken communities (Quarantelli and Dynes 1976). There is considerable variation in conflict after a disaster, although there tends to be relatively little in the emergency period and more in post emergency. Since disasters, at least natural disasters, come from outside the community they generate solidarity rather than increase already-present conflict. The cause of natural disaster is identifiable, unlike the source of many other difficulties, making it easier to take action. Community solidarity is likely to be increased as there is consensus on priorities, which are high on community rather than individual benefits, and the order in which they are to be accomplished. There is a focus, at least during the emergency period, on the present and a tendency for people to forget the past and future. The leveling of class distinctions often reduces the conflicts associated with them. The disaster too may strengthen community identification as it becomes an important event in its life history and provides an opportunity for wide participation in emergency activity which calls for innovation and adaptation.

As the community returns to "normal," hostility and conflict may appear. They seem to focus around the two problems of blame (discussed in more detail later in this chapter) and the allocation and distribution of resources. The search for a person or organization to blame is likely to be more intense in a manmade disaster. However, an attempt to blame may occur if it appears that the authorities could have, but did not, warn of the approaching disaster. Conflict may also develop as various community agencies struggle over the allocation and distribution of resources coming to the stricken area. This is especially likely to happen when there is an end to freely given aid. On an individual basis, there is an increase in hostility toward outsiders, especially nonlocal agencies and organizations.

Cross-Cultural Response

Until recently there has been relatively little cross-cultural disaster research. However, Dynes (1975) recently suggested that societies also can be divided into types on the basis of their response to disaster. The Type I society has a small population, a food-gathering economic system associated with a tenuous ecological base, and family, kin, and clan relationships are considered highly important. The social structure of the Type I society is fragile and lacks the resources to adapt to the extensive disruption that may be caused by disaster. A disaster can result in extensive social change or even destruction of the Type I society.

The Type II society is larger in population and is family and village based. It is limited in its ability to replace resources lost through disaster. There is poor articulation between various levels of social organization, family, village, and central government. Warnings of approaching disaster are difficult to transmit and often have little creditability. A charismatic leader may organize an effective response or the army—sometimes the most important governmental unit with resources, mobility and flexibility—may play an active part. Disaster in the Type II society usually results in less long-term social change than in the Type I society.

The Type III society is characterized by a large population sustained by an urban industrial base. The social structure is more complex and elaborate. In a disaster the complexity is itself likely to be associated with problems of coordination such as convergence, which is discussed below. In a disaster in Type III societies, the tendency is toward reduction of organizational autonomy in such areas as occupation, school, and housing in favor of increased interdependence. In Type III societies, as McLuckie's (1975) study of the degree of political centralization and its influence on response to disaster in Italy, Japan and the United States shows, there may be rather important differences. For example, in the politically more centralized countries, such as Italy and Japan, fewer persons in official positions are responsible for decision making in disasters, a situation which can lead to delay and less flexibility in response. Generally, individuals behave by their usual social roles, especially in the family. Usually disasters create little social change in Type III societies.

Convergence

In the United States, one of the most severe problems after impact is *convergence:* the "mass movement of people, messages, and supplies toward the disaster struck area" (Fritz and Mathewson 1957:1). The movement toward is usually more than the movement away from the impact area, and it presents a central problem of social control as it can substantially retard organized relief efforts. This usage of the term "convergence" is not to be confused with that discussed in Chapter II in which convergence refers to a theory of the crowd which holds that a crowd is a gathering of people who already share the same feelings, attitudes, and predispositions.

There are three general categories of convergence: (1) the physical movement of people toward the impact area, (2) the movement of information, and

(3) the movement of supplies and equipment to the area. It is also useful to think of "external convergence," movement from outside toward a disaster area, and "internal convergence," movement to specific points within the disaster area (Fritz and Mathewson 1957:3). The speed and fluidity with which convergence occurs is often unexpected and unanticipated by authorities. While efforts are being made to deal with the disaster, the convergence process begins and adds to the problem already created by the impact.

It may be useful to examine Figure 6.2 as a way of seeing how convergence might work in terms of spatial zones. In the center is the disaster impact area itself along with contiguous, proximate, and remote zones. Convergence, internal and exteral, is represented by arrows.

Personal Convergence

The convergence of persons to and within the impact area presents the most difficult problem of control found in many disasters (Fritz and Mathewson 1957:7). The central point of convergence is the impact area with its problems of rescue evacuation of the dead and injured. The establishment of relief and informational centers leads to the development of other internal points of convergence outside the immediate impact area including hospitals, morgues, and information centers.

At first, shortly after the impact, most convergence is internal and composed primarily of those looking for missing persons. But soon a number of other types of persons participate in the convergence process. These are often called "sightseers" or "curiosity seekers," but the situation is actually much more complex.

One category of convergers has been called the "returnee" which includes survivors who left or were evacuated, residents away when the disaster struck, nonresident property owners interested in the damage they may have suffered, and substitute returnees—friends and relatives of victims who are checking things for them. The motive of these returnees is that of helping others and assessing their own losses. Property values rank very low immediately after a disaster, but when concern for human life diminishes, interest in property returns. Members of families which have suffered high personal loss do not return as quickly as others. Friends and relatives of these persons may help by going to the site to collect and bring them various belongings. These persons may be and often are confused with looters. Persons also converge in order to be in familiar surroundings and to reestablish old social relationships.

Another category of convergers, labeled "the anxious," are friends and relatives of the victims. In a country of high mobility such as the United States, nearly everyone in a disaster has friends and relatives outside, and there are

FIGURE 6.2: A Spatial Model of Convergence Behavior

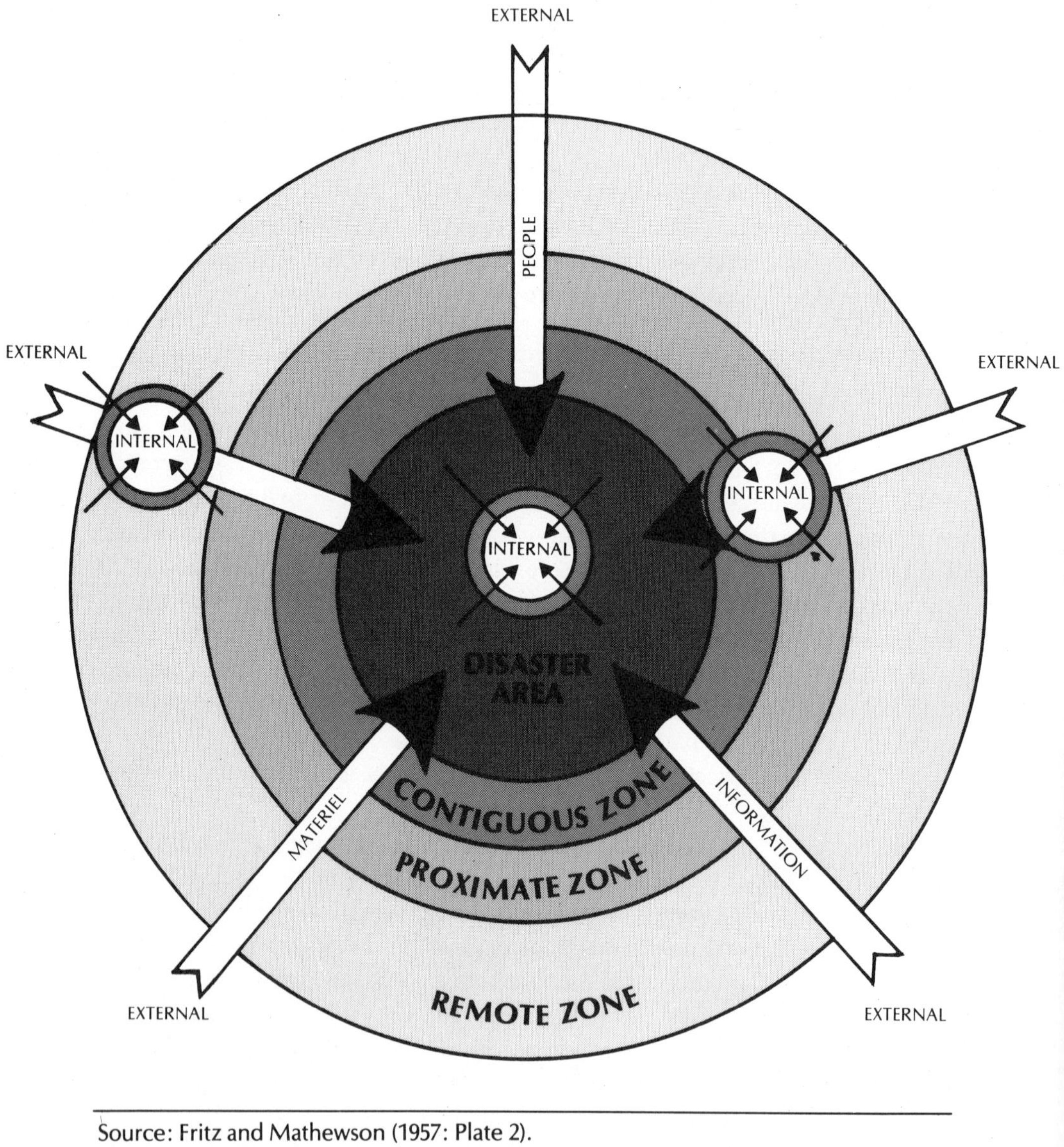

Source: Fritz and Mathewson (1957: Plate 2).

almost always some persons temporarily separated from one another. Thus a
disaster is, in some respects, a national or international affair. Anxiety over
friends and relatives is one of the major causes of convergence and leads to
congestion and confusion in the impact area as well as at medical and relief
centers in the contiguous and proximate zones.

Persons also converge to help the victims through volunteer assistance. A good deal of confusion may be created by the general pattern of informal help convergence.

There are people who are curious and who do come to see the sights. They have little or no personal identification with the disaster victims. The curious usually converge from relatively short distances and come in larger numbers if the disaster happened during a holiday or over a weekend.

Of course there are persons who exploit the victims, but their extent has been exaggerated and the stereotype of widespread looting is not likely to be found in reality. Disasters increase opportunities for exploitation, but reduce motivation, especially among the victims. Persons who do exploit are likely to be those who have no involvement with the disaster victims.

Looting, for example, does not have general community support after a disaster, as it sometimes does in civil disturbances. What looting does occur is often carried out by outside persons, who have entered for some other purpose. However, there is the stereotype that there will be widespread looting, and there is strong pressure to provide security forces. Since there is often an emergent norm in which rules on the use of private property are suspended, the use of such property for community purposes may appear as looting (Quarantelli and Dynes 1970). Perhaps more common is pilfering and souvenir hunting by persons who seek reminders of the event and proof of their having been there.

Other forms of exploitation are possible. There may be "relief stealers," persons who claim to be victims in order to receive relief services. There may be profiteering which takes advantage of victims' helplessness and needs, especially after rehabilitation has begun. But overall it is believed that such behavior is rare.

Informational Convergence

Information also converges on an impact area. The communication facilities of any community are designed for a normal load. After impact, communication facilities may be destroyed or damaged and rapidly become overloaded.

There is competition between the general public and the disaster relief agencies for the available communication facilities. If the general public is denied access, which it often is through the all-the-lines-are-taken technique, then an informal set of communication networks develops. Authorities may not be fully aware of these communication networks, the information being transmitted, or the communicators' needs. Furthermore, the two systems, formal and informal, may conflict.

An emergent form of handling at least part of the communication problem was discovered in a study of four flood-stricken communities (Waxman 1973). During normal times the radio stations have a system of "gatekeeping" in which professional newsmen control the flow of information by deciding what stories to follow up, what further information to gather, and how stories are to be presented. A marked change in the gatekeeping activities was noted after the floods. While the station's capabilities had decreased, demands had increased, and there was a shortage of the usual community news and information. The adjustment was to expand the usual five-minute news broadcast to around-the-clock information-giving about the disaster situation, a process that lasted almost a week in several of the communities. The norm emerged that necessary information on the dead and missing, the damage, food supplies, schools, and other matters was always announced to meet the demand for news. Thus news became as the public defined it, rather than as the previous gatekeepers defined it. This system developed strong feedback qualities as people with more accurate information contacted the stations when mistakes were made.

Outside the impact area the volume of communication convergence is a function of several factors. One is the accuracy and specificity of information concerning the geographic scope of the disaster and the population affected. Another is the speed with which the information is transmitted. If these two points are handled poorly by formal communication authorities, outsiders' anxieties are raised, and there will be a greater degree of informational convergence.

In the last few years, Citizen's Band radios have become widespread. While little or no research on their role in disasters has appeared, their use in such situations has been noted in some CB publications (CB-10-4 News, May, 1977). Use of the CB could help reduce the immediate confusion which can come with the breakdown and destruction of regular channels of communication. For example, they could lead to quicker identification and location of persons having various kinds of authority, aid in the more rapid establishment of central headquarters, and facilitate rescue work. On the other hand, their use could increase confusion through the transmission of inaccurate information and overload.

Material Convergence

The response to most disasters in the United States has been one of spontaneous generosity. Donated material begins to flow into the disaster area soon after people learn of it. Most of the material comes from close by, and much of it is helpful and valuable. However, there are often negative aspects of material convergence. Sometimes supplies come far in excess of need and a large percentage is worn out and unusable. The physical handling of the material often requires the services of a great many people and storage space which might better be used for something else. It can add to the congestion in the disaster area. It may also cause conflict relations between relief agencies or various segments of the population who may disagree over its allocation and distribution.

Controlling Convergence

Except in places which experience repeated disasters, there is usually very little planning for them. It is not likely that this is going to change, and convergence will probably remain a problem. But suggestions for its control have been made. One is that each community have an information specialist whose task is to inventory the situation after the disaster (Fritz and Mathewson 1957:66) and transmit the information to those who need it. It has also been suggested that a uniform code of disaster reporting be developed which might reduce sensational reporting in favor of accounts which are more moderate and verified. Plans or suggestions for controlling personal convergence include pleas through mass media asking the public to stay away, traffic barriers, and road blocks.

Controlling internal convergence can be very difficult. After impact, for example, demands made upon hospitals change both quantitatively and qualitatively. There is a convergence of casualties, the press, police, and medical personnel on the nearest or best-known hospitals while other relatively close hospitals may be virtually empty. The problem is not always one of scarce resources, but one of coordinating organizations and people. Disaster plans, about 75 percent of the hospitals in the United States have them, are intended to control these problems. But they tend to be poor and unpracticed, and their application is makeshift when there is a disaster (Quarantelli 1970, Stallings 1970).

Assignment of Blame

The disaster, especially if natural, is often considered unavoidable or an "act of God," and no attempt is made to fix blame. In disasters which seem to have been under possible human control, the victims and others often attempt to fix blame, punish those at fault, and undertake some preventive measures. Individuals are blamed when the situation is so well defined that responsibility can be assigned, when the persons at fault will not of their own free will take action to remedy the situation, and when the persons responsible are in opposition to basic values (Bucher 1957).

Several major views have been developed to explain the process of assignment of blame following disasters. One holds that the process serves to reduce guilt through an irrational search for scapegoats. Another approach argues that blame fixing is a rational process designed to prevent reoccurrence. A third view is that scapegoating serves to hide and obscure defects in the social system which may be more important than individual behavior. The focus on individuals delays or averts change in the social structure by leading people to believe that punishment or getting rid of guilty individuals will serve as a deterrent in the future (Drabek and Quarantelli 1967).

An example comes from the Coconut Grove Night Club fire in which the search for a scapegoat was conducted in the newspapers. A number of different people were chosen and rejected by the mass media, and as the facts became better known, the selection of the scapegoat became more rational. First was the bus boy who was soon considered blameless and was even admired as he frankly admitted lighting the match which started the fire, then attention focused on the prankster who removed the original light bulb, and the owners of the night club were also abused by the press. The final scapegoats were public officials who were believed to have been lax in their enforcement of safety ordinances (Veltford and Lee 1943).

In the Indianapolis Coliseum explosion of 1963 it became clear that the safety regulations had not been carefully enforced. As a result, there were a number of indictments, and public officials were villified. But the small financial appropriations for maintaining safety conditions made impossible all but minimal enforcement and safety inspections. Yet the reaction was such that individuals rather than the structure were blamed (Drabek and Quarantelli 1967, Drabek 1968:113–21).

In the United States, the overriding tendency is to blame individuals for almost everything positive or negative and to look less often for structural variables. In other cultures other causative agents for disasters may be identified. For example, the Hupa Indian Reservation was flooded in 1956 and 1966 because, in the victims' eyes, supernatural forces were punishing the white man for encroaching on Indian land, and some tribal members had violated certain ceremonial rules (Bushnell 1969).

Reestablishment of the Old System

As noted above, immediately after impact the community is characterized by a feeling of oneness. As the immediate problems are solved, this feeling begins to recede, former social distinctions reappear, and official control reemerges. This is especially true when the disaster impact is small. However, even small disasters may have lingering consequences as revealed in a recent study of differences in primary group relationships between victim and nonvictim families three years after the Topeka, Kansas tornado of 1966 (Drabek and Key 1976). It was found that kinship patterns, important in the immediate recovery process, were strengthened as were friendship patterns. There was a lessening of activity among neighbors and participation in voluntary associations, except for religious activity among victim families.

There is a tendency for persons to want to reestablish their old way of life. Even after extremely massive destruction, as from bombing raids, they prefer to move back and rebuild in their old homes (Haas, Kates, Bowden, 1977 and Iklé, 1954). The survivors want to regain what they can of their old associations. They still have property rights even though facilities may be destroyed, and there usually are some usable facilities left. It can be cheaper and more efficient to rebuild on the old sites rather than to start entirely anew. Indeed, a struggle may develop between those who wish to do so, as on a flood plain, and those who think it better to relocate for safety and other reasons.

Do disasters result in long-time change in the social structure? In disasters in which the impact is confined and small in scope, the answer is probably not. But, even after lesser disasters, consciousness of the event remains for a long time among those who experienced it. This is revealed in the way people refer to events as occurring "before" or "after" the tornado or whatever the disaster may have been.

Deeper and more extensive change may follow the impact of very destructive disasters especially if some vital institution is destroyed (Barton 1969:326 –32). There have been many cases in which the entire structure was upset by military invasions and occupations, epidemic diseases, and famines. The period of recovery, in such cases, may last for many years, or never occur.

Recovery or a return to pre-disaster conditions may occur relatively rapidly. It often involves a number of difficult decisions such as whether or not there should be a change in land use, the implementation of improved building codes, and whether or not the city should be made a safer and more attractive place. The pace is also influenced by variables as the amount of material wealth and assistance available, the loss in population and goods, and the level of technology present (Haas, Kates, Bowden, 1977).

The Persistence of Stress Symptoms

Some scholars believe that very little serious mental illness results as a consequence of disaster. The symptoms of stress, insomnia, digestive upsets, nervousness, and so on, observed immediately after impact seem to be transitory and disappear in a few days or weeks. It might even happen that there may be less disturbance as was observed in Great Britain during the World War II bombing raids (Titmus 1950).

Some argue, on the other hand, that the psychological reactions to disaster are significant and may persist for a long time. Feelings of fear and apprehension may also persist for some time (Kinston and Rosser 1974:443–4). After the 1953 tornado that struck Waco, Texas, for example, researchers found that many of the victims were quite conscious of the possibility of another, and observed clouds with extreme care (Moore 1958:256–91). Erikson (1976), in his study of the 1972 Buffalo Creek, West Virginia flood, found strong evidence of the disaster syndrome for as much as two years after the impact. The Buffalo Creek disaster and the reconstruction period was especially severe and led to both individual and collective destruction of the bonds of communality, or trauma. The victims, almost all of whom were damaged in some way, were reacting to both individual aspects of the disaster and having their meaningful community life destroyed.

In the case of children, in the early phases after the disaster, their reactions seem to be a function of the way in which reality is reflected to them through their parent's reactions. The dominant fear of children is being separated from their parents. If there is no separation and if the parents are able to cope well, then children show little awareness of danger and little anxiety (Kinston and Rosser, 1974:444–5). The aged may be especially vulnerable. The disaster might severely upset their limited contacts and give them a higher sense of deprivation.

The question of long-term reactions to the stress generated by disasters is still open. The consequences may be much more long term and severe than believed before, and the Erikson study has opened new questions which will probably lead to further research interest in this problem.

Conclusion

After the impact of a disaster an "emergency social system" emerges. It is composed of persons who attack the problems, such as rescue and debris removal, created by the disaster. Their activity is part of the "mass assault" and most of the immediate work is carried out by informal groups within the impact area. Most persons within the impact area rapidly recover from the initial shock and are able to perform effectively. Some individuals are faced with problems of role conflict as they may occupy a service position which requires that they remain on the job while they may wish to ascertain the condition of their families and help them, if necessary. In the immediate aftermath of impact there develops a strong sense of community and oneness among the survivors. There is a temporary destruction of the old status system and often the emergence of new leadership. Associated with this is a strong sense of altruism accompanied by a loss or diminishing of the usual property values.

Organizations of four types play a part in the after-disaster period. The Type I organization is expected, and at least somewhat prepared, to transfer its ordinary disaster-related activities to the new situation. Type II organizations, such as the Red Cross and Salvation Army, are expected to and plan to take part, but their ordinary activities are usually not so disaster related. They usually expand in size through the use of volunteers. Type III groups were in existence before the disaster but had nondisaster-related tasks and activities. They shift their functions to take part. Finally, Type IV groups are those that spontaneously emerge in and around the impact area. They deal with immediate problems and tend to disappear after they are solved.

One of the most difficult problems after a disaster is that of *convergence.* Large numbers of people, a great deal of information, and massive amounts of material begin to come into the disaster area. There is similar convergence within the impact area to key points such as hospitals. There is little looting, but there is a tendency to define private as community property and to use it as such.

If the disaster was caused by natural forces, there is usually little effort to assign blame. But if human agents are considered responsible, there may be a search for the guilty individual or individuals. This search usually focuses on individuals rather than the structure, thus interfering with the taking of effective preventive action.

Persons try to reestablish a situation as much like the old as possible. In the case of small-scale disasters it may be possible to do so without much noticeable difference between the old and new. In disasters of extremely large impact, it may take many years to recover and, if a vital institution has been destroyed, complete recovery may never occur.

The long-term psychological consequences of disasters are not fully understood. In the view of some scholars the effects are relatively transitory. Recently, it has been suggested that the consequences may be deeper and longer lasting than previously thought.

Most disaster research has focused on short-term and small-scale disasters in the Western World. There has been much less on large-scale and long-term disasters which involve the destruction of some vital institutions. Nor has there been enough cross-cultural research to permit us to speak with much confidence about disasters outside the Western World.

*

PART III Crowd Violence

C rowds are groups of people in face-to-face contact for transitory periods of social interaction. Blumer (1951) described four different types of crowds: (1) the *casual* crowd, (2) the *conventionalized* crowd, (3) the *acting* crowd, and (4) the *expressive* crowd. The casual crowd is illustrated by a sidewalk gathering which forms to watch something of special interest. Casual crowds have a short existence and little or no sense of unity. The composition of the crowd is characterized by a high rate of turnover since its members come and go as they like.

The conventionalized crowd, as defined by Blumer, is typified by the kind of group found in sporting events. In the conventionalized crowd, individual excitement is expressed in established, regularized patterns of behavior. The acting crowd, typified by lynch mobs and riots, occurs, according to Blumer, when members of acting-aggressive crowds yield to hostile impulses because they have lost their sense of reflexive self-consciousness and their capacity for self-control. The acting crowd exists in the transitory present as a nonmoral group in the sense that its traditional normative restraints have been temporarily suspended. This supposedly happens because the members of acting crowds get caught up in the emotional excitement of what they are doing.

Blumer's fourth type of crowd, the expressive crowd, is a group in which collective excitement is manifest as a form of release. Behavior is characterized by high emotionalism and physical agitation or by rhythmical movements of the body. This form of activity is performed as an end in itself, rather than as a means to some goal. Rock music festivals, for example, sometimes produce expressive crowd behavior today, while historically the same response was often elicited through certain religious ceremonies.

The next three chapters of this book are devoted to what Blumer called *acting* crowds, and in particular, to riots. Chapter VII concerns the *preconditions* of riots with special attention given to indicators of situational stress, Chapter VIII focuses on crowd *formation* and *boundaries* during the riot process, and Chapter IX concludes the section with a discussion of crowd *confrontation and control.*

143

Fire blazes (top) in Detroit following the riots there in July 1967. Michigan's governor called out the National Guard to quell the riots.

CHAPTER VII

Preconditions

The Detroit riots, which began on July 23, 1967, left 43 dead, 342 injured, 5,000 homeless, 7,000 jailed, and roughly $50 million of property damage. Before the ordeal ended after five days, the authorities had called in 5,000 national guardsmen and 2,700 paratroopers to support local and state police. The assassination of Martin Luther King, in April of 1968, led to major riots in Baltimore, Chicago, and Washington, D.C., as well as minor riots in at least 100 other cities. On September 9, 1971, inmates rioted at New York State's Attica Prison. The official report of the New York State Special Commission on Attica (1972) called the assault that ended the riot "the bloodiest one-day encounter between Americans since the Civil War." Thirty-nine citizens were killed by the gunfire of law enforcement personnel. The objective of this chapter is an analysis of the context in which these events occurred emphasizing social conditions creating situational stress.

Social Deprivation and Frustration

The United States has a well-established tradition for riots both in its cities (Brown 1969) and in its prisons (Garson 1972a). Between the 1830s and 1850s, for example, there were thirty-five major riots in only four cities: Baltimore (12), Philadelphia (11), New York (8), and Boston (4). The myth of domestic tranquility in this country is more an ideal than a fact. Riots are a longstanding social problem and they have been the subject of numerous special reports that in recent years were often based on explanatory models developed in the social sciences. One of the most widely accepted explanations of riots places the blame on social conditions that cause human misery and deprivation.

The *deprivation-frustration-aggression (DFA) hypothesis* suggests that social deprivation leads to frustration, which in turn leads to aggression. McPhail (1971:1058) observes that this single general hypothesis has dominated research on riots and has "explicitly or implicitly guided or provided a basis for ex post facto interpretation of the majority of findings." The DFA hypothesis has been extremely popular and, at least in some quarters, has approached consideration as a fundamental social law (Gurr 1968). Prison administrators, for example, have generally accepted the principle that poor institutional conditions cause disturbances. Insufficient funding, so the argument goes, is responsible for bad food, confinement in small, poorly ventilated cells, hour-after-hour of boredom, ill-trained prison guards, and overcrowding. Such oppressive conditions supposedly create a "powder keg" easily triggered by an incident which sparks frustration into rebellion.

The so-called powder keg hypothesis linking social deprivation (poor prison conditions) to prison riots usually implies that only two factors must be present for an uprising to occur: (1) deprived living conditions and (2) a precipitating incident. But this simple scheme is not without opponents. Clarence Schrag (1960) has drawn attention to a number of important limitations.

Schrag has argued that poor prison conditions, inmate dissatisfaction and "sparking" incidents cannot be the sole explanation of prison riots, because these factors are neither restricted to prisons where riots have occurred nor are they necessarily present in prisons where riots have occurred. Schrag also argues that even though prison improvements have been painfully slow in coming, there has been consistent progress made in upgrading prisons since World War II. Since this is the case, prison riots should have become relatively less frequent rather than more frequent. Another criticism of the powder keg hypothesis is that prison riots have been relatively infrequent in the South, where prison conditions are very poor. (e.g., Murton 1972). Finally, Schrag astutely observed that the powder keg hypothesis places the blame for prison uprisings on conditions for which administrators cannot be held accountable. Prison officials, after all, are not responsible for inadequate operating budgets. Operating funds are usually the prerogative of budget-minded federal and state legislators.

Despite these criticisms, there is a possibility that the powder keg hypothesis may be correct in emphasizing the violent consequences of overcrowding. Prisons, particularly state institutions and county jails, are almost always seriously overcrowded. Corridors have been made into large bull pens for the daily overflow of people being held over for grand jury indictments or transfer to other institutions. Ethologists, who study animal behavior, have some evidence that the overcrowding of animals results in the breakdown of normal behavior and population decline (e.g., Calhoun 1962). But studies done with rats cannot provide unequivocable evidence for a link between overcrowding and human aggression, particularly since experiments involving human subjects have yielded inconsistent findings. One study found that men became more aggressive when crowded together, but that women did not. Men may become uncomfortable when their personal space is compromised, whereas high density and physical contact among women may be less uncomfortable (Freedman et al. 1972). Another study found that density had no effect on aggressiveness (Price 1971) and still another found that men are sometimes less aggressive under high density conditions than under low density conditions (Smith and Haythorn 1972). In short, the popular assumption that overcrowding is bad or has negative effects on human behavior is not unassailable. In addition, the effect of overcrowding may depend on a number of important situational variables which have not yet been adequately investigated. The length of time a person is crowded may influence his behavior, just as involuntary confinement may influence a person's reactions to crowded places. Further research along these lines may show that people indeed become more aggressive when crowded together. An important consequence of the belief in the powder keg theory is that convicts have been released by state officials who sometimes prefer not to risk the presumed consequences of overcrowding.

The evidence for social deprivation as a sufficient cause of urban riots is equally uncertain. One prominent study (Lieberson and Silverman 1965) found little support for the popular belief that race riots are simply an outgrowth of urban slums. Many highly educated people believe that urban riots are caused by dilapidated and overcrowded housing in black ghettos. But when cities that experienced a riot sometime between 1913 and 1963 are compared with riot-free cities of similar size and region, it is impossible to statistically distinguish these cities on the basis of housing conditions. The sad truth is that dilapidated housing is so common in most American cities that it cannot be used to account for why riots occur in some cities but not in others. Moreover, housing conditions were actually improving for urban blacks in the period between 1940 and 1970. As shown in Figure 7.1, nearly 40 percent of all black households lived in crowded conditions in 1940, but by 1970 the percentage was less than 20. For the most part, people were less crowded in the 1960s than in the 1950s, yet the riots occurred in the 1960s rather than the 1950s. Bad housing isn't likely to make people happy, but bad housing in itself cannot explain the occurrence of riots.

The data reported by Lieberson and Silverman (1965) also cast doubt on the popular notion that unemployment is an adequate explanation of urban riots. Once again it is impossible to distinguish between riot cities and riot-free cities on the basis of black unemployment rates. Figure 7.2 shows black unemployment rates improving between 1961 and 1969, whereas they had been deteri-

**FIGURE 7.1: Households Living in Crowded Conditions,
by Race, 1940, 1960, 1970**

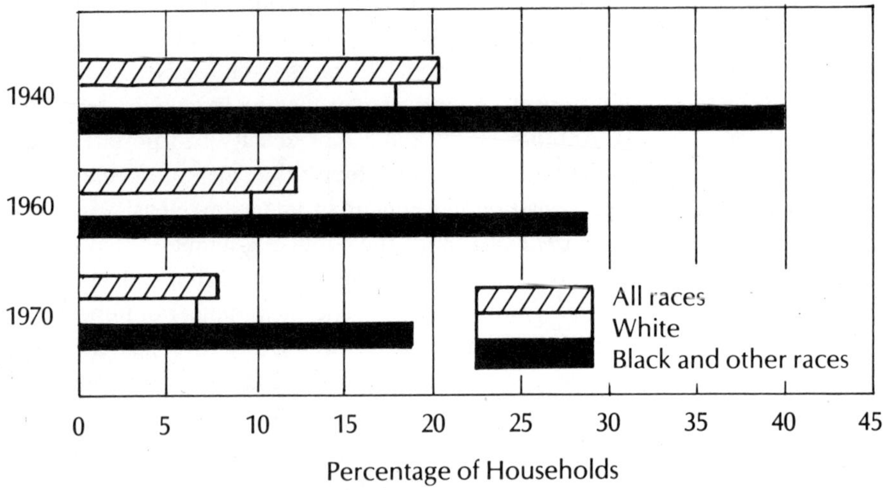

Source: Executive of the President, OMB, Social Indicators, 1973, USGPO, Washington, DC.

orating between 1953 and 1958. Such findings as a whole lend little support to the idea that deprivation necessarily leads to frustration which in turn causes aggression.

The results of ten research reports on five riots that occurred in the late 1960s suggest a similar conclusion. These ten research reports yielded a total of 287 coefficients of association between various "predictors" and "indicants" of collective violence (McPhail 1971). The majority of these coefficients (173) had something to do with the DFA hypothesis and are found in one of the categories as shown in Table 7.1.

The indicators grouped under Attitude Statements are essentially opinions abouts politics, housing practices, and race relations. Of the 79 coefficients included in this category only 6 were of at least a moderate magnitude (>.30). The objective indicators listed under Socioeconomic Attributes were even less productive since only 1 of 57 coefficients was of at least moderate magnitude.

Relative Deprivation and Frustration

Up to this point, social deprivation has referred to the objective living conditions of a group of people. *Relative deprivation* refers to *a perceived gap between a group's actual standard of living and its desired* standard of living. Groups can define a *desired* standard of living by comparing their current

FIGURE 7.2: Unemployment Rates by Race, 1948-74

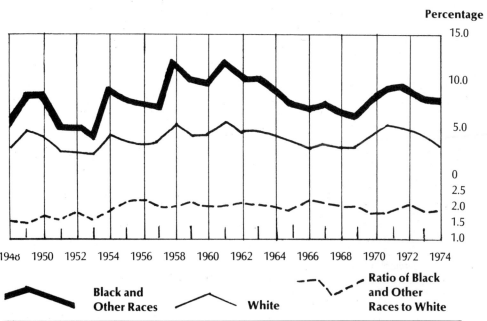

Source: Executive of the President, OMB, Social Indicators, 1973, USGPO, Washington, DC, 113.

living conditions against either the social conditions of their recent past or the standard of living enjoyed by some comparison group. The distinction between absolute social deprivation and relative deprivation is important because it allows for circumstances in which a group feels relatively deprived even though its objective standard of living is improving.

It is frequently argued that the black minority's growing awareness of the gap between its standard of living and the standard of living enjoyed by the white majority in this country led to the riots of the 1960s. When conditions are generally improving a group that sees itself being left behind is likely to become increasingly angry. Consequently, urban blacks who saw a widening gap between themselves and the white majority should have been disproportionately represented among the rioters of the 1960s. On the other hand, the growing success of the black middle class should have been seen as a source of satisfaction in as much as it implies a reduction in the gap between blacks and whites.

Two of the coefficients listed under Attitude Statements in Table 7.1 are directly relevant to the preceding logic. "Black Atts. re: whites" and "Black Atts. re: blacks" are attitudinal measures based on questions which asked: "Is the gap in income between Negroes and whites increasing, decreasing, or not

Table 7.1: Independent Variables — Frequency of Use and of Different Magnitudes of Association with Riot Participation

Independent Variables	f	%	n.s.	.00 .09	.10 .19	.20 .29	.30 .39	.40 +	Total
ATTITUDE STATEMENTS (I)									
1. Political Attributes	42	15	9		21	10	2		42
2. Job/housing Atts. & Expects.	22	8	8	1	5	4	2	2	22
3. Blacks' Atts. re:whites	10	3	1		7	2			10
4. Blacks' Atts. re:blacks	5	2			3	2			5
SOCIAL RELATIONS & INTERACTIONS (II)		20%							
5. Blacks social contacts w/whites	25	9	17		6	2			25
6. Other relations & inter.*	23	8	6	2	12	2	1		23
7. Marital status	6	2	1		1	4			6
8. Structure-Family of Orientation	4	1	2		2				4
SOCIOECONOMIC ATTRIBUTES (III)		19%							
9. Attribute Consistency	23	8	11		5	7			23
10. Education level	10	3	1	1	3	4	1		10
11. Income level	8	3	5		2	1			8
12. Employment	7	2	2		3	2			7
13. Underemployment	3	1			2	1			3
14. Occupational level	3	1	1	1	1				3
15. Other SES Indicators**	3	1	2		1				3
EXPERIENCE/OPINION OF DISCRIMINATION (IV)		17%							
16. Exper./Opinion of Police Malpractice	40	14	13	1	17	4	5		40
17. Exper./Opinion of Discrimination	10	3	2	1	7				10
DEMOGRAPHIC ATTRIBUTES (V)		10%							
18. Age	9	3			4	2	1	2	9
19. Place of Birth/Length of Residence	8	3	2		4	1	1		8
20. Region of Socialization	6	2	1	1		4			6
21. Sex	5	2	2	1	1			1	5
22. Ethnicity	1	0						1	1
POLITICAL PARTICIPATION (VI)		5%							
23. Voting Behavior	12	4	5		5	2			12
24. Civil Rights Discussion/ Activities	2	1			1	1			2
TOTALS	287		91	9	113	55	13	6	287
		100%	32%	3%	39%	19%	5%	2%	100%

*See fn. 5;** see fn. 6.

[5]This included number of group memberships, type of group membership, interaction with neighbors, church attendance, living alone or with others, organization membership and a social isolation index which combines information on organizational membership, living alone or with others, marital status and length of residence in riot city.

[6]This included SES level of residential area of the respondent, condition of the respondent's residence, and respondent's judgment of his personal economic status during the past few years.

Source: McPhail (1971:1061).

changing?" and "Is the gap between those Negroes who are better off and those who are poorer, increasing, decreasing, or not changing?"

The coefficient based on the first question was not significant, whereas the coefficient based on the second question was of significant magnitude. Both of these results are inconsistent with the DFA hypothesis: blacks who participate in riots should especially resent an increasing gap and they do not, while at the same time black rioters were particularly sensitive to where they stood in relation to middle-class Negroes (Caplan and Paige 1968:20). These negative findings tend to substantiate the results reported by Lieberson and Silverman (1965): the discrepancy between black and white median incomes was larger in cities without riots in 10 out of 12 possible comparisons. Moreover, they also found that median black income was just as likely to be higher in cities with riots than in those without riots. These findings contradict the notion that riots are a direct outcome of either low income or large black-white discrepancies in family income. But why did the riots of the 1960s occur in a period of generally increasing prosperity for blacks?

Social Prosperity and Rising Expectations

The *J-curve of rising expectations* (Davies 1969) is an attempt to explain why riots and revolutions occur *not* when social deprivation is extreme, but rather in periods of improving social conditions. When social conditions are generally improving, people supposedly expect further improvements in the future. A rising standard of living promotes a sense of optimism and the belief that "tomorrow will bring better things than today." Unfortunately the rising expectations of many deprived groups may outstrip their capacity for achievement just when some ultimate goal appears to be close at hand. Desired improvements can rarely be achieved quickly enough to avoid an "intolerable gap" between what people want and what they can actually get. According to Davies, the development of an intolerable gap is a direct cause of collective violence.

The J-curve of rising expectations (see Figure 7.3) was derived by Davies from his studies of the Russian and French Revolutions, but he has applied his analysis to student protests and the black rebellion of the 1960s. He explicitly contends that J-curve analysis is an assertion "about the state of mind of individual people in a society who are likely to revolt" (Davies 1969). Nevertheless, the data presented by Davies are aggregate statistics based on *national units*. Rising expectations are inferred from rising economic indicators of national prosperity, and gaps are inferred from nationally based indicators of sharp economic reversals. For example, the French Revolution of 1789 followed a period of growing prosperity as indicated by increasing farm productivity in the first half of the eighteenth century and rapid economic growth between 1763 and 1770. The war in America gave the French economy a further boost between 1778 and 1781, but this period was followed by a severe economic crisis in France. In 1788 a bad harvest combined with an unfavorable trade agreement with the English. The next year was even worse. High unemployment, a breakdown in food supply, and an inflationary rise in bread prices lead to the outbreak of revolution on July 14, 1789.

FIGURE 7.3: Need Satisfaction and Revolution: The J-Curve.

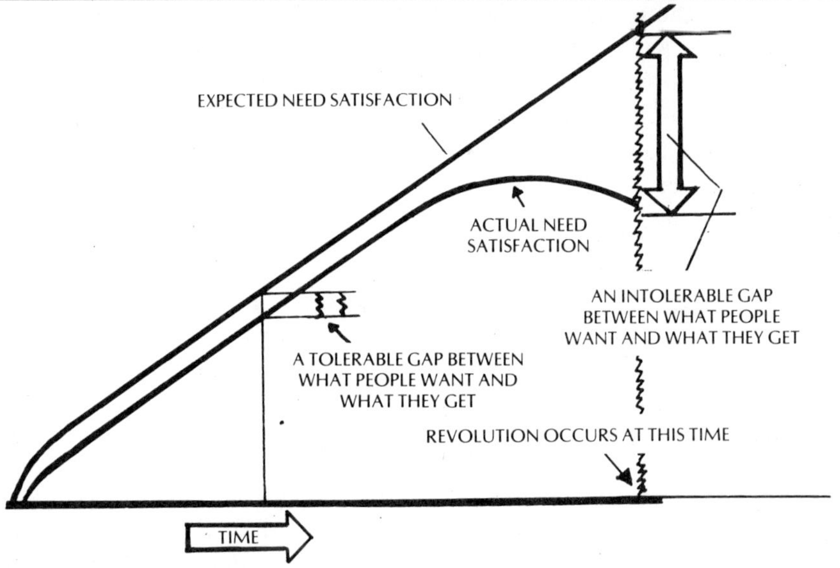

Source: Davies (1969: 691).

Davies' application of similar reasoning to the urban riots of the 1960s was fairly straightforward, except for one important modification to be noted later. Up until World War II the living standards and general health of American blacks showed little improvement above subsistence levels. Day-to-day survival was a constant concern accentuated by high mortality and short life expectancy. In the 1940s things began to change: (1) in 1941 an executive order ended discriminatory hiring in defense industries and opened jobs for over one million blacks, (2) the admission of blacks into the category of commissioned officer during the war years, (3) the beginning of Supreme Court desegregation decisions in 1946, capped by the 1948 decision for the integration of public housing and the 1954 decision ordering the massive integration of public schools, (4) the complete integration of all black army personnel into unsegregated units by 1954, and (5) the civil rights acts of 1954 and 1964 which protected and enforced the right of blacks to register and vote (Davies 1969). These signs of progress were unmistakable, and it is reasonable to suppose that the massive migration of southern blacks to the industrialized north reflected, at least in part, an expectation that standards of living could be dramatically improved.

Up to this point Davies encountered no serious problems with his scheme, but there was an important difficulty ahead. The difficulty stemmed from an index of "nonwhite economic satisfaction" that predicted the peak of black unrest should have occurred in the mid 1950s rather than between 1965 and 1967. Davies side stepped this problem by proposing that the rising expectations of black Americans were not really challenged until 1963, after a resurgence of white violence against blacks. The resurgence of white violence "affronted the dignity" of black people and "quickly frustrated rising expectations" for social equality. Thus Davies proposed a kind of gap for the black rebellion that was substantially different from the economic gap used to account for the French Revolution of 1789. Davies may have been historically accurate in making this change, but the modification itself opens his work to the criticism that J-curve analysis cannot be refuted since it only leads to the post hoc discovery of "new" gaps. This is a serious criticism and emphasizes the importance of stating the J-curve argument in testable form before data are even collected. Even so, Snyder and Tilly (1972) have challenged Davies' position on empirical grounds alone.

Snyder and Tilly studied collective violence in continental France during the period from 1830–1960. They plotted both the number of disturbances and the number of participants in disturbances across five-year intervals as shown in Figure 7.4. The greatest conflicts occurred when power was changing hands in France. For example, in 1851–52 the "crucial events were Louis Napoleon's *coup d'etat*, the widespread but unsuccessful insurrection it incited, and the installation of a police state under the man who was to become Napoleon III" (Snyder and Tilly 1972:523). At the same time, none of the models tested by Snyder and Tilly, using econometric time-series techniques, demonstrated significant relationships between indicators of economic deprivation and the magnitude of collective violence. They concluded instead that collective violence "tends to occur when one group lays claim to a set of resources, and at least one other group resists that claim" (1972:526). Government-sponsored repression, they suggest, accounts for the "major part of the damaging and seizing which constitutes the collective violence" of recent French history. In fact, Snyder and Tilly found that extent of *governmental repression* and *degree of political activity* provide a partial explanation for fluctuations in the magnitude of collective violence in France between 1830 and 1960.

The position outlined by Snyder and Tilly moves away from social psycho-

When riots erupted in Washington, DC following the assassination of Dr. Martin Luther King, Jr. on April 4, 1968, President Johnson called out federal troops to protect the city. The presence of troops may lead, however, to the formation of crowds.

**FIGURE 7.4: Disturbances and Participants in
Disturbances, 1832-1958**

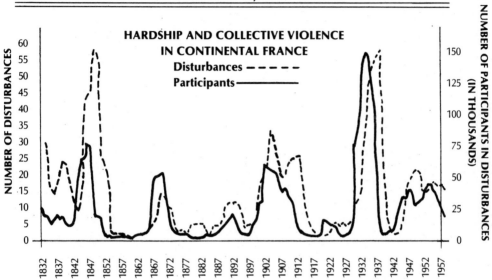

Source: Snyder and Tilly (1972: 523).

logical interpretations to a more sociological analysis of urban riots. Their viewpoint suggests that the riots of the 1960s were an expression of a political struggle between conflicting interest groups. Black Americans were making their claim on scarce resources traditionally denied to them because of racial discrimination and "blocked opportunity." There is no doubt that *discrimination* and the black minority's perception of *social injustice* were an important aspect of the social context of the 1960s.

Discrimination and Protest

Spokespeople for black Americans in the 1960s frequently saw the discrepancy between black and white standards of living as the result of racial discrimination and blocked opportunity. Correspondingly, they interpreted the riots themselves as an expression of political protest. Data from Detroit and Newark are consistent with this reasoning. For example, "96 percent of the rioters but only 50 percent of the non-rioters in Newark said racial discrimination constituted the major obstacle to better employment" (Caplan and Paige 1968:20). The rioters in both Detroit and Newark were also more likely than nonrioters to see themselves as victims of discrimination and express significantly higher levels of racial pride and identity with the black community.

Furthermore, data from Los Angeles (Sears and Tomlinson 1968) clearly refute the myth that blacks viewed the urban riots of the 1960s as a haphazard expression of disregard for law and order.

As shown in Table 7.2, majorities of black respondents felt that the riots "did have a purpose, that it was a black protest, and that those outsiders attacked in the riots deserved what they got" (Sears and Tomlinson 1968:489). It is significant that 38 percent of the black respondents living within the Los Angeles curfew zone and 45 percent of the "Arrestees" described the collective violence in Watts as a "revolt," "revolution," or "insurrection" even though the mass media consistently portrayed the same events as simple riots. The data presented by Sears and Tomlinson also refute the myth that urban blacks viewed the riots with alarm. Most of the black Los Angeles respondents (54%) anticipated "predominantly beneficial" effects from the disturbances, and only a minority (26%) expected unfavorable effects (1968:490). In contrast, 75 percent of the whites questioned in the same Los Angeles study felt that the riots had hurt the "Negro's Cause," an opinion which was explicitly denied by the majority of blacks: 38 percent of the respondents living in the curfew zone felt the riots had helped, and 54 percent of the arrestees agreed. The riots were undeniably a source of optimism for many blacks.

It is reasonable to suppose that collective violence is sometimes noninstrumental and without ideological meaning (Marx 1970), but this was not the case for most of the riots occurring in the 1960s. The black community generally viewed those events within an ideological framework emphasizing racial discrimination, economic exploitation, and the legitimacy of political protest. The riots were also seen within a social context that reflected a growing disillusionment with the progress being made by the civil rights movement in the United States.

By the mid-1960s the legal victories won by the National Association for the Advancement of Colored People (NAACP) which were initially a source of optimism in the black community had gradually become a source of discontent. "Free by 63!", a slogan popularized in 1957, was replaced by "Freedom Now!" in 1963. "Freedom Now!" was in turn replaced by "Burn, Baby, Burn!" in 1965. "Burn, Baby, Burn!" was generally interpreted as a call to arms and the Los Angeles riot of 1965 was in fact a turning point in the civil rights movement that marked significant changes in its leadership, goals, and tactics (Killian 1968). At a national level, Stokely Carmichael and H. Rap Brown were gaining in prominence while men such as Roy Wilkins and Dr. Martin Luther King were receding. The strategy of non-violent protest advocated by the Southern Christian Leadership Conference (SCLC) and other organizations was being replaced by a strategy of violent confrontation supported by the Black Panther Party. "Black Power" had emerged as a dominant slogan by

Table 7.2: The Riot As Protest

	Percent Whites	Percent Negroes (Curfew Zone)	Percent Arrestees
What word or term would you use in talking about it?			
Riot	58	46	44
Revolt, revolution, insurrection	13	38	45
Other (disaster, tragedy, mess, disgrace, etc.)	27	8	10
Don't know, no answer	2	8	2
Total	100%	100%	100%
Why were targets attacked?*			
Deserved attack	—	64	75
Ambivalent, don't know	—	17	21
Did not deserve attack	—	14	0
No answer	—	5	4
Total		100%	100%
Did it have a purpose or goal?			
Yes	33	56	56
Don't know, other	4	11	13
No	62	28	29
No answer	—	5	2
Total	99%	100%	100%
Was it a Negro protest?			
Yes	54	62	66
Don't know, other	3	12	15
No	42	23	16
No answer	—	2	3
Total	99%	99%	100%

*This question was not asked of white respondents.
Source: Sears and Tomlinson (1968:489).

1967 and it symbolized the black minority's frustration in achieving political and economic self-determination. After 1965, even the more conservative black leaders in this country were beginning to suggest that violence was an understandable, if not fully justified, course of action. The fact that most whites disagreed with this assessment of the situation is important but cannot discredit the black viewpoint.

Prison riots in the 1960s were also race-related disturbances and unquestionably reflected the political influence of the civil rights movement in the United States. Between 1968 and 1971 there were at least 37 major prison riots, frequently led by black inmates and other minority group members (Pallas and Barber 1972, Flynn 1973). The origin of these riots is now recognized as the racial and political tensions of our society as a whole. The report of the New York State Special Commission on Attica notes that prisons were not insulated from the growing mood of anger and alienation that was so characteristic of the 1960s. The young black inmates at Attica in 1971 were products of conditions found in the cities where "pervasive discrimination and segregation, continued black in-migration . . . and poverty converge . . . to destroy opportunity and enhance failure" (New York State Special Commission on Attica [NYSSCA] 1972:115). From 1966 to 1970, 73 percent of all inmates received in New York prisons came from urban areas, 65 percent were black or Puerto Rican, and 43 percent were under 30.

In the late 1960s, militant young blacks were joined in prison by a new type of white inmate: young, well educated, involved with drugs, and often characterized by the establishment as a politically-motivated agitator. The bond between militant blacks and the new type of white inmate was their common rejection of established authority and their denunciation of the wages, programs, hygiene, medical care, and censorship typically found in state institutions (NYSSCA 1972:118). Together they challenged one of the oldest codes of the prison: "Do your own time." Inmates demanded the right to form associations for religious and political purposes. They joined organizations which stressed ethnic identity, such as the Muslims, the Black Panthers, and the Young Lords. They began to consider themselves political prisoners, even though the majority of them had not been convicted of a politically-motivated crime. Many claimed that the responsibility for their actions belonged not to them—but to a society which failed to provide adequate housing, equal educational opportunities, and an equal opportunity to compete in American life. Believing themselves to be victims, prison inmates frequently claimed that the public should concentrate its efforts on the rehabilitation of society. The prison programs which existed in most institutions were ridiculed as preparations for a submissive role in a racist and unfair society (NYSSCA 1972:117–8). In this context, the most recent series of prison riots was a part of a broad underclass challenge to the status quo and traditional authority.

Political interpretations of prison riots, and of crowd violence more generally, have the advantage of focusing on broad social conditions rather than on the subjective states of individuals. But even so, many questions are unanswered by a purely political interpretation of collective violence. Why do riots occur at certain times, for example, and how do they get started? More to the point, situational stress, whether as a consequence of social deprivation, rising expectations, or social injustice, is in itself an incomplete background for crowd violence. *Rumors* and *precipitating events* are also important preconditions of riots.

Threatening Rumors

Rumors play an important part in the riot process before, during and *after* the outbreak of collective violence. Rumors, defined in Chapter III as "unconfirmed message(s) passed from one person to another in face-to-face interaction," are likely to occur in periods of social crisis because people define a new social reality whenever they fail to perceive a stable and unambiguous environment. The greater the situational ambiguity the greater an individual's need for information from other people—a need further increased by the perceived importance of events. The spread of rumors is also inversely related to a group's capacity for evaluating rumored information in a particular set of circumstances. The more threatening the circumstances and the greater the perceived need for immediate action, the less likely it is that a group of people will spend time deliberating the merits of rumored information.

In periods preceding riots, *rumors can enhance situational stress* by predicting the outbreak of violence which in turn can lead to fear and overreaction. The crisis at Attica prison was inflamed by the spread of threatening rumors predicting the outbreak of violence. In August of 1971, Commissioner Oswald and his staff at Attica were "constantly receiving warnings from almost everywhere in the prison system that serious trouble was at hand" (Oswald 1972:-41). Prison officials, like the police, often rely on information from informants and consequently they are particularly prone to accept rumors at face value. Rumors are rampant within prison populations and Oswald attempted to keep abreast of only the most serious: (1) the riot would begin at Attica no sooner than the end of August or in September, (2) the riot would occur instead on November 2 and would be "tied in somehow to California, where Angela Davis was then being held on murder charges," (3) the riot would be coordinated with outside groups who would storm one of four state institutions by "killing the correction officers in the towers, and bringing in firearms and explosives," (4) the riot would be "coordinated with kidnappings of prominent people, who would then be exchanged for prominent militant leaders." According to Commissioner Oswald, a plan to kidnap Caroline Kennedy, John F. Kennedy's daughter, had to be abandoned by the "revolutionaries" because she was too well guarded at her school in New York City (1972:41).

In response to each of these rumored plots, the commissioner and his staff planned counteractions with the "appropriate law enforcement agencies." State officials who recognized the unreliability of their informants, nevertheless failed to make any attempt to verify rumors. The uncritical acceptance of rumored information by state officials hampered decision making at Attica throughout the entire crisis. Rumors of different kinds appeared and reappeared and were nearly always accepted at face value. One explanation for this noteworthy pattern of behavior is that the rumors reconfirmed what state officials already believed. The rumored information received by Commissioner Oswald and his staff was completely consistent with their interpretations of events at Attica and elsewhere in the country. Specifically, it appears that a significant number of state officials were committed to a "conspiracy theory" of prison rebellion. Prison riots, according to the prevailing conspiracy theory, were part of a grand revolutionary plan to overthrow the national government. The riots were intended "to polarize the people of the United States," and become a symbol of "establishment repression" (Oswald 1972:28–33). It was feared that collective violence would spread from the nation's prisons to its city slums. The Attica inmates constituted the vanguard of a new revolutionary army, and the prison itself was the first line of national defense.

Commissioner Oswald feared that some of the more dangerous militants lodged at Attica were making plans for the anticipated riot. A number of inmates were singled out as potential ring leaders. One was Richard X. Clark. Clark had been transferred to Attica from New York's Auburn Prison where he had allegedly taken part in a prison riot. Herber X. Blyden was also singled out as a potential riot leader. Brother Herbert, as he was called at Attica, had been one of five men who signed "The Attica Liberation Faction Manifesto of Demands and Antidepression Platform" which Oswald received in July. More important, Blyden had arrived at Attica with the reputation of being a riot leader. He was under indictment on 75 counts for his alleged role in a major riot at the Tombs, a New York City jailhouse. Another potential leader of the upcoming riot was believed to be Samuel Melville, who was also known as the Mad Bomber. He was one of the few authentic revolutionaries at Attica. Melville had been convicted for a series of explosions in New York City and had been sentenced for 6 to 18 years on a charge of first-degree arson. For state officials, the mere presence of these men at Attica seemed to confirm rumors predicting the outbeak of violence.

The situation at Attica became so tense that correction officers from all of New York's institutions demanded an "emergency meeting." By the end of August, 1971, they feared their institutions were about to "explode." The correction officers from Attica felt they were understaffed and, as their apprehensions were escalated by still more rumors, they compounded problems by calling in sick. When they did show up for work there was a tendency for the older and more experienced officers to choose job assignments at a safe distance from the inmates.

A second way in which rumors can enhance situational stress is by *crystalizing intergroup hostility.* In the 1960s rumors were vehicles for the expression of racial prejudice. Certain themes in rumors are closely associated with outbreaks of collective violence. Knopf (1975) calls these themes "hostile belief systems." For example, rumors spread among whites typically suggest that blacks are inherently violent, promiscuous, and continually conspiring against whites and white property. Blacks, on the other hand, believe that whites are inherently violent, that the police and other agents of "white authority" abuse their power, and that the white establishment's "system" is forever conspiring against them (Knopf 1975:145). Murder, rape, and castration are frequently the substance of the rumors.

In the period preceding the Detroit riot of 1967, there were several inflammatory rumors circulating within the city. One story was about a black couple assaulted by white youths and in a second story a man was killed with a gun. A third rumor was based on an incident that occurred about three weeks before the riot. The city administration had initiated an aggressive campaign to end prostitution in the Twelfth Street area of Detroit and rumor had it that police officers involved in the crackdown had brutally beaten one of the prostitutes and her "boyfriend" (Singer et al. 1970:36). One week later a prostitute was killed and it was rumored that she had been murdered by the police (Locke 1969).

A third way in which rumors can increase situational stress is by *escalating the significance of otherwise minor incidents*. Rumors occasionally transform a series of minor incidents into events that precipitate riots. The Harlem (New York) race riot in 1935, for example, began as the result of a routine police action: a 16-year-old youth was arrested for stealing a knife from a department store. In the process of making the arrest the boy's hand was cut and he began to bleed. To avoid spectators, the police took their suspect to the basement of the building to await the arrival of an ambulance. A woman began to scream that the police had taken the boy to the basement to beat him up. This was not the case, but the arrival of the ambulance "confirmed" the woman's accusation and the rumor spread that the boy was "near death."

A similar process took place at Watts in 1965, at Newark in 1967, and at Detroit in the same year. In Watts a young man was stopped on suspicion of drunken driving, an argument developed, and a young lady in pink hair curlers intervened on his behalf. A scuffle ensued and the rumor spread among bystanders that the police were abusing a pregnant, black woman. In Newark a black cab driver was arrested and the rumor spread that he had been badly beaten by the police. The story was that witnesses had seen the driver being dragged into the police station in a paralyzed state (National Advisory Commission on Civil Disorders 1968). In Detroit the police made a routine raid on an after-hours drinking club and rumors of police brutality quickly spread throughout the black community: a young man was allegedly pushed down a flight of stairs and a female prisoner was supposedly "manhandled" by the police (Knopf 1975:204).

One of the most striking aspects of the preceding rumors is the involvement of the police. What is not so clear is how rumors can link various incidents together and *define events in the light of community grievances*. In Detroit, for example, the rumors preceding the outbreak of collective violence on July 23, 1967 were tied together by an underlying theme of police brutality that reinforced the black community's antipathy toward "white" law enforcement. This linkage of ordinarily trivial events, according to the National Advisory Commission on Civil Disorders (1968), contributed to a "cumulative process" of mounting tensions that ultimately "spilled over" into violence. The Commission found that a *series of tension-heightening incidents* preceded each of 24 riots that it investigated in 20 cities and at 3 universities. These *precipitating events* occurred in a period of weeks or months before the outbreak of collective violence and were "linked in the minds of many Negroes to a preexisting reservoir of underlying grievances."

Precipitating Events and Community Grievances

The 24 riots surveyed by the National Advisory Commission on Civil Disorders (1968) were each preceded by a series of at least 3 precipitating events. Of all of the incidents identified by the Commission, some 40 percent involved a police action, 22 percent involved black protest activities, and an additional 17 percent involved white racist activities. The white racist activities included 15 cross burnings in New Jersey and the killing of a Negro boy by a group of white youths in Detroit. Police actions were identified as the final incident preceding 12 of the 24 riots. A common element in most of the incidents (about 93%) was confrontation between blacks and whites in which members of both groups felt "wronged" by the other group.

In many of the incidents, urban blacks felt that they were treated unfairly because of racial discrimination. A typical incident took place in Bridgeton, New Jersey five days before the outbreak of collective violence in that city. Two police officers were sent to question a young man about a complaint for nonsupport. A fight began and the young black was critically injured and partially paralyzed. Acting for the injured man's family, a Negro minister asked for the suspension of the two officers pending an investigation of the incident. This request was denied even though the same procedure had been used when three policemen had been accused of "collusion" in the robbery of a white-owned store.

There is no doubt that a significant number of police in the 1960s were racists. In that decade it was not uncommon to hear patrolmen and even police officials referring to blacks as "animals in a zoo," and housing projects as "nigger hatcheries." In Los Angeles and other cities the police both feared black people and openly expressed their contempt. Stark's monograph, *Police Riots*, gives this picture of what some Los Angeles police were like:

(They) greet each other with the old Luckey Strike slogan: LSMFT— Which they translate as "Let's Shoot a Mother-Fucker Tonight." Many policemen call their night sticks and riot batons "nigger knockers." Nor has it been all talk. Reports from many cities, including Detroit, San Francisco, Chicago, New York, and Oakland indicate that police officers have attacked or shot members of the black community, often Black Panthers, at offices, social events, at home in bed, and even in the halls of a courthouse (Stark 1972:98).

In Los Angeles members of the Black Panther Party complained bitterly that they were being harassed by the police simply because they had placed "Black Panther" stickers on the rear bumpers of their cars. The Panthers were afraid of losing their drivers' licenses because they were getting so many traffic citations from the overzealous police. The police denied that they had been picking on the Black Panther Party and observed that its members were "irresponsible" citizens who by implication were likely to ignore traffic regulations. A field experiment reported by Heussenstamm (1971) seems to have resolved this disagreement in favor of the Black Panthers.

For Heussenstamm's experiment 15 students, all of whom had no traffic violations for the previous 12 months, put Black Panther bumper stickers on their cars. They were told to drive their cars just as they had in the past and were admonished to obey all traffic regulations. Nevertheless, within only four days one subject was forced to drop out of the experiment because he had already accumulated three traffic tickets. Within the first week of the experiment three other people had also received three citations and were withdrawn from the study. Altogether, the 15 drivers received 33 tickets in 17 days. Such findings do little to dispel the black community's allegations of police harassment and brutality in the 1960s.

According to Stark (1972), the racist attitudes of many white policemen did in fact combine with what he described as police attitudes favoring the routine use of excessive violence. Naturally there is controversy over the question of when violence becomes "excessive." Nonetheless, a series of crime commissions have pointed to the problem of police brutality. And the accusations of these commissions have been generally substantiated by both interview data and systematic observation of the police in action (Stark 1972:83). Even if this evidence is inaccurate, there is no doubt that many urban blacks *believed* in the reality of police brutality. As Table 7.3 shows, a survey study of South Central Los Angeles found that 65 percent of the Negro respondents believed that the police used unnecessary force in making arrests, and nearly 37 percent said that they had seen the police use unnecessary force.

The hostile attitude of many white police toward black Americans in the 1960s was complemented by their exaggerated belief in the danger of their

Table 7.3:   Ghetto Perceptions of Police Brutality
Percent Distribution of Negro Responses to 24 Questions
About Police Brutality (N = 586)

	Lack of respect, insulting language	Roust and frisk	Stop and search cars	Search homes	Unnecessary force in arrest	Beat up in custody
Do you think it happens to people in this area?						
Yes	71.3%	71.9%	68.5%	42.5%	65.5%	65.2%
No	11.8	12.2	14.1	24.4	14.0	11.1
Don't know	15.5	15.2	16.0	31.7	19.5	22.3
No answer	1.4	.7	1.4	1.4	1.0	1.4
Has it happened to you?						
Yes	23.0	20.9	19.3	5.1	7.8	3.9
No	58.2	58.8	58.8	65.4	68.5	69.8
Don't know	.2	0.0	0.0	.2	0.0	0.0
No answer	18.6	21.2	21.8	29.4	23.7	26.3
Have you seen it happen?						
Yes	38.6	41.1	39.9	15.2	36.9	20.8
No	40.2	38.9	38.6	54.8	41.6	54.4
Don't know	0.0	0.0	.2	.2	0.0	0.0
No answer	21.2	20.0	21.3	29.8	21.5	24.8
Has it happened to someone you know?						
Yes	41.5	37.9	37.4	20.8	32.1	34.4
No	38.4	41.6	39.6	49.2	42.5	40.0
Don't know	.2	.5	.2	.2	0.0	.2
No answer	20.9	20.0	22.8	29.8	25.4	25.4

Source: Raine (1967).

occupation and a growing reliance on weaponry. The cognitive orientation of the police, in short, led them to anticipate violence; and their anticipation of serious trouble, in turn, frequently led to overreactions in situations where no real danger was imminent (Marx 1970:41). Black neighborhoods in New Jersey were occupied by police before any disorders occurred, and other blacks living in New Jersey were angered by tear gas which had blown into their homes after a police training session on "riot control" techniques. This kind of approach often created confrontations and a focal point for the process of *crowd formation* discussed in Chapter VIII.

Summary and Conclusions

The *deprivation-frustration-aggression hypothesis* suggests that social deprivation causes frustration which, in turn, leads to aggression. But when deprivation is treated in *absolute* terms and refers to objective standards of living as indicated by overcrowded housing, unemployment, and low family income, it is not possible to account for the outbreak of collective violence in the 1960s. Poor housing and high unemployment, for example, are long-standing historical problems common to most American cities. They are closer to being a constant feature of urban areas than to being a variable feature. Furthermore, both housing conditions and unemployment rates were improving rather than worsening for Black Americans in the 1960s.

When deprivation is treated in *relative* terms as a perceived gap between blacks and whites it is still not possible to account for the urban riots of the last decade. One study shows that riots were more likely to occur in cities with small black-white discrepancies in median family income rather than in cities with large discrepancies. And a second study indicates that it is impossible to distinguish between rioters and nonrioters on the basis of their perception of an increasing economic gap between blacks and whites. Interestingly, it was found that the urban rioters of the 1960s were distinctive in their perception of an increasing gap between themselves and middle-class Negroes.

These negative findings, on the whole, suggest that deprivation is not a sufficient explanation for the urban riots of the 1960s. Nevertheless, social deprivation was an important source of *situational stress*. Situational stress, in itself, does not necessarily lead to collective violence. Other factors must also come into play as in Smelser's value-added model.

Davies developed the J-curve of rising expectations to account for the occurrence of revolutions and riots during periods of social improvement. The central assumption of his work is that a group's expectations will outpace its capacity for achievement when confronted with sharp economic reversals. Intolerable gaps between what people thought they could get and what they actually achieve are direct causes of collective violence. With respect to the "black rebellion" of the 1960s, Davies argues that the gap which triggered the outbreak of violence was the black community's recognition of continued social inequality despite a series of legal victories and improving social conditions. It was a recognition forced upon them by the resurgence of white violence towards blacks after about 1963. The frustration of the black community was its realization that "nothing had really changed."

Survey data suggest that the collective violence of the 1960s was a form of political protest. Urban blacks commonly interpreted the riots as protests against racial discrimination, economic exploitation, and unequal opportunity. This protest theme is reflected in their view of "white authority," in their allegations of "police brutality," and in the rumors that circulated among them.

Rumors were a significant part the riot process typically observed in the 1960s. Rumors enhanced situational stress by *predicting the outbreak of vio-*

lence, by *crystalizing intergroup hostility,* and by *escalating the importance of otherwise minor incidents.* Rumors linked ordinarily minor incidents together and *defined events in the light of existing community grievances.*

A *series of tension-heightening incidents or precipitating events* generally preceded the riots of the 1960s, confrontation between blacks and whites in which members of one group felt "wronged" by the other was an element in many of these incidents. Police actions accounted for roughly 40 percent of all the incidents identified by the National Advisory Council of Civil Disorders (1968).

J curve impt –
Rumors –

To what extent may rising expectations explain the looting that took place in New York City after the power outage in July 1977?

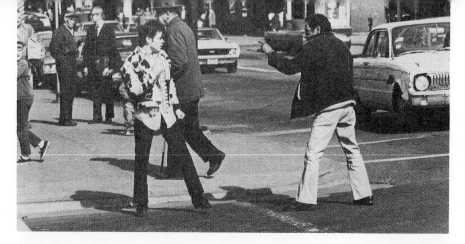

Racial incidents such as this street corner fist fight between a white from Appalachia and a native American can sometimes precipitate the formation of a crowd and more violence.

CHAPTER VIII

Crowd Formation

The existence of a crowd is often assumed in discussions of riots, but the problem of *how* crowds form should not be taken for granted. Crowds are neither "omnipresent nor continuous" (McPhail and Miller 1973). The objective of this chapter is an overview of the process of crowd formation. Special consideration is given to each of the following factors: (1) the size of *proximate populations,* (2) *assembling instructions,* (3) *crowd composition,* and (4) *crowd boundaries.*

Crowd Formation and Proximate Populations

Precipitating events frequently provide a focal point for the development of crowds. One factor underlying the process of crowd formation is the size of *proximate populations* of people. Large, proximate populations are conducive to crowd formation. A majority of the urban riots of 1967 began at or near pedestrian intersections, while the majority of campus demonstrations occurred at large universities rather than small colleges.

It is extremely difficult to extract a uniform pattern across different cities and events. Nevertheless, some generalizations are possible. Of the 24 disorders extensively surveyed by the National Advisory Commission, in all but two cases the disturbances began between 7:00 P.M. and 12:30 A.M. Moreover, 50 or more persons were generally in the immediate vicinity of the first outbreak of disorder. Collective violence, therefore, seems to be dependent upon the proximity of a large number of people. Several other facts are consistent with this premise. The urban riots of the 1960s tended to occur in July

(60%), June or August, on the weekends, and especially when the weather was hot and the interiors of slum buildings were even more unbearable than usual. Finally, seven-eighths of the major disturbances surveyed by the National Advisory Commission occurred in cities with populations in excess of 250,000 people.

The demographic composition of the rioters also suggests the critical importance of the proximity of people as a determinant of crowd formation. The rioters were just the sort of individuals you would expect to congregate outside on a hot summer night: the young, the single, and the divorced. Over 86 percent of the rioters in Detroit and Newark were between 15 and 35 years of age, and 61 percent were between 15 and 24 years old. The comparable percentages for nonrioters in these same age brackets were 38 and 23 percent. Young, single, or divorced persons have fewer obligations to other people, consequently they have more discretion in the use of their own time. In addition, it is probable that many younger members of ghetto communities were employed on a part-time rather than full-time basis.

The preceding remarks suggest a linear relationship between the number of disorders experienced by various American cities and the size of their black populations. Incidents occurring in cities with large black populations would be more likely to spark crowd formation than incidents occurring in cities with only small black populations. The larger the black population, one would suppose, the larger the number of urban riots. But Spilerman's research (1971) has specified the form of the relationship as an S-shaped curve. There is both a *threshold* effect and a *ceiling* effect for the size of proximate black populations.

As shown in Table 8.1, there were no disorders in 261 cities with black populations of less than 1000 people. This suggests that the "human resources" required for riots were insufficient in small communities, that there is a threshold population size below which rioting crowds will fail to form. It is also evident from Spilerman's data that the number of disorders per city increased with the size of the black population living within a city. There were 1.62 riots per city for the 21 cities with black populations between 50,000 and 100,000 people and 4.95 riots per city for the 19 communities with more than 100,000 blacks. But more significantly, row 5 of Table 8.1 indicates that the number of disorders per 1,000 blacks in a city increased up to a black population size of 5,000 people and then began to drop off. Spilerman suggested two explanations for this drop off.

First, he proposed a "saturation effect." As the number of disorders within a city increased and intervening time periods decreased, it would become more and more likely for disorders to be counted as a single, major riot. The second possibility is that the riots occurring in large black ghettos tended to involve

Table 8.1: Disorder Data for Cities with 25,000 or More Inhabitants, by Negro Population Size, 1961–1968

	Negro Population of City (in thousands)							
	0.00–1.00	1.00–2.50	2.50–5.00	5–15	15–25	25–50	50–100	100+
(1) Number of Disorders*	0	11	31	85	37	49	34	94
(2) Number of Cities	261	93	80	118	44	37	21	19
(3) Aggregate Negro Population (1,000s)†	92	151	300	1,076	846	1,289	1,490	6,212
(4) Disorders per City	0	.118	.388	.720	.841	1.324	1.619	4.947
(5) Disorders per 1,000 Negroes	0	.073	.103	.079	.044	.038	.023	.015

*Sources of the disorder data are *The New York Times Index*, Congressional Quarterly's *Civil Disorder Chronology* (1967), and the Lemberg Center's *Riot Data Review* (1968).

†1960 Census of Population.
Source: Spilerman (1971:431).

many individuals in major disturbances rather than relatively small numbers of people in several "minor" disorders. In either case, the number of disorders in a city (D) would be constrained by a ceiling effect. Spilerman fitted the curves shown in Figure 8.1 to a general S-shaped function:

$$D = e^{\left[a - \beta \frac{(e^{-\gamma N})}{N^2} - \delta \frac{(1 - e^{\gamma N})}{N}\right]}$$

where a, β, γ and δ are parameters. The proportion of variation in number of disorders accounted for by the curve for non-South cities was 73 percent. The nonlinear regression for cities in the South was considerably less efficient (34 percent). Nonetheless, both proportions are substantial and reflect the overall importance of the size of proximate populations in the development of crowds. Additional work suggests a connection between crowd size and the availability of proximate populations.

Coleman and James (1961) have developed an equilibrium model of crowd size based on the assumption that the "acquisition rate" for a crowd is "proportional to the number of single individuals available to be 'picked up'." They based their mathematical model on the premise that free-forming crowds are the result of a "natural process" in which there is a tendency for people to break away from a crowd in proportion to its size. To some extent, the loss rate and acquisition rate counterbalance each other, but crowd size is ultimately dependent upon the number of persons in the vicinity. One difficulty of this model is its assumption that people are as equally likely to join a small crowd as a large one.

FIGURE 8.1: Relationship Between Racial Disturbances During 1961-68 and Negro Population Size

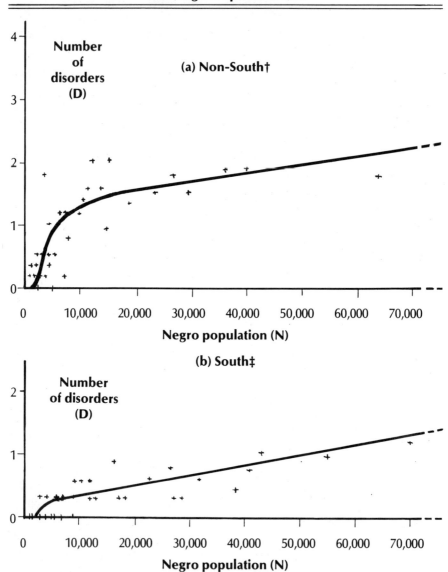

*Each point represents five cities that are adjacent in Negro population size. The group value for Negro population is the anti-log of the mean of the logged figures. The group value for number of disorders is the arithmetic mean. (Grouping is for presentation purposes only; all analyses were performed on the individual city values.)

†Parameter values for the non-South are: $\alpha = 2.649$, $\beta = 1.708 \times 10^7$, $\delta = 3.271 \times 10^5$, $\gamma = 6.95 \times 10^{-6}$

‡Parameter values for the South are: $\alpha = 1.270$, $\beta = 2.103 \times 10^6$, $\delta = 6.615 \times 10^4$, $\gamma = 5.23 \times 10^{-5}$

Source: Spilerman (1971: 432).

A study completed by Milgram, Bickman, and Berkowitz (1969) has investigated the "drawing power" of large and small crowds. The subjects (N = 1,424)
were New York City pedestrians who happened to use a 50-foot length of
sidewalk on two winter afternoons in 1968. A stimulus crowd (groups of
experimental confederates) entered the target area, stopped, and looked up at
the sixth floor of a building on the other side of the street. Their focal point
was dimly perceived and exceptionally unexciting: two people standing at a
window. The "crowd crystals" (Cannetti 1962) were each composed of 1, 2,
3, 5, 10, or 15 people. The purpose of this exercise was to determine how many
pedestrians who passed through the observation area would either look up at
the window or stop and join the crowd. As shown in Figure 8.2, only 4 percent
of the passersby stopped alongside a single individual compared to 40 percent
who stopped alongside a stimulus crowd of 15. According to this study, large
crowds have greater drawing power than small crowds.

Several other factors affect the assembling process in addition to the size of
the proximate population and the size of the stimulus crowd. Variations in

**FIGURE 8.2: Mean Percentage of Passersby Who Look Up and Who
Stop, as a Function of the Size of the Stimulus Crowd**

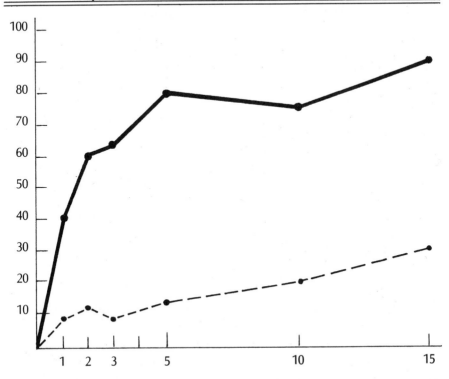

Source: Milgram, Bickman, and Berkowitz (1969: 80).

assembling instructions (McPhail and Miller 1973:107) have an important effect. Rallies and demonstrations are sometimes preceded by flyers and public announcements. In fact, crowd formation is usually structured by assembling instructions.

Crowd Formation
and Assembling Instructions

The formation of crowds at rallies, demonstrations and parades and at the scenes of fires, accidents, or arrests is dependent on assembling instructions that direct people to a particular location at a particular point in time (McPhail and Miller 1973). People have to know about an event in order to become part of an assembling crowd. Sometimes they receive "short-range" notice, and at other times people learn about events through "long-range" notification (McPhail and Miller 1973).

When sights and sounds (e.g., smoke, police sirens) indicate that "something is happening" someone will usually suggest "going to see what's happening." Such suggestion constitutes *short-range assembling instructions*. The subsequent movement of people toward the scene of an event amounts to a *nonverbal* assembling instruction for still more people. And the greater the *social density* of people in the vicinity of the event the greater the diffusion of assembling instructions. (McPhail and Miller 1973, Lewis and Carlson 1977). People converge on a crowd from more distant places after there has been time for "long-range" notification through television, radio, leaflets, newspapers, or rumors. The times and locations for rallies and demonstrations are typically announced in flyers and newspapers in advance of their occurrence. Television and radio play a more important part in notifying people of spontaneously developing events. In the 1960s, many people were seen with pocket radios which they used to "keep up with the action." Others were not so well informed; they have been called the "know-nothings."

The "know-nothing" hypothesis states that no matter what the nature of a crisis a "hard core" of persons in a community will remain "chronically uninformed" (Spitzer and Denzin 1965). The hypothesis has been supported primarily in studies that involved events of limited magnitude and importance (Bogart 1950, Medalia and Larsen 1958). When a president is shot almost everyone, even the chronically uninformed, will hear about the event. Nonetheless, some people will know little about an event even when they have heard of it. Spitzer and Denzin's study (1965) of news flow after the assassination of President Kennedy found that low levels of information were characteristic of *older* rather than *younger* persons. The underrepresentation of older people among the rioters of the 1960s might therefore be partly explained by lack of knowledge rather than lack of sympathy.

As could be expected, people who learn about an event from a large number of sources are more likely than others to follow assembling instructions (McPhail and Miller 1973, Lewis and Carlson 1977). But people don't always follow instructions. They are not always "free" to attend rallies and look in on fires and arrests; time is often committed to other activities, and time is given up reluctantly. As shown in Figure 8.2, the percentage who stopped in the study on crowd size and drawing power was always smaller then the percentage who looked up at the sixth-floor window. Looking up takes less time than stopping. Campus demonstrations tend to occur in the afternoons and evenings when fewer classes are scheduled. The urban riots of the 1960s tended to occur in the evenings of weekends when people had more free time. Moreover, riot participants were disproportionately drawn from categories of people with the fewest social commitments. But even people with time to spare are not necessarily available for recruitment into crowds.

Some people are reluctant to do anything without a companion. Not surprisingly, "a fair proportion of the participants (in a crowd) are likely to have specifiable kinship or friendship ties to one or more other participants ..." (Milgram and Toch 1969:523). Aveni (1977), for example, found that people celebrating a football victory at Ohio State University were doing so with one or more friends. People may also be unavailable because they lack access or transportation to an event. Other people may simply refuse to attend rallies and demonstrations or show any curiosity about local incidents. Some people may be "joiners" while others are not. The motivational theorists in collective behavior (Zygmunt 1972) have put much effort into identifying what kinds of people are *predisposed* to join crowds and into motivational analyses of *crowd composition*.

Crowd Composition

Hoffer's (1951) model of "mass discontent" suggests that participation in political movements and collective violence is an escape from the "futility of spoiled lives." Talents and other ascribed status attributes are never distributed equally in any society, and this circumstance, according to Hoffer, means that there are always a large number of "losers" in a system where success is based on competition. Life's losers, the misfits of a society, fall into two types. Unemployed college students, young people without clearly defined occupational careers, and adults between jobs are life's "temporary misfits." They may agonize over their indefinite futures and worry that the best years of their lives are passing without bringing fulfillment, but these people are not really part of the hard-core of discontent. The hard core is made of "permanent misfits:" the uneducated, unskilled, unemployable, physically infirm, and mentally retarded.

For all social misfits, the promise of collective behavior is an escape from themselves, an escape from botched lives, an escape from failure. When our own lives fail we have time left over to meddle in the affairs of other people, to gossip, and concoct plans to undermine the game in which we could not succeed. The seething frustration of discontent, according to Hoffer, will express itself as hostility and aggression whenever an opportunity is available. Local issues and community incidents are the occasion for collective violence, not the cause of it. The idyllic promises of an "infallible leader" who is seen as a bearer of hope transforms "action programs" into a chance to lose oneself through total involvement in "communal affairs." In short, life's losers, Hoffer's misfits, are always ready for mobilization—ripe for political and economic exploitation.

As harsh and exaggerated as this viewpoint may be, it nevertheless had its full share of champions in the 1960s; and it continues to draw support from some groups even today. Hoffer's statement of mass discontent is an implicit defense of the status quo and an explicit indictment of individuals. Faults in the economic and political institutions of a community are overlooked in favor of a sweeping attack on the real or imagined inadequacies of the socially maladjusted. Obviously, this kind of orientation will have strong appeal to civil authorities struggling to find a politically acceptable explanation of urban riots. After all, how can an electorate blame a state governor, mayor, or local chief of police for the violent outbursts of discontented social misfits? Hoffer's work reflects a commonly held, one-sided, and venerable viewpoint—a conservative viewpoint which happened to accommodate the political expedients of the 1960s and found its reembodiment in 1965 as an official account of the famous Watts riot.

One week after the Los Angeles riots had ended, California's Governor Pat Brown appointed an eight-man commission of leading citizens to "probe deeply the immediate and underlying causes of the riots" and to "develop recommendations for action designed to prevent a recurrence of tragic disorders." John A. McCone, a former head of the C.I.A., was chairman of the group which therefore came to be known as the McCone Commission. The Commission's report (Violence in the City—An End or a Beginning) is a slender 86-page volume which cost $250,000 to produce. It was hardly off the press before being attacked by its own consultants. Robert Blauner, for example, chastised the Commission under the headline "Whitewash Over Watts"

(1966). The report is, in fact, a hastily completed and deficient analysis of the Los Angeles riot. Blauner objected to its "narrow legalistic perspective," its consistent "protection" of the police and city administrators, and its eager acceptance of the "conventional position" that the circular connection between education and employment is the "crux of the dilemma of the Negro poor" (Blauner 1966:4–5).

By background and training McCone and his personally selected collaborators were pragmatists who were disposed to see the Commission's social science consultants as "dreamers and visionaries" (Jacobs 1971:298). Consequently, the McCone Commission intentionally confined its investigation to "objective facts," ignored the "speculative opinions" of its consultants, and ultimately imposed its own preconceptions of law enforcement, violence, and slums on its final analysis. The report's conclusions provide an unambiguous and succinct summary of contemporary "riff-raff theory."

The McCone Commission "found" that the Los Angeles riot was essentially an apolitical, meaningless outburst of collective violence. The rioters were marginal people, and the frustrations that led to rioting were simply a consequence of chronic personal failure. What provoked the riot was not the social conditions of a black ghetto (i.e., consumer exploitation, police harassment, overcrowding, and poor public services) but rather the personal inadequacies of recently migrated ghetto residents, (i.e., inferior education, insufficient skills, social maladjustment, and criminality). The rioters were portrayed as marginal people in the sense that they supposedly represented only a small percentage of the total Negro population of Watts and were not supported by the majority of the black community. In short, the riff-raff theory contends that urban riots are the product of a relatively small group of social misfits: the unemployed, the uneducated, the maladjusted, and, of course, the criminals. The discontent of this "underclass" was supposedly flamed into violence by the "irresponsible agitation" of black leaders (Fogelson 1971:308). Extending the internal logic of this approach led the McCone Commission to its general recommendation that there were no serious problems in Watts which could not be handled by "elevating the riff-raff." Its proposed solution was to improve education in the black community and instill "achievement motivation in the ghetto poor so that they might embark upon the educational and occupational careers that exemplify the American success story" (Blauner 1966:54).

Testing Riff-raff Theory

Clark McPhail's (1971) survey of research on riot participation identifies five different ways in which riot behavior has been measured: (1) arrestee status, (2) respondent's reported status, (3) respondent's witness of others' behavior(s), (4) respondent's reported status and witness of others' behavior(s), and (5) respondent's reported status and behavior(s). The most frequently employed measure is a respondent's arrestee status. McPhail reports that at least six studies have compared a sample of respondents arrested on riot charges with a control sample of persons (who were not arrested) living in the same community. Arrestee status yields a larger proportion of moderate (r > .30 to .59) and high (r > .60) correlations between riot participation and its presumptive "causes" than any of the other four approaches. But arrestee status is without doubt a crude measure of riot participation.

What are its faults? First, arrestee status really tells us only that a "person was in an area when and where the police were arresting people" (McPhail 1971:1067). Crowd bystanders are sometimes mistaken for active participants and a person's being picked up in a mass arrest may only mean that he or she is slow of foot, mentally deficient, or physically small. Second, arrestee status tells us very little about a person's pattern of riot participation over a period of time. The same person on different occasions can be a bystander, an active participant, or an active counterrioter. He or she may stand by in a crowd while watching a store being looted, throw rocks at the police when they arrest looters, and later help a fire department to save the same store from flames. In short, "arrestee status," as well as most of the other indices of riot participation used in current research may fail to adequately distinguish between crowd bystanders, active participants, and counterrioters. The Kerner Commission Studies recognized the importance of this problem, but were only partly successful in developing an improved measurement technique.

In 1967, 20 major American cities reported some form of collective violence ranging from minor disorders to major disruptions. Special research teams, under the auspices of the Kerner Commission, were dispatched to 10 of these cities where they interviewed both public officials and riot participants. The research teams also collected 1500 pages of sworn depositions. Respondents were classified as "rioters" if they reported that "they were active or reported breaking windows, looting, firebombing, or other 'anti-social' behaviors." Respondents who reported that they had stayed home or had watched the riot from in front of their own homes were classified as "not involved," and those who reported "trying to stop the riot, calling the fire department or engaging in some other 'pro-social' behavior" were classified as "counter-rioters" (McPhail 1971:1060). But even this classification scheme fails to accommodate the person who intermittently engages in legal and illegal (prosocial vs. antisocial) behaviors during the course of an urban riot. A more serious limitation of the scheme used in the Kerner Commission Studies is the classification of individuals as "counter-rioters" even if they reported committing illegal acts in addition to prosocial acts.

One of the most cogent empirical tests of the riff-raff theory was undertaken by the Institute for Social Research (ISR) at the University of Michigan on behalf of the National Advisory Commission on Civil Disorders (the Kerner Commission). In 1968, results in part were published by Nathan S. Caplan and Jeffery M. Paige as an article written for *Scientific American.* The data were from interviews conducted in Detroit and Newark following riots in the summer months of 1967.

In both cities "the sampling area was defined as those 1960 census tracts in which violence and damage had occurred" (Caplan and Paige 1968:15–6). A two-stage area probability sample was used in which each city block in the sampling area had a probability of selection proportional to its number of dwelling units and each dwelling unit had a probability of selection inversely proportional to the size of its block. The probability of selection for any dwelling unit in the sampling area was the product of these two probabilities and each unit therefore had an essentially equal chance of being included in the study. Trained Negro interviewers were used in both cities, and they were ultimately successful in obtaining responses from two-thirds of their subjects. In Detroit every person over 15 years old living in a selected dwelling unit was listed on a sheet, and every other person was selected as a subject from this listing. In Newark the interviewers listed black males between 15 and 35 and interviewed them all. Individuals in each city were counted as rioters if they reported "that they were active or that they had been involved in breaking windows, looting, or firebombing, and so on" (Caplan and Paige 1968:16). People who reported that they had stayed home or watched the disturbance from their own yards were classified as nonrioters.

The first riff-raff hypothesis tested by Caplan and Paige concerned the question of whether or not the Detroit and Newark rioters were more likely to be *unemployable* than nonrioters. The rioters were supposedly among the hard-core unemployed because they lacked both trade skills and education. If this were true, if the rioters were a part of the chronically unemployed, they should have been found at the bottom of the income ladders for the black communities in both cities. But the interview data from Detroit (N = 393) and Newark (N = 233) are inconsistent with this prediction. There was not a significant difference in annual income between rioters and nonrioters in either city. In Detroit, 39 percent of the rioters versus 30 percent of the nonrioters reported annual incomes of less than $5,000, but this small differential disappears when the data are age controlled. The income differential for rioters and nonrioters found in Newark was even smaller; 33 percent of the rioters reported annual incomes below $5,000 compared to 29 percent of the nonrioters (see Figure 8.3).

The data on unemployment are more difficult to interpret. In Detroit about

**FIGURE 8.3: Annual Income Reported by Rioters and Nonrioters
in Detroit and Newark, 1967**

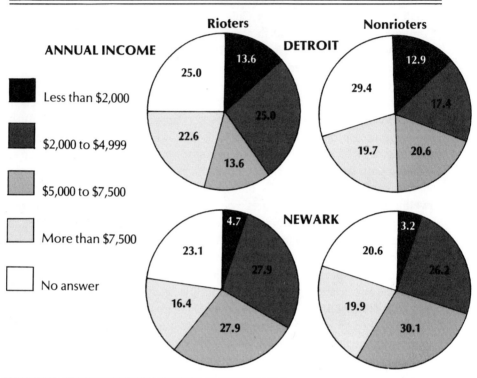

Source: Caplan and Paige (1968: 15-21)

30 percent of the rioters reported that they were unemployed, compared to 32 percent of the nonrioters. Although about 30 percent of the Newark rioters also reported that they were unemployed, only 19 percent of the nonrioters in Newark said they were unemployed. So in Newark, rioters were more likely to be unemployed than nonrioters, but there is no evidence that this was so because they had given up hope or lacked education. On the contrary, occupational aspirations were higher among the Newark rioters than among the nonrioters; and 98 percent of the rioters compared to 86 percent of the nonrioters had attended high school. In both cities Caplan and Paige found a significant relationship between education and rioting, but it is in the opposite direction from the one predicted by the riff-raff theory; it was the rioter who was better educated than the nonrioter (see Figure 8.4).

A second hypothesis central to riff-raff theory suggests that urban rioters are disproportionately drawn from populations of *unassimilated migrants*. Urban migrants unaccustomed to city life were presumably unable to cope with urban

**FIGURE 8.4: Educational Levels Reported by Rioters and
Nonrioters in Detroit and Newark, 1967**

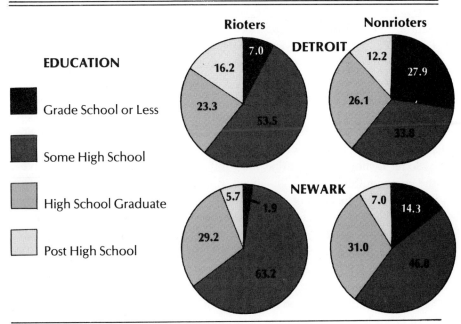

Source: Caplan and Paige (1968: 15-21).

complexities and problems such as drugs, poverty, and crime. Bewilderment,
frustration, and despair combined with the absence of well-developed social
support networks would supposedly predispose unassimilated migrants to riot
in American cities. But what are the facts?

It is true that Black Americans have migrated from the rural south to
northern cities in unprecedented numbers since World War II. This makes the
riff-raff hypothesis regarding urban migrants seem plausible, yet it is clearly
refuted by the ISR data. Caplan and Paige found that the Detroit and Newark
rioters were disproportionately drawn from among the long-term residents of
the cities. In Detroit 59 percent of the rioters and only 35 percent of the
nonrioters had been born in the city. Nearly 75 percent of the rioters in each
city reported that they had been raised in the North, a claim which could be
made by only 64 percent and 48 percent of the nonrioters in Detroit and
Newark respectively. The idea that it was black southern migrants, who had
failed to adjust to the ghetto life of the city, who rioted in the 1960s is not based
on fact. In Detroit and Newark, the people who rioted came from among the
long-term residents of the North rather than from a mass of unassimilated
newcomers.

A third hypothesis derivable from riff-raff theory can also be considered in the light of the ISR data. Caplan and Paige reported that several indices of social maladjustment failed to distinguish between rioters and nonrioters. The data did not indicate that the rioter is "alienated from or peripheral to the larger Negro community." Rioters were as likely to be members of community organizations as nonrioters and they were significantly more likely to visit daily with their neighbors than were nonrioters. It is also important to note that the rioters were just as likely to report the presence of an adult male in their home during childhood as were the nonrioters (75% vs. 77%). Some speculators have tried to suggest that both urban crime and collective violence are a product of "broken homes" in the black ghetto.

So far it should be clear that the 1960s rioters were fairly representative of the communities in which they lived. Rioters could not be distinguished from nonrioters on the basis of annual income, years of urban residence, or social maladjustment. And they could not be distinguished on the basis of inferior education and achievement motivation as indicated by levels of occupational aspiration. A fourth riff-raff hypothesis suggests, however, that rioters are disproportionately drawn from the criminal "element" in black communities. But once again, the best available data do not support this contention.

The information gathered in 1967 by the National Advisory Commission on Civil Disorders constitutes one of the most comprehensive data sets on urban riots. Among other things, the commission gathered approximately 20,000 arrest sheets from police departments all over the country and turned them over for analysis to Robert M. Fogelson and Robert B. Hill of Columbia University's Bureau of Applied Social Research. Fogelson and Hill found that a majority of the arrestees had prior criminal records (Fogelson 1971:40); this does not necessarily mean that the rioters were criminals or that they were any more likely to be criminals than nonrioters. Fogelson and Hill observed that in the United States people have criminal records after being arrested even if the arrest is not followed by a conviction; probably no more than 25 percent of all people arrested are convicted for a major crime. Moreover, Fogelson (1971:4) found that the President's Crime Commission estimated that "50 to 90 percent of black males living in the ghettos have criminal records." This is not a surprising estimate since it is well established that "categoric risk" for black ghetto males is high. Categoric risk refers to the greater probability for members of some groups to be stopped and arrested by police on the grounds of "probable suspicion" of a crime having been committed.

A last critical element of the riff-raff theory of collective violence is the contention that the rioters represented a very *small percentage* (2%) of the black communities of various cities in which disturbances occurred. The only available data regarding this assertion come from the ISR studies of Detroit and Newark and the U.C.L.A. survey of the Los Angeles riot. The problem is to determine both how many blacks could have rioted and how many blacks did riot. Unfortunately, given the limitations of the sampling frames (the exclusion of females, of boys less than 15, of men over 35, etc.) and the difficulty of defining riot boundaries, the answers to these questions are necessarily tentative. Fogelson (1971) has calculated the ratio of rioters to arrestees, standardized by age; for Los Angeles it was approximately 6:1, in Newark it was 5:1, and in Detroit the ratio was 3:1. If these estimates are even roughly accurate it means that the proportions of blacks who participated in the Los Angeles, Newark, and Detroit riots were 14 percent, 15 percent, and 11 percent respectively. Fogelson reports that the proportion of blacks participating in an urban riot was as low as 2 percent in only one city, Philadelphia. He is correct in emphasizing the speculative character of these estimates, yet we can see that the best available data indicate the urban rioters of the 1960s represented a sizable minority of the black communities in which disturbances occurred.

Five of the central hypotheses derivable from riff-raff theory have been assessed and rejected for lack of empirical support. The rioters were not poorer than nonrioters living in the same ghetto communities; they were not disproportionately representative of recent migrants from the South; they were not distinguishable from nonrioters on the basis of inferior education or achievement motivation; they were not any more likely to have criminal records than nonrioters living in black ghettos; and finally, the rioters were something more than a cantankerous fringe element, they were sizable minorities of black communities.

So, what is the best tentative answer to the question of who rioted? The urban rioters of the 1960s were typical young adults born and raised in the northern ghettos of the United States. They were the people most likely to be in the immediate vicinity of the events which triggered collective violence in that tumultuous decade. The young people of the 1950s and 1960s had reached maturity in a period when black communities were experiencing a heightened sense of racial pride and political awareness. Ultimately, it was the availability of these young people that set the stage for collective violence. They took the lead in rioting and engaged in the most serious forms of civil disorder (Fogelson 1971). Even their patterns of looting reflected the grievances of an upcoming and more militant generation of blacks.

Looters and Looting: The 1960s

Between 1964 and 1968 approximately 60,000 people were arrested for looting. These people were young and old, male and female. Looting during the riots was a public, collective enterprise which can be viewed as a "primitive political protest mechanism" (Quarantelli and Dynes 1970:176). Looting occurred in almost all major disturbances and was most likely in disorders explicitly focused on protest. It was a subculturally *legitimated* form of *collective behavior* in several ways. First, looters in civil disorders often worked together in pairs, family units, or small groups; second, the looters were selective in their choices of places to loot; and third, the looters were apparently acting on the basis of a collective redefinition of property rights.

The mass media legitimated looting within the black community by showing that many people looted with impunity while the police were simply standing around. Looting occurred in daylight hours, and, in some instances at least, spectators were actually handed goods by looters and told where to find more. Food, furniture, clothing, and liquor stores were selected as targets whereas factories, schools, churches, and private residences were generally avoided. Moreover, some kinds of stores were more vulnerable than others: One chain store in Washington, D.C., had 19 of its 50 stores looted while supermarkets of other companies located in the same neighborhoods were left untouched. Such massive action obviously is not a matter of individual but of collective definition of "good" and "bad" stores from the viewpoint of ghetto dwellers (Quarantelli and Dynes 1970:175). Familiar neighborhood stores with a reputation for high prices, anti–civil rights attitudes, or known white ownership were deliberately ransacked while others, particularly those owned by blacks, escaped unharmed (Berk and Aldrich 1972). Finally, it seems that many residents of the black community felt justified in taking goods from ghetto stores. Ordinarily people think of property as a thing, but it is in actuality "the *rights* held by individuals ... to certain valuable things, whether material or intangible" (Quarantelli and Dynes 1970:176). In this sense property rights are shared norms about "who can do what" with the valuable resources of a community. The seemingly incomprehensible claim of some looters that they had a "right" to take portable television sets is understandable when it is recognized that among many blacks there was a belief that years of discrimination and consumer exploitation had established the priority of their moral claim to the goods of society. The looters felt that they were only taking what would be rightfully theirs in a just world.

The preceding account of looting in the 1960s, although based on empirical evidence, may be difficult to accept because it challenges conventional wisdom about the criminality of riot participants. Quarantelli and Dynes (1970:176) begin their discussion of looting with the observation that many people, including governmental officials, have an invalid conception of looting behavior during civil disturbances. It is something more than "blowing-off" steam in a stressed environment. Looting in the 1960s was not the result of simple greed.

A massive power failure north of New York City on the night of July 13, 1977 set off a spree of looting in the city which led to more than 3,000 arrests.

And yet, it is necessary to understand that these generalizations apply to looting during a civil disturbance and not to looting during a natural disaster. The importance of this distinction was evident in the New York City blackout of July 13, 1977.

At 9:34 P.M. 9 million New Yorkers lost electricity and it was suddenly Christmas time for tens of thousands of looters. In what *Time* magazine called an "orgy of looting," blacks and Hispanics poured out of local ghettos to steal merchandise ranging from clothespins to jewelry and automobiles. Adults strolled home with shopping bags stuffed with steaks and roasts while baseball fans at New York's Shea Stadium amused themselves by singing *White Christmas*. Most New Yorkers, in fact, refused to believe that another technological failure had overtaken the Big Apple. But the reality of the situation soon overcame any lingering disbelief. The nude cast from *Oh! Calcutta!* finally gave up its performance in resignation and went home in borrowed clothes. Besieged bars ran out of ice and liquor.

In a period of a little less than 36 hours the city fire department fought 65 serious fires and responded to 1,700 false alarms while 2,000 stores were plundered and 3,776 suspected looters were arrested by city police. In contrast to the 1960s, stores owned by blacks and Hispanics suffered the same fate as those operated by whites (Dellinger 1977:42). Furthermore, the ideological dimensions of looting in the 1960s appeared to be absent in the hot summer evening of 1977. Looting in the New York City crisis was little more than an opportunistic response and not an expression of political and economic grievances. And although many arrested suspects justified their behavior by pleading poverty, there was little evidence that the most needy were actually involved in the looting.

Crowd Boundaries

Crowds generally form rings because the circle is the most efficient arrangement of people around a common point of interest (Milgram and Toch 1969:-518). Even when walls, roads, fences, and other physical barriers are present, it is usually possible to discern *arc segments* in crowds. In fact, crowds grow "in the form of accretions to the initial circular core" (Milgram and Toch 1969:520). People who arrive early tend to be near the center of a crowd and people who arrive late tend to be on its boundary. *Crowd boundaries* define the limits or extent of crowds.

As indicated in Chapter I, patterns of social relationships allow groups to be recognized as entities with discrete boundaries. Couch (1970) has identified seven "dimensions of association" useful in analyzing social interaction in crowds: monitoring, acknowledgment, alignment, role taking, identifying, directing, and evaluating. All coordinated action requires that people *monitor* or "pay attention" to the actions of each other. If an individual wants to remain part of a group, that person must be able to *align* his or her acts with the behavior of other group members. In crowds, monitoring tends to be *global* and *visual* rather than particularistic and auditory (Couch 1970:460). In bureaucratically organized groups we primarily monitor the behavior of specific people by paying attention to what they say to us; in crowds we pay attention to many people simultaneously by watching what they are doing.

Particularistic monitoring often implies face-to-face interaction in which it is difficult not to acknowledge the presence and attention of a specific person. Global monitoring in crowds, however, does not require the acknowledgment of a particular individual because it does not entail paying attention to specific people. To acknowledge the presence and attention of another person implicitly makes an individual accountable or responsive to that person. Crowds inhibit "particularistic monitoring and the claims for acknowledgment that commonly accompany it." (Couch 1970:461) People in crowds can experience a sense of freedom because they have not acknowledged the presence of any specific individuals, and consequently they are not accountable to anyone in particular.

But even in crowds individuals must assess the intentions of other people and anticipate their behavior. *Parallel role taking* is an empathetic process in crowds (Couch 1970:463) in which a person simply "adopts" the viewpoint of other people. It differs from *reciprocal role taking* because it does not involve the identification of different kinds of people in a crowd. In fact, members of crowds typically take each other into account by assigning some common identity to everyone (e.g., students, blacks, women), while reciprocal role taking depends upon a person's success in differentiating the identities and roles of other people.

Parallel role taking is associated with *parallel alignment* of behavior in crowds. Activity in crowds is to some extent coordinated simply because everyone's behavior is identical or at least similar. In contrast, in bureaucratically organized groups we rely on reciprocal role taking to fit our own actions into the various activities of other group members. This process of *reciprocal alignment* involves particularistic monitoring, the acknowledgment of specific individuals, and the identification of their discrete, personal identities.

The combination of global monitoring, parallel role taking, and undifferentiated identification may tend to reduce an individual's level of selfconsciousness in crowds. People are unlikely to feel self-conscious when their identities are undifferentiated and their presence in a group has not been acknowledged (Couch 1970:467), and they are less likely to be influenced by other people's evaluation of their behavior. Consequently, they may be willing to follow the directions of crowd leaders even when their "directives" are certain to meet with the disapproval of outsiders.

The people who issue directions in crowds are usually the most involved members. They tend to be located near the center of a crowd (Milgram and Toch 1969:520) and therefore serve as an ideal focal point. As the distance from this focal point increases in concentric circles, the proportion of people turned toward it, or *polarized*, will drop off. Polarization is one of the best ways to operationally specify the borders of a crowd.

Milgram and Toch (1969) use circle diagrams in a simple geometric procedure to specify degrees of crowd polarization and identify the functional boundaries of crowds. Polarization is highest in the center of crowds and tends to be degenerate over time. One of Milgram and Toch's most interesting comments is that casual observers tend to believe that the members of crowds are much more involved with what is going on than is actually the case. The significance of this is that the alleged homogeneity of crowds might be nothing more than a perceptual distortion of crowd observers.

Crowd boundaries have two key properties: *sharpness* and *permeability*.

Sharpness is a function of how precipitously polarization drops off, and of the extent to which the perimeter of a crowd contains mixed elements (members vs. nonmembers). Boundaries are sharpest when crowd members are highly polarized, when nonmembers lack any degree of polarization, and when there are few nonmembers mixed among the members of a crowd at its edges.

Permeability refers to the extent to which people feel free to enter a crowd from an external point and move toward its center. Crowds generally grow by accretion at their boundaries, but accretion does not imply the penetration of the crowd itself. Some crowds will not allow movement from peripheral to central points; others inhibit movement from central to external points. A recent study (Lindskold et al. 1976) presents data supporting the principle that the *permeability of crowd boundaries is a function of the amount of interaction occurring among crowd members.* It was hypothesized that a crowd watching something would have a less permeable boundary than a nonpolarized aggregate, and that a crowd merely watching the same thing would have a more permeable boundary than a crowd of actively interacting people. It was found that other people were most reluctant to intrude on interacting crowd members and least reluctant to intrude on an aggregate of nonpolarized individuals.

Summary and Conclusion

Large populations of people in the vicinity of precipitating events were conducive to crowd formation in the 1960s. Seven-eighths of the major disturbances surveyed by the National Advisory Commission occurred in cities with populations in excess of 250,000 people. The urban rioters of the 1960s were primarily young adults born and raised in the northern ghettos of the United States. Ultimately the availability of so many young people with time to spare and smoldering grievances set the stage for collective violence.

Spilerman's research (1971) has specified the form of the relationship between the size of proximate black populations and the number of disorders in American cities as an S-shaped curve. There is a threshold population size below which rioting crowds fail to develop. Cities with black populations of less than 1,000 people apparently lacked the human resources needed for crowd formation and collective violence. The number of disorders per 1,000 blacks in a city increased up to a Negro population size of 5,000 people, then began to drop off. The proportion of variation in the number of disorders accounted for by the curve for non-South cities was 73 percent. The nonlinear regression for cities in the South was considerably less, 34 percent, but still of substantial magnitude.

Additional work suggests a connection between *crowd size* and the availability of proximate populations. Coleman and James (1961) have proposed that

In this photograph of students at the University of Minnesota who were protesting the invasion of Cambodia in 1970, crowd boundaries and parallel alignment of behavior are evident.

the "acquisition rate" for a crowd is "proportional to the number of single individuals available to be 'picked up'." One difficulty of this model is its assumption that people are equally likely to join a small crowd as a large one. Research reported by Milgram, Bickman, and Berkowitz (1969) suggests that large "crowd crystals" have greater *drawing power* than small crowd crystals. Variation in *assembling instruction* will also have an effect on crowd formation and size.

Assembling instructions direct people to a particular location at a particular time. They provide a space and time frame for crowd formation. The greater the *social density* in the vicinity of a precipitating event the greater the diffusion of assembling instructions. Rumors and mass media are important in the long-range notification of people who are some distance from the scene of an event. The "know-nothing" hypothesis states that no matter what the nature of a crisis a "hard core" of people will remain "chronically uninformed" (Spitzer and Denzin 1965). Low levels of information are characteristic of older rather than younger persons, which may partly explain the underrepresentation of older people in the initial stages of the 1960s riots.

People who learn about an event from a large number of sources are more likely to comply with assembling instructions than others (McPhail and Miller 1973). But people are not always *available* for recruitment into crowds. Some people have committed their time to other activities and some people are reluctant to do anything without a friend. Other people may be unavailable because they lack access or transportation to an event or because they simply are not joiners. The motivational theorists in collective behavior have put a great amount of effort into explaining what kinds of people are likely to join crowds.

Hoffer's (1951) model of *mass discontent* suggests that participation in political movements and collective violence is an escape from the "futility of spoiled lives." The uneducated, unskilled, unemployable, physically infirm, and mentally retarded are life's hard-core losers. They are the *social misfits* found in any society, always ready for mobilization in crowds, and ripe for political and economic exploitation. Hoffer's analysis is a one-sided and therefore distorted viewpoint which happened to accommodate the political expedients of the 1960s and found its sentiments echoed in an official account of the Watts riot.

The McCone Commission "found" that the Los Angeles riot was essentially an apolitical, meaningless outburst of collective violence. What provoked the riot was not the social conditions of a black ghetto (i.e., consumer exploitation, police harassment, overcrowding, and poor public services), but rather the personal inadequacies of recently migrated ghetto residents. The *riff-raff theory* of riot participation contends that rioters are a relatively *small group of marginal people:* the unemployed, the uneducated, the maladjusted, and, of course, the criminals. The discontent of this "underclass" was supposedly flamed into violence by the "irresponsible agitation of black leaders."

One of the most cogent tests of riff-raff theory was undertaken by Caplan and Paige (1968) on behalf of the National Advisory Commission. Data from interviews conducted in Detroit and Newark following the summer riots of 1967 contradict the central tenets of riff-raff theory. Rioters could not be distinguished from nonrioters on the basis of annual income, years of urban residence, social maladjustment, or criminality; nor could they be distinguished on the basis of inferior education and achievement motivation as indicated by levels of occupational aspiration. Furthermore, the rioters were something more than a cantankerous fringe element, they were sizable minorities of the black ghettos in which they lived. The rioters of the 1960s were fairly representative of the communities in which they lived. They were the young people who had reached maturity in a period when black communities were experiencing a heightened sense of racial pride and political awareness. It was this upcoming and more militant generation of blacks that took the lead in joining the violent crowds of the 1960s.

People joining crowds generally position themselves in rings because the circle is the most efficient arrangement of people around a common point of interest (Milgram and Toch 1969:518). *Crowd boundaries* define the limits of crowds and are recognizable to us because of the distinctive patterns of social interaction found within crowds. Social interaction in crowds is characterized by a predominance of global monitoring and *parallel role taking* in which the *personal identities* of crowd participants are *undifferentiated.* Behavior is coordinated in crowds through *parallel alignment* in the sense that everyone is doing identical or similar things. Since the presence of specific individuals is not acknowledged in crowds, people may be less likely to feel self-conscious and may be less restrained by the evaluations of outside observers.

Crowd boundaries have two key properties: *sharpness* and *permeability.* Boundaries are sharpest when crowd members are highly *polarized* or turned toward a common point of interest, when nonmembers lack any degree of polarization, and when there are few nonmembers mixed among the members of a crowd at its edges. Permeability refers to the extent to which people feel free to enter a crowd and move toward its center. Permeability of crowd boundaries is a function of the intensity of social interaction between crowd members. People are most reluctant to intrude on highly polarized crowd members who are interacting, and least reluctant to intrude on a simple aggregate of nonpolarized individuals who are not interacting.

The entrance to the Attica State Correctional Facility in Attica, New York.

CHAPTER IX

Confrontation and Control

In the current literature there are two major approaches to the study of riots: (1) survey designs which focus on the attributes of individual "riot participants," and (2) research designs which focus on the attributes of "riot communities" (Stark et al. 1974). Both approaches share a common bias in sociology (Cohen 1965) toward the analysis of *inputs* and associated *outputs*, thus neither approach yields much information about the riot *process* itself. This is an important gap in our understanding of crowd violence that requires the study of group behavior *during the course* of a riot. The objective of this chapter is an analysis of what happened at New York State's Attica prison in September of 1971. The dynamics of crowd confrontation and the failure of traditional control strategies are the central topics of discussion.

Attica: The Social Context of Confrontation

Attica was hailed as an ultimate in maximum security prisons when it opened in 1931. It was designed to be the most escape-proof institution in the United States complete with unbreakable toilets and washbasins. It is, in fact, a modern gothic fortress surrounded by a wall 30 feet high, 2 feet wide, and 12 feet down. The wall at Attica is an intimidating sight for new arrivals and visitors. It is "massive, sand colored, and ugly" (Wicker 1975).

Behind the wall, four main cellblocks are grouped around a large quadrangle (see Figure 9.1). The cellblocks are linked to each other by enclosed corridors which meet at right angles in a central location called "Times Square." Each of the four cellblocks houses approximately 500 men. The inmates live on three floors of each block. The floors are divided into two areas by a central hallway,

193

with two rows of cells (called galleries) in each area. Each gallery holds a "company" of men and there are 12 companies per cellblock. Additional buildings are located outside of the quadrangle formed by the four main blocks.

FIGURE 9.1: Attica Prison

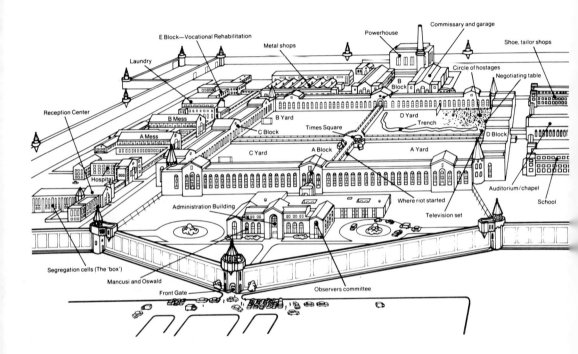

Source: Wicker (1975: Inside Cover Design).

It is said that "prisons aren't hotels" and Attica is no exception to this cliché. In 1971 it was an unutterably grim place. The cells at Attica are small cubicles, approximately six feet wide, nine feet long, and seven feet high. It is impossible for inmates to see down the galleries without using small, hand-held mirrors. Messages and books can only be exchanged by hand-to-hand delivery from one cell to the next. And because of inadequate wiring there is only an unshaded, 60 watt bulb in each cell. In 1967 people were confined in these dingy quarters from 14 to 16 hours a day.

The initial violence of the Attica riot and its suppression by State Police and correction officers are nearly inexplicable without appreciation of the mounting tensions at the institution. Deprivation is an ordinary part of life in prison, but the summer months immediately preceding the Attica riot were especially marked by anxiety, growing frustrations, and deepening fears. Inmates, correction officers, and prison officials were living together in an explosive atmosphere which they could neither comprehend nor control. There were three major sources of situational stress within the institution: (1) inmate harassment, (2) racial conflict, and (3) an inequitable parole system.

Inmate Harassment

Ordinarily prison life is imagined to consist of highly disciplined, routinized behavior carefully circumscribed by rules and regulations; life should be highly predictable in a prison, and in some ways it is. Situational ambiguity, on the other hand, means that life is problematic. When social interaction is unpredictable, people commonly experience both anxiety and frustration: anxiety because it is difficult to avoid unanticipated risks, and frustration because it is harder to achieve important goals. Whether social interaction is predictable in any particular setting is a function of an individual's relevant knowledge from past experience and of what he can learn from his current situation. At Attica many of the inmates had relatively little prior experience with maximum security institutions, and their introduction to Attica's distinctive set of rules was haphazard at best.

An inmate handbook had been revised in 1968, but after November of 1970, none of these rulebooks were distributed to inmates at Attica. Consequently, inmates often learned rules only after they had broken them. In theory, correction officers were to explain prison regulations to new inmates on their arrival at all state institutions. At Attica this was difficult for two reasons: first, young correction officers didn't have a firm grasp of the rules themselves; second, many of the Attica inmates spoke only Spanish. Given these two problems it was only natural for an informal policy of denying inmate requests to develop within the institution: "When in doubt, say no!" *This informal policy was both confusing and infuriating.* Somtimes a request denied by a young officer was subsequently approved by an older officer.

It was also difficult to learn Attica's rules because the prison staff was allowed a considerable degree of discretion in enforcing institutional regulations. Some officers were uptight and insensitive, while others were more patient and tolerant. For example, some officers insisted on complete silence during roll call and others did not. Could an inmate remain in bed during roll call? The answer depended upon who the officer was. Consequently, the inmates were required to "master the idiosyncrasies not of two or three officers but of dozens during a year. From day to day, they could never be sure what to expect" (NYSSCA 1972:75).

Two other factors impeded the learning process at Attica. The rules were often petty and senseless, and they were used for harassment. Nobody paid much attention to "dumb" rules, and harassment created hostility. Black Muslims were required to attend meals even when their religion forbade them to eat. Instant coffee was sold at the commissary although water heaters were forbidden in the cells. On top of these irritations, the Special Commission found that the cells of disfavored prisoners were searched repeatedly to uncover rule violations which were routinely ignored for others. The inmates regarded their cells as a last refuge for privacy and were particularly angered by cell searches. Books and other carefully kept personal possessions were typically thrown on the floor. Beds were torn apart. Thus, it was possible for a handful of officers to make life miserable for hundreds of inmates simply by enforcing stringent versions of repressive prison rules.

Rules regulating correspondence with the outside world were considered especially repressive by Attica inmates. Prison administrators determined who could visit inmates, who could write them letters, what could be said in those letters, and what magazines and books were permitted within the institution. Unfortunately, the rules were never adequately explained, and when an inmate's letters from approved correspondents violated prison regulations, they were simply left undelivered. Newspapers were censored with scissors, and it angered inmates to receive mutilated copies after straining their tight budgets to include subscriptions. All packages were inspected for contraband and were subject to strictly enforced prison rules, rules which often seemed arbitrary and silly to the inmates. They could receive socks and underwear, for example, if these items were not blue. Only correction officers were allowed to wear blue underwear (NYSSCA 1972:45).

Racial Conflict

The most intense source of social stress at Attica was *racism.* Attica had a history of racial segregation which existed into the mid 1960s. There were black and white sport teams, different barbers for black and white inmates, and separate ice buckets for blacks and whites at July 4 picnics. In his book, *Attica—My Story,* Russell G. Oswald, the New York Commissioner of Corrections in 1971, insists that racism was not a problem at Attica. After assuring his readers that he himself "never viewed a black man as any less nor any more than a white man," Commissioner Oswald stated his belief that "In no way . . . was Attica a white massacre of blacks" (1972:17–8). But the facts speak for themselves; the tragedy at Attica was tinged with racial overtones from its beginning to its desperate conclusion.

Job discrimination at Attica prior to the riot was clear-cut. White inmates held the best jobs in the institution. Although only 37 percent of the prison population was white, white inmates constituted 67 percent of the clerks and 70 percent of the "runners" (office errand help). By contrast, 76 percent of the inmates in the notorious metal shop were black, and blacks constituted 80 percent of the undesirable "grading companies" which were used for heavy manual labor. Correction officers at Attica defended this informal and unstated policy of discrimination by suggesting that "It is hard to find coloreds who can do good clerical work." But there were about 200 blacks and Spanish-speaking inmates at Attica who had high school educations, and none of the jobs required more than that (NYSSCA 1972:40).

Racism among the officers at Attica was probably no worse than it was in the communities surrounding the institution. Citizen observers, including Tom Wicker of The New York Times, have bitterly recalled the treatment of minority group members at local motels and restaurants (Wicker 1975:187-9). The typical correction officer was from a rural, white background and had little or no previous contact with blacks and Spanish-speaking groups who live predominantly in major cities. In September of 1971, nearly 80 percent of the Attica inmates had been committed to the institutions from urban areas, and 43 percent were from New York City alone. Fifty-four percent of the prison population was black and nine percent was Puerto Rican (see Table 9.1). None of the 380 correction officers were black.

Some correction officers at Attica actively discouraged black-white friendships at the institution. White inmates who were friendly towards blacks were often called "nigger lovers," and were "sometimes the target of snide remarks implying that there must be a homosexual basis ... for such an unnatural relationship" (NYSSCA 1972:81). White inmates told the Special Commission that they had been denied privileges for having friendships with blacks.

The Parole System

In 1971 there were three tickets out of Attica: (1) maximum expiration of sentence, (2) conditional release, and (3) parole. By 1971 conditional release and parole were the most common grounds for leaving the prison. Under conditional release an inmate is let out after serving his maximum sentence less his accumulation of "good time." Inmates are typically given credit for days of good time in which they have not violated prison regulations. Credit for good time is allowed in order to encourage satisfactory conduct. The practice, however, means that rule infractions can carry a double penalty. Confinement in a disciplinary cellblock is one sanction, and it is often combined with a loss

Table 9.1:   Characteristics of Inmates at Attica, 9/9/71

	Percent Total Population	Percent D-Yard Population	Percent Spanish-Speaking	Percent White	Percent Black
Race					
White	36.6	25.3			
Black	54.2	63.8			
Puerto Rican	8.7	9.5			
Other	0.5	0.4			
Age					
60–	2.7	2.1	0.5	5.3	2.2
50–59	7.1	5.5	2.5	8.4	6.8
40–49	17.4	16.0	14.4	17.2	18.2
30–39	33.6	33.8	48.8	30.0	33.7
25–29	22.1	21.7	21.6	23.8	20.8
21–24	14.6	17.6	10.2	14.8	15.2
–21	2.5	3.3	2.0	1.5	3.1
Level of Education					
Illiterate	2.4	2.6	9.7	0.5	2.5
Elementary School	11.6	13.0	17.4	10.0	11.5
Junior High School	36.7	37.0	44.5	38.1	34.2
Some High School	27.2	27.9	19.1	20.7	33.0
High-School Graduate	7.7	6.7	5.1	9.4	7.0
High School Equivalency	8.2	7.4	2.6	12.8	5.9
Beyond High School	4.1	3.5	0.5	5.8	3.8
Not Stated	2.1	1.9	1.1	2.7	2.1

Source: New York State Special Commission on Attica (1972:490).

of good time. Violating unexplained and selectively enforced rules was, therefore, not a trivial risk at Attica. Moreover, unintentional rule violations were particularly frustrating for inmates trying to establish a good record for parole hearings.

It is commonly assumed that judges determine how long a person will be confined in prison, but this assumption is mistaken. In New York, as in most areas, it is the Parole Board that determines how long a person will remain in prison. The first parole system for releasing and supervising adults was developed in 1877 at Elmira, New York. The Elmira system established the precedent for using an indeterminate sentence. Under New York penal law, criminal offenders could be sentenced to a minimum and a maximum term of imprisonment, rather than a fixed term. If the parole board approved, an inmate could be released after serving his minimum time. In 1967 New York Penal Law was further modified so that sentencing judges were only required to specify a maximum sentence. They could leave it to the Parole Board to determine an "optimum release" for individual felons (except for murder and kidnapping convictions). The Parole Board was thus given the broad authority to set a minimum sentence for an inmate, and the responsibility of determining if an inmate should actually be released when he becomes eligible for parole. Each month a three-man panel of the Parole Board met at Attica to set minimum sentences and grant or deny parole.

The difficulty with the procedure was that nobody could really explain what criteria were used by the Parole Board in making its decisions. Prison officials and parole officers sometimes gave inmates pointers on things which might impress the board, but they never got beyond "meaningless generalities." Consequently, inmates sometimes waited years for a few minutes with a parole board which they knew nothing about. They could only speculate on how to favorably influence its members, and they often rehersed answers to questions which were never asked. When the big day finally arrived, the average time allowed for an inmate's hearing was only six minutes, which included his "interview," the "reading" of his file of up to 150 pages, and the "deliberation" of the panel members.

After attending Bible classes, professing a guilty conscience, and enrolling in prison rehabilitation programs, the Attica inmates were often surprised when their requests for parole were denied. They could not understand the Parole Board's behavior, yet they knew that its decision either sent them home or kept them imprisoned for up to two more years. The ambiguity of the situation was further complicated by the seemingly arbitrary decisions of the board. The New York Special Commission commented that "some inmates who have had good behavior records in prison are 'hit' (denied parole), while others with many infractions are granted parole" (1972:97). By 1971, *parole and conditional release* had become major sources of inmate anxiety and frustration (NYSSCA 1972:91).

The Precipitating Incidents at Attica

On August 22, 1971, the inmates at Attica stage a memorial demonstration for George Jackson who had just been killed at San Quentin. The inmates regarded the official version of the shooting as a "flagrant insult." California officials said that Jackson had attempted to escape with a gun which he had concealed in his hair. The Attica inmates were justifiably skeptical. It was rumored that Jackson had really been the victim of a political "execution." The inmates demonstrated their sympathy for Jackson by wearing black armbands and marching silently to the prison Mess Halls where they refused to eat breakfast. The young correction officers who found themselves confronted by silent hostility were badly frightened. Commissioner Oswald, on the other hand, considered the Jackson memorial "an impressive display of inmate unity" and a sure sign of effective planning.

One week later, the apprehensions of the prison staff soared again when the

Inmates at Attica Prison (below) raise their hands in clenched fists as a show of unity during their uprising in September 1971. Commissioner Russell G. Oswald (left) negotiates with a group of prisoners in the top, right photo. In the bottom, right photo a group of inmates, who are stripped for searching, stand in line for the return to their cell block after authorities recaptured the prison.

inmates staged a sick-call strike. On August 30 about 300 inmates signed up for sick-call and seated themselves throughout the hospital area of the prison to dramatize their grievances regarding medical care at Attica. Coincidentally, on the very next day, correction officers from all state institutions met with Commissioner Oswald in an "emergency meeting." They feared that their institutions were about to explode and exaggerated the ominous significance of the recent events at Attica (Oswald 1972:209). Oswald agreed that a grave crisis had developed and he prudently included an "urgent warning" to Governor Rockefeller in his August report. But it was far too late. The spark for Attica was only a few days away.

On September 8, 1971, Leroy Dewer was enjoying his first day in "A" yard after seven days of confinement for "insolence, abusive language, and disobeying an order." It was 3:30 p.m. On a late summer afternoon there were usually 400 to 500 men from cellblock A in the recreation yard. Dewer and another inmate were sparring with each other in a friendly manner, but the officers in charge, who were standing on a platform about 100 yards away, couldn't tell whether their activity was good-natured horseplay or a fight. Two officers walked across the yard to summon the sparring inmates, and Dewer returned with them. The other man had slipped into a crowd of inmates which had formed to watch the proceedings. When Dewer reached the door of cellblock A, an older lieutenant ordered him to his cell. Dewer asked "what for" and the officer responded by repeating his order. Dewer refused, turned around, and walked back toward the waiting crowd. The lieutenant stepped down from the door and moved after him. Dewer instinctively spun around and taunted the older man. Then he hit the officer lightly on the chest. It was an unthinkable act; no one at Attica had ever seen an officer struck before. That night Dewer and another inmate were removed from their cells and taken to HBZ, the disciplinary cellblock. The Attica inmates were convinced that both men would be beaten by the prison "goon squad." A rumor to this effect was widely accepted by the following morning.

The Initial Confrontation:
September 9, 1971

Everything appeared to be normal on the morning of September 9, 1971, inspite of the apprehensions of the prison staff. And it was until "5 company" returned from breakfast. As the men filed down the enclosed corridor toward cellblock A, they were approached by a correction officer who had been involved in the previous day's incident. As the lieutenant walked by he was struck on the side of the head. A number of inmates joined the attack when he fell to the ground; but many of the men were too surprised to move. Moments later, however, some of the inmates rescued the officer from his attackers, and he was eventually hoisted to his feet. The lieutenant ran down the corridor toward cellblock A pursued by about 20 inmates. The inmates snatched a telephone from his hands and proceeded to demolish the cellblock's administrative area. During the rampage the keys to A block's galleries and recreation yard were discovered. All of the men confined in cellblock A were now freed to join the rioters.

Fifteen minutes later a group of inmates returned to Times Square. By locking the iron gates at the Square it was possible to isolate each of the four main cellblocks from the rest of the prison (see Figure 9.1). For the men rioting in cellblock A there was no way out except through Times Square, and the area had been secured. Then a gate gave way under the force of their combined weight. No one knew that years of painting had hidden a cracked weld in one of its hinges. Officer Quinn was quickly overpowered, and the gates sealing off the remaining cellblocks were subsequently opened. Now the conflagration spread quickly throughout the institution. The speed of the prison takeover convinced Commissioner Oswald and the administrative staff at Attica that they were being confronted by a carefully rehearsed and well-organized group.

Structural Conduciveness and the Riot Process

The testimony assembled by the New York State Special Commission on Attica led it to conclude that the uprising was an unplanned, spontaneous event. The argument offered by the Special Commission is convincing. First, the men who subsequently emerged as inmate leaders and negotiators were not involved in the initial outbreak of violence. Second, if they had planned the riot they would not have chose an enclosed corridor for its beginning. A mess hall seating 768 men is a much better place. In fact, mess halls are almost traditional starting points for prison riots. Third, the inmate leaders, whoever they might have been, could not have known that the gate at Times Square was defective; and fourth, the initial behavior of the inmates was inconsistent with logical planning. They failed to capture the prison's power house, they burnt the commissary before removing all of its food stuffs, and they destroyed the metal shop before removing volatile fluids which could have been used in bombs. Finally, the Special Commission determined that the inmates rioting at Attica were completely disorganized until after midday on September 9, 1971.

Accepting the judgment that the Attica riot was not a planned operation, how was it possible for the inmates to win control of a major share of the prison so quickly? What organizational features made their early success possible? First, the *ratio of inmates to custodial staff was high*, as it is in any maximum-security prison. A single correction officer cannot be expected to contain the aggression of 20 inmates, especially if correction officers are not armed with guns. At Attica, they were not armed because of their vulnerability in the prison. It would be a relatively easy matter for inmates to arm themselves by taking weapons from the correction officers. A second factor promoting early success may have been the *inexperience of some correction officers*. The officers in direct contact with the inmates were among the youngest and least experienced working at Attica. Job rotations at the prison were governed by a seniority system which allowed the older and more experienced officers to choose positions at a convenient distance from the inmates. As tensions mounted at the prison, fewer experienced officers were immediately available in case of a crisis. The young correction officers grew increasingly apprehensive and worried that they were understaffed. They compounded the problem by calling in sick. A third organizational factor contributing to the initial success of the Attica inmates was an outdated and completely *inadequate communications system*. There were too few telephones throughout the prison and the phones that did exist were on a single line. The prison warden could talk with only one person at a time, but most of the time his line was hopelessly jammed by an overload of calls. Apparently no one knew what they should do because a contingency plan for riot control in the institution had never been implemented by prison officials. Some administrative officials may not have known a plan even existed. The *lack of an effective organizational plan for riot control* was almost certainly a fourth factor contributing to the rapid spread of disorderly behavior.

Emergent Organization in the Riot Process

By 10:30 a.m., nearly 1,300 of Attica's 2,243 inmates had assembled in D yard. It was a chaotic, completely disorganized scene. Inmates milled around searching for close friends, discovering old friends, telling jokes, and asking questions. It was an exhilarating experience for many of the inmates who converged on D yard. For Richard X. Clark it was close to euphoria:

> It was black in that corridor, and now suddenly the sun was shining and everyone was smiling. There was a warmth there I had never felt before at Attica. For the first time since I had been in the joint, I felt liberated, I had a sense of freedom (1973:29).

The sense of excitement described by Clark spread quickly throughout the assembled body of inmates. Although some were at first reluctant, they began to share in the booty from the prison commissary. The inmates had "liberated" candy bars, cigarettes, and food, and had transported them to D yard in wheelbarrows. With an unaccustomed exuberance they experimented with pills and drugs taken from the prison's medical supplies. The party atmosphere was contagious. Homosexuality prospered. Stragglers arriving in D yard were sometimes shocked by the wild scene; it seemed so unreal. Any misgivings initially experienced by the inmates were washed away by the euphoria of the moment. A vague sense of unease would have been incompatible with the bright panorama of activity in D yard on that unforgettable September morning.

After about an hour of chaos and disorganization, Roger Champen, a well-known jailhouse lawyer, climbed onto a table and called for attention by using an officer's bullhorn. He told his fellow inmates, "We've got to pull ourselves together," and began to issue instructions. One group of inmates was dispatched into the cellblocks for blankets and bedding, another began to break up tables and benches for firewood, and still another group was sent to collect water cans. While these initial steps were being taken other inmates began to speak. The new speakers included more "inmate lawyers," inmate leaders of political and religious groups, and inmates who had had experience in uprisings at other institutions. In short, the inmate leadership in D yard emerged from the leadership structure of the inmate population as it existed prior to the riot.

Strict rules were laid down: drugs were forbidden and drugs or syringes were to be surrendered in the center of the yard; homosexual relationships were outlawed as demeaning; fighting among inmates was prohibited; and, most important, the hostages captured by the inmates were not to be harmed. The Black Muslims in D yard organized themselves as bodyguards for the hostages. Although 50 hostages were taken by the inmates, 11 were released because of injuries. Officer Quinn was one of the hostages released by the inmates. The remaining hostages were herded to the center of D yard where they could be seen by state officials.

The cooperation of the inmates on following rules, protecting the hostages, and completing job assignments was enforced by an inmate "security guard." From Thursday morning through Monday morning as many as 300 inmates acted as part of the security guard at one time or another. The security guard was organized into squads which were designated by different colored armbands. The squads patrolled different areas and performed somewhat different functions. Security guards with green armbands were responsible for escorting Commissioner Oswald into D yard for negotiations; security guards on night patrol wore white armbands. "One of the most significant functions of the security guard was to make sure that the inmates remained in D yard" (NYS-

SCA 1972:200). It seems that some of the inmates in D yard would have returned to their cells, if it had not been for their fear of the security guard. Inmates caught breaking rules were forced to dig sanitary ditches. State officials later mistook these ditches for defensive works filled with volatile chemicals from the metal shop.

The Failure of Negotiations

Much to his credit, Commissioner Oswald had decided to negotiate with the inmate leaders in D yard even before he arrived at the prison. By 2:00 p.m. when Oswald and Deputy Commissioner Walter Dunbar reached Attica, the inmates in D yard were well entrenched and had already drawn up a list of reform demands. Since hostages were involved the Commissioner was determined to follow a policy of restraint and was willing to make a number of important initial concessions. He allowed representatives of the news media to enter the prison, and he gave his approval for a panel of "citizen observers" to assemble and oversee the negotiations. Both of these decisions were costly in the end.

The presence of news media transformed the negotiation sessions into a political theatre for debating revolutionary politics. Various political factions among the inmates competed for TV exposure and filled the night air with rhetoric. The citizen observers became a liability because they never determined their own role. Should they be neutral bystanders or should they serve as a conduit between the prison officials and the estranged inmates? Should they become advocates for the inmates or champions of state authority? Nothing was ever decided along these lines because the panel of "citizen observers" was far too large (over 30 members at one point) and represented several antithetical viewpoints. The observers' inability to reach consensus among themselves severely undercut their role as mediators in the dispute, and some of the citizen observers added to the rhetoric of the occasion by delivering inflammatory speeches.

The negotiations between prison authorities and the D yard inmates were crammed into a 30-hour period between 7:00 p.m. Friday and 1:00 a.m. Sunday. In the early hours of Sunday morning the inmates rejected a compromise proposal of 28 points for institutional reform which had been approved by Commissioner Oswald. Most of the 28 points were standard reform demands which had already surfaced at other prisons throughout the country. The package was rejected by the inmates because it did not include everything they wanted. Commissioner Oswald, in consultation with Governor Rockefeller, would not approve three key demands: (1) he would not provide transport for inmates who wished to leave the country, (2) he would not fire Attica's

Superintendent, Vincent Mancusi, and (3) he would not obtain a grant of criminal amnesty for the rioting inmates. The last provision was critical for the Attica inmates who feared blanket indictments on criminal charges based solely on their presence in D yard. Officer Quinn's death from injuries sustained in the Times Square skirmish hardened the inmates' position on this issue and produced a stalemate.

By Sunday afternoon D yard had undergone a melancholy change. Rain had turned the ground into a sea of stinking mud and the air was cold. Still, the inmates continued to demand both a grant of criminal amnesty and transport out of the country. Although many of the prisoners were personally demoralized, they persisted in the collective view that the hostages gave them unlimited power and protection. The inmates wanted Governor Rockefeller to come to Attica, and many believed the fiction that it was only a matter of time before the state capitulated. After all, the inmates considered themselves objects of public sympathy, and they were enjoying a novel sense of power. They had seen themselves on TV; famous politicians, radical lawyers, and newspaper columnists had responded to their summons. But the situation was changing more rapidly than they realized.

By Monday, September 13, there were 587 state police, 250 deputies from nine counties, and over 300 correction officers on hand to retake the prison. Many of the correction officers had brought their personal hunting rifles with them. The State Police had been issued Ithaca shotguns and Winchester .270 caliber rifles equipped with telescopic sights. The .270 Winchester is a commercial hunting rifle and the ammunition made for it is intended to expand greatly upon impact for maximum "stopping power."

Riot Control: The Traditional Strategy

The standard administrative procedure for ending prison riots follows a policy of *forceful suppression* rather than one of restraint. With only a few exceptions, the strategy of force pursued by prison officials has resulted in inmate deaths (Garson 1972b). Cannons, machine guns, tear gas, and even tanks have been used to subdue rioting inmates. In 1927 more than a thousand inmates at California's Folsom Prison rioted after a frustrated escape attempt in which two guards were stabbed and one inmate was accidentally shot. The inmates took control of a cellhouse, held seven hostages captive, and refused an ultimatum to return to their cells. Rather than accept a prolonged state of seige, the prison officials ordered a full scale assault. Eight inmates were killed and one guard died of "excitement" (Garson 1972b:413). When tanks arrived on the scene, the remaining inmates released their hostages unharmed and surrendered. Riots at Leavenworth Penitentiary, Kansas, in 1929, and at Joliet Penitentiary in 1931 were also forcefully suppressed. Two inmates were killed and a number of others were wounded.

The traditional policy of suppression was accepted into the 1950s as a matter of proper administrative procedure even though the record of the 1920s and 1930s had shown that force resulted in the deaths of 19 inmates. None had died in the same period when a policy of restraint had been followed (Garson 1972b). Moreover, the implementation of force in the 1950s belied the official belief that the professional training of police and prison guards would temper their use of firearms. Several incidents proved the contrary. When officials at Lincoln Penitentiary, Nebraska, chose to suppress rioting inmates with force in 1955, one inmate was shot in the back, and a photograph of the riot showed "half a dozen guards or police aiming at fleeing convicts in the prison year" (Garson 1972b:416). Earlier in 1953, rioting inmates at Monroe, Washington, had protested the death of a prisoner who had been shot while allegedly waving his undershirt in an attempt to surrender. The guards involved in the shooting claimed self-defense. Such episodes are especially tragic when it is recognized that "even though twenty-five prison riots in the 1950's involved the taking of hostages, no hostages were killed regardless of whether the riot was ended by force or restraint" (Garson 1972b:415).

Public outrage against the use of force finally intensified in the 1950s, at least in part, because of a revival of public interest in prison reform. As early as 1946 James Bennett, Director of the Federal Bureau of Prisons, noted significant public interest in prison problems. He issued a 16-point list of evaluative standards for the use of reform-minded citizens. In 1950 Adlai Stevenson was the keynote speaker at the Annual Convention of the American Prison Association. Stevenson, who was then Governor of Illinois, endorsed prison rehabilitation and praised reforms in his own state. "Detention or Correction?" was a slogan symbolic of the conflicting views of wardens, prison guards, and the increasing numbers of psychologists, psychiatrists, and social workers involved in prison management. Humanitarian ideals briefly resurfaced in the course of the 1950s debate.

By 1968 the traditional policy of forceful suppression of prison riots had been modified, but still not abandoned. A strategy of *restraint and negotiation* was followed when hostages were involved, and a strategy of force when they were not (Garson 1972b:418). When riots involving hostages could not be concluded through negotiation or voluntary dispersal, force was used as a last resort. A state of seige was not seen as an acceptable alternative to forceful suppression; prolonged restraint was apparently rejected as a useful administrative strategy for several reasons:

Restraint ws considered 1) a risk to hostages . . . , 2) a risk to further property damage, particularly through fire, 3) a futile response to unacceptable inmate demands for escape (Garson 1972b:414).

Other factors favored the forceful suppression of prison riots into the late 1960s and early 1970s. Restraint had become an unpopular political course of action. Law and order was a significant conservative cause which the White House under Richard Nixon was promoting. Spokesmen for the early Nixon Administration justified violence by arguing that "acquiescence to the criminal element only begets greater violence." Violence against prison inmates flourished in the permissive context of this kind of thinking, especially since prison officials proved to be receptive to the idea that suppression was necessary to save hostages.

Correction officers and state police were understandably sympathetic with fellow officers being held as hostages, and many felt obligated, if not morally required, to suppress rioting inmates as quickly as possible. Finally, many prison officials frequently expressed the belief that if riots were not expeditiously suppressed they would spread to other institutions. Although there is some evidence that riots tend to spread from one prison to another, there is no correlation between the duration of a riot and the spread of rioting to other institutions. The occurrence of a riot is a sufficient cause for its spread to other places; short riots are just as likely to initiate the diffusion process as long-lasting riots (Garson 1972b).

The Final Confrontation At Attica

In spite of abundant evidence that force resulted in inmate deaths, and in spite of the past success of restraint, prison administrators in the late 1960s and early 1970s were strongly inclined toward the use force in dealing with riots. In 1968 about 350 prisoners at the Ohio State Penitentiary rioted in protest against "sadistic" prison guards. Nine guards were taken as hostages. The Governor of Ohio, in response, ordered 500 National Guardsmen to free the hostages. The National Guard and police blasted a hole in the prison wall and went in shooting. Five inmates were shot to death and 11 wounded. Following the Ohio Penitentiary riot there were nine others involving hostages which were ended by either force or the threat of force. Six of these nine riots occurred in New York and four of the New York riots were ended by ultimatums. The Attica inmates received their final ultimatum on Monday, September 13, 1971.

At 7:40 a.m. Commissioner Oswald sent the inmates a last warning that they must accept the terms of the 28 points which he had already approved. The citizen observers were infuriated by Oswald's letter which they interpreted as an "ultimatum," but Oswald's own staff criticized the note as too "soft." In any case, the Commissioner's note did not make clear the consequences of rejecting the 28 points. The note did not say explicitly that D yard would be attacked by heavily armed men. The inmates in D yard were therefore never really warned that the State was about to retake the prison. The men in D yard believed the hostages guaranteed their safety, and they simply could not conceive that state authorities would endanger the hostages. For 30 of the inmates this proved to be a fatal assumption. State officials were growing more and more anxious to reassert their authority, and the Attica riot was increasingly viewed as a challenge to state sovereignty and even to national security. Governor Rockefeller and Commissioner Oswald worried that the inmate radicals had to be confronted before the riot could spread to other prisons and then into the urban slums of America. State authorities consistently overestimated the potential danger of the riot, just as they repeatedly exaggerated the dangerous intentions of the Attica inmates. Commissioner Oswald was personally convinced that the inmates would go through with their threat to kill the hostages. When the State decided that something had to be done, that the riot was intolerable, the lives of the hostages became expendable (NYSSCA 1972:-329). The inmates never realized that the hostages could lose their protective charm and rejected the commissioner's ultimatum at 9:30 a.m.

The assault was launched by "Jackpot 1," a National Guard helicopter equipped with a tear gas disperser, at 9:44 a.m. The helicopter's appearance was the inmates' first notice that the assault was actually underway. Even so, many thought that Governor Rockefeller had finally arrived. Two rifle teams had moved into position on the roofs of A and C blocks, but they had been under orders to keep out of sight. On the third floor of A block 11 state troopers and about 11 correction officers unobtrusively pointed guns out of windows in the direction of D yard. The plan of attack made no provision for effectively controlling the firepower of these rifle teams. The decision to use firepower was left to the judgment of the riflemen themselves with the instructions that they were to "fire at the first sign of an overt, hostile act against a hostage" (NYSSCA 1972:351).

At about this time the inmates decided to stage an elaborate bluff. Several of the hostages were taken to the roof of Times Square where they would be in plain view. Each hostage was held by an inmate who had apparently been chosen as an "executioner" in case of an attack. The hostages were forced to scream for mercy with knives at their throats. Testimony from both inmate executioners and the hostages themselves make it reasonably certain that the inmates brandishing knives had no real intention to kill their victims. But the damage was done. The menacing actions of the inmate executioners were easily mistaken for serious attacks by the rifle teams. When Jackpot 1 arrived and released a cloud of gas the inmates on the roof of Times Square instinctively ducked down, dragging the hostages with them. The fusilade began with the misperception of this action.

When the shooting ended, 10 hostages and 29 inmates were dead or dying. Three hostages and 85 inmates had suffered nonlethal gunshot wounds. None of the hostages had been killed by the inmates; all were killed by the overfire of the assault force. One instance was a classic case of perceptual distortion under stress. Inmates ran toward the hostages thinking it would be safer in their vicinity, but the assault force saw this action as an attempt to kill the hostages before they could be saved. State police fired at the fleeing inmates and inadvertently killed several of the hostages.

Even after the shooting was over violence continued unchecked. Inmates were beaten by correction officers, stripped, and forced to crawl through the sanitary trenches. Often inmates were forced down a gauntlet of correction officers in A block. A National Guardsman carrying an inmate told this story.

"I was assigned to one stretcher on which there was a large black man. There were gun wounds in his legs and rearend. . .

A small nonuniformed man (later identified by the inmate as a correction officer) came up to us and asked what was wrong with this particular prisoner, and I told him the inmate had gunshot wounds in his legs. My telling him seemingly went unnoticed. He told us to put the inmate down. (The man then) picked the head end of the stretcher up and dumped (the inmate) onto his feet. The (inmate) fell over onto his shoulder and really bounced off the floor.

Then this nonuniformed man pulled out a Phillips screwdriver and (said to the inmate), who was lying on the floor on his back, 'If you don't get moving—if you don't get up on your feet you are going to get this right up your ass.' Then he did stick this man right in the anal area five or six times" (NYSSCA 1972:436–7).

The Failure of Control Strategy

How did the situation at Attica get so completely out of hand? There is no definitive answer, but a number of factors clearly contributed to the tragedy: (1) *the strategy* implemented at Attica *was poorly planned* and badly administrated, (2) there was a clear *failure of discipline* within the assault force itself, (3) there was an *over reliance on excessive firepower*, and (4) there was *too little regard for situational determinants of collective violence.*

Poor Planning and Administration

It appears that no one really wanted the responsibility of commanding the assault force. The Superintendent of the State Police allegedly saw no need for his involvement and drove to his lodge on Lake George. Monday was his usual day off (NYSSCA 1972:342). And even though several top ranking state officials were at Attica, the burden of planning the assault fell on local law enforcement personnel. Their previous experience and training left them unprepared for what they considered to be a novel problem in crowd control The plan they devised was deficient in a number of areas: (1) it made no provision for screening the men who should take part in the attack, (2) it made no provision for preventing reprisals, (3) it made no provision for adequate control of firepower, (4) it made no provision for moving the inmates out of D yard after the assault, and (5) it made no provision for adequate medical aid. State troopers testified that the objectives of the operation were not made clear. The command hierarchy was never outlined, so it was impossible to really know who was in charge of whom. Prison officials, for example, had decided that correction officers were too emotionally distraught to take part in the attack, but no one ever told them. This failure was serious in itself, but the State's failure to maintain discipline in the assault force was even more so.

Failure of Discipline

The riot control tactics used in the 1960s and early 1970s were borrowed from military strategy; but generally speaking, the police "could not perform at the minimum levels of teamwork, impersonality, and discipline which these military doctrines take for granted" (Stark 1972:126). Top police officials in Detroit secretly testified that the city's police were for all practical purposes out of control by the third or fourth day of the 1967 riots. The contrast in Detroit between the performance of the police and guardsmen, on the one hand, and the performance of the regular Army troops, on the other hand, is revealing. In the area overseen by the police and guardsmen thousands of rounds of ammunition were expended, 30 people were killed, and the rioting lasted for days. By comparison, the regular Army troops fired only 201 rounds of ammunition, one person was killed, and order was restored in a few hours. The Army units had been trained as combat units, while the training of the police did not prepare them for this kind of situation. Consequently, the Army maintained its discipline and police did not.

> The Army ordered the lights back on and troopers to show themselves as conspicuously as possible; the police and guardsmen continued shoot-

ing out all lights and crouched fearfully in the darkness. The police and guardsmen shot wildly often at one another. The troopers were ordered to unload their weapons, and did so. The guardsmen were so ordered, but did not comply (Stark 1972:129).

A similar lack of discipline was also manifest at Attica. What happened at the prison was unique only in the number of people killed in a single encounter. The failure of state officials to prevent unnecessary shooting and deaths was profound. The plan of attack did not include a prearranged signal for either initiating or ceasing gunfire. The men in the assault force were told simply to fire at the first sign of hostile acts, and that they were to fire rather than engage in hand-to-hand combat. Such wide discretionary latitude in the use of guns undoubtedly contributed to an excessive use of firepower in retaking the prison.

Excessive Use of Firepower

Including "00" buckshot pellets, at least 2,200 lethal projectiles were discharged in D yard. Almost ten percent of the men in D yard were struck by the gunfire. What is "obvious from the evidence" is that "any inmate moving on the catwalks or running in the yard was likely to be shot" (NYSSCA 1972:403). There was a great deal of completely unnecessary shooting. "Troopers shot into tents, trenches, and barricades without looking first" (NYSSCA 1972:335). Statements made later in explanations of this kind of behavior were "in many cases exaggerated, embellished, and even fabricated." Photographic evidence contradicts official justifications for particular incidents of violence.

The state police defended their choice of the .270 Winchester on the grounds that a bullet would not pass through a body and strike an innocent bystander. But this logic is inconsistent with the use of "00" buckshot in Ithaca shotguns. Each pellet is larger in diameter than a .22 caliber bullet and one round of nine-pellet buckshot, fired at a distance of 50 yards, will release three to five pellets which "cannot be expected to hit their intended target" (NYSSCA 1972:355). The wounds caused by the shotguns and .270 Winchesters were so extensive that inmates bled to death before receiving medical aid. As noted, the plan for retaking the prison did not include the preparation of medical supplies or the proximity of medical personnel. The deficiencies of the plan were further compounded by ignoring situational factors promoting collective violence.

Situational Determinants of Collective Violence

Aside from inept planning and organization, the *social context* of the assault promoted unrestrained violence. The assault force had been assembling for over three days prior to the attack. By Monday the men were under *extreme stress;* they were tired, restless, and frustrated. Many of the correction officers, troopers, and deputies felt that they were being forced to stand by while "convicted felons were lionized, pandered to, and offered concessions." The men were bored because they had nothing to do. A few state troopers made slingshots and "amused themselves by firing at inmates in D yard (NYSSCA 1972:308). Correction officers spent part of their time on the roofs of A and C blocks pointing out inmates "who were known troublemakers." As the men milled about just outside the prison wall, they were increasingly enraged by the delay. Self-control became more tenuous as time wore on, and the rumors circulating among the state troopers, deputies and correction officers further inflamed their excitement and rage.

Information about what was going on in D yard was sketchy. Disquieting *rumors flourished.* The hostages were supposedly being castrated, sexually molested, and beaten by their captors. One rumor falsely reported that Officer Quinn, who died of wounds sustained at Times Square during the initial skirmish, had been killed when his head was deliberately crushed in an iron gate. A sick inmate released from D yard reported that the inmates were building a gallows to hang the hostages. According to another rumor, a dead hostage had had his testicles cut off and stuffed into his mouth. Dr. Warren Hanson, a surgeon who had been making daily visits to D yard, heard on Saturday night that a group of "inmates had forced two hostages into a bathroom, thrown wood in after them and set the place on fire." This "report" supposedly came from Robert Douglas, Governor Rockefeller's representative, Commissioner Oswald and his Deputy, Walter Dunbar (Knopf 1975: 268). Such rumors increased the anxiety of the assault forces and at the same time reinforced existing racial stereotypes.

The content of the rumors was drawn from the hostile *stereotypes* held by each of the antagonistic groups. The inmates were brutal savages from one point of view; and prison administrators and state officers were treacherous, white racists from the other. While inmate leaders and prison officials were engaged in futile negotiations, a wave of malignant rumors had hopelessly polarized the conflict.

When other people have been degraded or dehumanized, the inhibitions against brutality are reduced. There is evidence that at least some American soldiers, for example, began to think of the Vietnamese as subhuman. The names they used, "gook," "dink," and "slope" indicate their lack of regard for the Vietnamese as people (Middlebrook 1974). At Attica the inmates were degraded to the point where troopers and correction officers were eager to begin the attack. They were repeatedly overheard asking each other, "When are we going to go coon hunting?" (NYSSCA 1972:311). The inmates were "asking for it," and deserved to be punished. In a sense, violence was considered to be morally justified.

In general, any *situational factors which decrease the fear of punishment will increase the chances of aggression and excessive violence.* Controlled experiments have shown that *anonymity* will significantly increase aggression among college students (e.g., Zimbardo 1969, Baron 1970). Just being a member of a large assault force may make individuals feel anonymous and less vulnerable to punishment. At Attica anonymity was guaranteed.

The attackers were wearing uniforms, gas masks concealed their faces, and a cloud of gas surrounded them. Although there is some photographic evidence from the assault, the assault forces were not aware of cameras in the yard. The deterrent effect of photography was lost. The troopers should have been advised that there would be "police photography details" at work during the attack. In short, there were no procedures established to insure individual accountability for unnecessary shooting. No records were even kept of the serial numbers of rifles and shotguns distributed to the assault force. Weapons were passed from hand to hand for days without any serious attempt to keep track of who had what gun. Moreover, "buckshot pellets cannot be traced ballistically to the gun which fired them" (NYSSCA 1972:362).

Aside from anonymity, blind *obedience to orders* may have played a significant role at Attica. If an individual feels that he is not personally responsible for aggression and is simply carrying out orders, he may experience little guilt and become excessively violent. Milgram's classic experiment on interpersonal aggression (1963) found that subjects acting "under orders" would apparently inflict intense electric shocks on another person. When told to do so, 65 percent of Milgram's subjects delivered what they believed to be a 450-volt shock: a shock intensity reached long after a mock victim complains of the "pain," pounds on the wall in apparent agony, and begs to be released from the experiment. Replications of Milgram's experiment have found that up to 85 percent of the experimental subjects would inflict the maximum level of shock available (Rosenhan 1969). In the context of this research tradition, the blanket order to shoot threatening inmates at Attica may have served the latent function of sanctioning unrestrained fire power. A national survey found that 51 percent of its respondents felt they would obey an order to shoot the inhabitants of a Vietnamese village—including old men, women, and children (Kelman and Lawrence 1972:45). Given this general public viewpoint, it seemed likely that most people would obey the order to shoot "threatening" inmates at Attica.

Aftermath and Postscript

Long after the full scope of the Attica tragedy was established, New York Deputy Commissioner Walter Dunbar still maintained:

> Control of the prison and of the recalcitrant inmates was established, in short order, by a unique and well-planned effort. . . . Excellent direction and self-discipline were demonstrated. Such was borne out by the facts that control was established in short order, and that there was a minimum of casualties (Dunbar 1973:10).

Despite this viewpoint, the hours and days following the assault were filled with questions and allegations. Was the force used by the state necessary? Why weren't the inmates warned that an armed attack was imminent? Why wasn't limited amnesty for the inmates given more consideration? Some observers were even calling the attack a "massacre." All of these questions and allegations were initially greeted by official silence. In the late afternoon of Monday, September 13, however, a group of newsmen and legislators were taken on a tour of the prison.

The tour group was shown a naked inmate lying on a table with a football tucked under his chin. Deputy Commissioner Dunbar reportedly introduced the inmate as the "castrator" of a hostage; and according to Assemblyman Arthur O. Eve and Congressman Herman Bedillo, he claimed that the castration "had been filmed from a helicopter as well as observed from a rifle's telescopic sights." The Special Commission concluded that the initial response of the state officials at Attica was a resort to rumors as justifications for their actions:

> Officials' public statements that the hostages had been maimed and murdered, which were issued before the results of the autopsies were known, reflected their apparent eagerness to provide the media with 'facts' which would justify an armed assault in which 39 men were killed and over 80 more wounded (NYSSCA 1972:456).

Although rumors were used to justify the assault at Attica, they were not necessarily part of a deliberate attempt to mislead the public. State officials believed in their "facts," and the information which they passed on to the press was consistent with their original perception of what had happened at Attica. Given the strength of commitment to their vision, it was easy for them to misinterpret events. They saw things as they expected to see them. For example, it was later determined that the castration rumor was given credence because a hostage was carried out of the prison bleeding heavily from a gunshot wound in the groin.

When the manner in which the hostages had died was eventually clarified, the credibility of prison officials in New York was so weak that a special panel of citizens (the Goldman Panel) was sent to Attica to insure the humane treatment and civil rights of the inmates. Inmate charges of continuing brutality combined with the prison's regrettable delay in identifying the inmates killed in the assault had aroused public concern. The numbering and impersonalized tagging of inmate corpses seemed to be symbolic of the status of inmates at Attica.

When the Goldman Panel arrived at the prison on Friday, September 17, 1971, it found severe overcrowding and a need for the improvement of "personal and human rights":

1. The inmates had not had baths for a over a week.

2. Many inmates had no writing paper to write to their families.

3. Toothpaste and personal articles. Many inmates had complained that they had lost their eyeglasses during the disturbance. Inmates were in need of shoes and socks, toothpaste, and tobacco.

4. Food. Inmates were only receiving two meals a day in their cells.

5. The need for greater access for counsel (Report of the Goldman Panel to Protect Prisoners' Constitutional Rights 1971:4).

In addition to these concerns, the Goldman Panel found that the Wyoming County District Attorney and the Deputy Attorney General of New York were "concerning themselves solely" with the responsibility of investigating charges against inmates and were not investigating the charges of inmates against correction officers. By September of 1973 a grand jury had handed up 42 indictments which charged 62 inmates with more than 1,400 crimes. In September of 1975 it appeared that the Attica prosecution was "slowly running out of steam," but 18 cases involving 34 defendants were still pending (New York Times, September 21, 1975). It would still be more than a month before a single indictment would be handed up against state employees at Attica. Ironically, in late September of 1975 New York Governor Hugh Carey was at last considering the possibility of amnesty for the Attica inmates if still another investigation showed that the law was selectively enforced against inmates (Toledo Blade, September 25, 1975b).

Summary and Conclusion

Attica never was and never will be a decent place to live. In the summer of 1971 the three major sources of *situational stress* at the institution were

harassment, racial conflict, and an inequitable parole system. Prison regulations were inadequately explained, selectively enforced, and were contradictory and even silly. Correction officers at the institution expressed racist
attitudes to the New York State Special Commission, and parole procedures
were ambiguous because the criteria used in making decisions were never
specified and the decision-making behavior of the Parole Board was sometimes
inconsistent.

Rumors played a significant part before, during, and after the tragic confrontation on September 13, 1971. In the months preceding the initial outbreak
of violence, rumor-prone state officials planned "countermeasures" for rumored inmate plots. They failed to verify their information before acting on
it throughout the crisis. During the riot itself the unconfirmed rumors that
hostages were being beaten, castrated, and cruelly murdered were believed
because of the official belief that the inmates were capable of these atrocities.
The decision-making process at Attica was seriously hampered throughout the
confrontation by the uncritical acceptance of rumored information.

The riot itself was precipitated by the misperception of an event which
occurred in D yard on September 8, 1971. Correction officers at Attica were
under a great deal of stress by the end of the summer months, and they were
expecting trouble. Two inmates sparring with each other were accused of
fighting, and later that evening were taken to the prison's disciplinary cellblock; the rest of the inmates were certain that they would be beaten by the
prison "goon squad." The riot broke out the following morning when "5
Company" was returning to A block after breakfast. Prison officials consistently maintained that this initial confrontation was a carefully orchestrated operation planned by "revolutionary" inmates at the institution. The bulk of
available evidence, however, indicates that *the riot was a spontaneous outburst
of collective violence.* The two strongest pieces of evidence are as follows: (1)
inmate leaders would not choose to start a riot in an enclosed corridor, and
(2) they could not have known that the gate in Times Square was defective.
Moreover, the initial behavior of the rioting inmates was inconsistent with
logical planning. The inmate leadership which eventually developed in D yard
emerged from the leadership structure of the inmate population as it existed
prior to the riot. But these leaders were not a part of the initial outbreak.

Negotiations with the inmates were impeded by several factors. First, the
continuous presence of the news media transformed D yard into a stage for
political rhetoric and inflammatory speeches. The citizen observers, though
well intentioned for the most part, proved ineffective. They were not given a
clearly defined role to play, their number was too great, and they spent far too
much time in political debate among themselves. Finally, the negotiations
stalled completely when it became clear that criminal amnesty for the inmates

was the dominant issue. The inmates feared blanket indictments for criminal offenses based solely on their presence in D yard, and state government officials may have feared the political repercussions of appeasing the rebellious prisoners.

As the stalemate in negotiations wore on, the inmates never seemed to have realized that the hostages would eventually lose their protective charm. The inmates could not conceive that the state would endanger the hostages simply to regain its sovereignty over the prison. This misunderstanding was compounded by the failure of state officials at Attica to issue a clear warning that an armed attack was minutes away. This failure was only one aspect of the generally inept riot control strategy implemented by the state.

Perhaps the most serious deficiency in the assault plan developed by local law enforcement personnel was its omission of an effective *mechanism for controlling the firepower* of the assault force. There was no signal for a cease fire and the decision to shoot was left to the discretion of the individuals involved. Members of the assault force were simply told to shoot at any inmate who in their judgment was threatening either to themselves or one of the hostages. Such general guidelines allowed too much latitude in a situation in which an excess of violence was not only possible, but likely. Violence was likely not because of malicious people, but because of the *social context* which had developed at Attica.

Situational determinants of violence played an important part at Attica. Members of the assault force were frustrated by the delay when prison officials negotiated with the inmates. During the stalemate in negotiations rumors spread which portrayed the inmates as subhumans, reduced inhibitions against interpersonal aggression, and supplied rationales for "punishing" the inmates. The circumstances of the attack virtually guaranteed a sense of *anonymity* for the attacking force. Individuals were submerged in a large group, they wore uniforms, had gas masks on their faces, and were surrounded by a cloud of gas. They were not told that photographs would be taken of their conduct and no procedures for individual accountability for weapons and ammunition were implemented.

*

PART IV *Social Movements*

S ocial movements, discussed in Part IV, play a role of great importance in the world today and few, if any, people escape being influenced by them. In Chapter I, collective behavior was defined as "relatively unorganized patterns of social interaction in human groups." *Social movements are collectivities with a degree of leadership, organization, and ideological commitment to promote or resist change.* As such they are transitional and fall between relatively uncoordinated crowd action and institutionalized bureaucratic activity. When social movements become fully institutionalized, they cease to be social movements. For this reason, the change-oriented programs of well-established organizations, such as labor unions, are not considered social movements. The leadership patterns and organizational characteristics of labor unions resemble those of other formal organizations, consequently, they are unlike those found in social movements.

The leaders of social movements are usually self-appointed rather than elected and unsalaried rather than salaried. The leaders of social movements often act without a mandate from their constituency, and in many cases, under conditions of economic and social insecurity. It is true that funding available from foundations, churches, and the government may be creating a new professional class whose careers involve leadership of social movements (McCarthy and Zald 1973). But even in these cases, the leaders of social movements do not have offices vested with authority. They must persuade rather than order their memberships to follow a certain course of action. For the most part, the membership of a social movement consists of partisans rather than employees or dues-paying members. Leaders of labor unions can coerce their membership by withholding benefits and jobs from individuals who refuse to follow union policy; most members of social movements cannot be forced to fulfill certain duties, conform to specific regulations, or even attend meetings. Moreover, the leaders of institutionalized organizations know their membership, while the identities of the followers of a social movement are often unknown.

The next three chapters consider social movements as *deliberate collec-*

tive enterprises. Chapter X, "Preconditions," begins with a review of the types and stages of social movements and considers *stress situations* associated with the *preconditions* of social movements. It briefly discusses the possibility of predicting social movements from stress conditions.

Chapter XI, "Mobilization," treats the problem of *how social movements get started.* It begins with a discussion of *ideologies* and how they rationalize, justify, and motivate behavior in social movements. The chapter considers leadership and membership, and the process of recruitment and conversion, then ends with a discussion of the organization of social movements.

Chapter XII, "Success and Failure," deals with the *strategies and tactics of social movements* and the public reactions and social control efforts of the host society. The problems of success and failure are considered as well as the impact of social movements in society as a whole.

A perceived crisis in the social and spiritual condition of the urban poor in England led evangelists William and Catherine Booth to found the Salvation Army in 1878 as a way to help the needy and to reform society.

Supporters of the Equal Rights Amendment express their views at a rally in Austin, Tex.

CHAPTER X

Preconditions

O ne of the major concerns of collective behavior theorists has been the development of *typologies for social movements.* After discussing several of these schemes, the principal objective of this chapter is a review of the conditions that give rise to social movements. Indices of situational stress are given special attention.

Types of Social Movements

One of the best known and most influential typologies of social movements is that of Herbert Blumer (1951:199–220). He distinguishes between: (1) the *general* social movement, (2) the *specific* social movement, and (3) the *expressive* social movement. The general social movement has vague goals, lacks a coordinated program, and is rather formless and inarticulate. Such a movement develops gradually out of cultural drifts and slow changes in social values. It creates a supporting literature and gains leaders and spokesmen over a substantial period of time.

Specific movements grow from general movements and may be of a reform or revolutionary character. Reform movements accept the basic social order in which they find themselves and seek to change only some part of it. Indeed the reform movement may be considered as an affirmation of the values of society. Both reform and specific movements have well-defined goals, a definite leadership, an organization with a division of labor, an ideology, and a "we consciousness." A revolutionary movement, on the other hand, has the purpose of introducing an entirely new set of values to replace the prevailing ones.

Expressive social movements, rather than attempting to change society, release the tension and unrest out of which they grow in expressive behavior of some kind. Religious movements, for example, provide for a release of tension without a push for social change. Features of expressive movements and specific movements may be combined in millenarian movements. In this kind of movement the expressive functions of religion are combined with an expectation that the dawn of a new world or millenium is at hand in which current suffering will give way to an ideal social order and personal salvation.

Millenarian movements are often found as a consequence of the contact between more complex and less complex cultures or in times of rapid social change involving urbanization, rapid population growth, and economic disturbance. Millenarian movements are sometimes followed, in areas of colonial domination, by movements of national liberation or revitalization movements as the pressure of the dominating powers both destroys the indigenous cultures and reveals their relative backwardness. In recent years, many movements of national liberation have been successful in casting out colonial domination, but revitalization movements are usually not successful in restoring old ways of life (Roberts and Kloss 1974:77–98, Wilkinson 1971:70–75).

Roberta Ash Garner (1977:6–7) recently developed a five-part typology of social movements. First is the *class-conscious revolutionary movement* whose goal is to seize the state, including its social control forces. Its aim is to change the state's class system, so it must use nonlegitimate (from the state's point of view) strategies and tactics. A second type are the *class-conscious movements without a program of immediate revolution.* These movements are likely to work, at least partially, within the structure of the host society. They may wish to change the class system, but choose activities such as running candidates in elections rather than attempting revolution to gain control of the state. The *reform movement* is the third type. The reform movement uses legitimate strategies and tactics and does not attempt to change either the class system or the means of production. The fourth type is the *counterrevolutionary movement* which attempts to reestablish a prior class structure. Finally, the *coup d'etat* is a movement which attempts, through nonlegitimate means, to replace one set of rulers with another, without making any change in the prevailing class structure.

Still another typology was developed by Aberle (1967) who divides social movements along two dimensions: the *locus* of change sought, and the *amount* of change sought. Each of these dimensions is divided into two categories. The locus of change can either be in the individual or in the social structure of a society, while the amount of change sought can either be partial or total. Cross-classification on these two dimensions generates four possible types of social movements (see Figure 10.1). *Transformative* movements aim at the total change of a social structure, and they generally envision a cataclysmic upheaval as a precondition for the occurrence of such an all-embracing change.

Millenarian movements and revolutionary movements fall into this category. *Reformative movements* aim at only the partial change of a social structure. They do not anticipate cataclysmic violence and are more circumspect in their goals. The Women's Christian Temperance Union (WCTU), for example, was interested in outlawing the production and sale of alcoholic beverages and later expanded its goals to include women's suffrage. *Redemptive movements* aim at the total change of the individual since they explain social problems by blaming personal weaknesses among those involved. The early Salvation Army accounted for alcoholism and prostitution by blaming moral failure and spiritual bankruptcy. Its members believed the solution to these problems was salvation through Christ. *Alterative movements* seek only limited changes in individuals. The Zero Population Growth (ZPG) movement attempted to persuade people to limit the size of their families, but did not advocate sweeping changes in life style or the establishment of legal penalties for having large families.

FIGURE 10.1: A Classification of Social Movements

		LOCUS OF CHANGE	
		Supraindividual	Individual
AMOUNT OF CHANGE	Total	Transformative	Redemptive
	Partial	Reformative	Alterative

Source: Aberle (1967: 316).

The Stages of Social Movements

In addition to the development of typologies of social movements, considerable attention has been paid to their stages. This developmental approach is sometimes called the "natural history" method.

One of the most influential treatments of the stages of a social movement was developed by Rex D. Hopper (1950:270–9), who identified four stages. First is the preliminary stage characterized by *mass excitement and unrest.* Those caught up in the excitement and unrest are susceptible to milling or circular interaction. They may be influenced by activities such as agitation, suggestion, imitation, and propaganda. The leaders who emerge at this time are skilled in the use of these techniques, indeed this stage belongs to the agitator. The dominant social form is the "psychological mass" composed of anonymous persons who have little or no interaction with one another and little or no organization. They are people from all walks of life who respond to common influences.

Next is the popular stage of crowd excitement and unrest in which unrest, discontent, and dissatisfaction result in *collective excitement*. Participating individuals become aware of one another and resistance develops. Intellectuals transfer their allegiance from the established system to the movement. A social myth develops which leads people to think that they are on the way to a new order. Milling becomes intensified, less random and aimless, and changes to social contagion and collective excitement. Leaders at this stage attempt to develop esprit de corps as a way of generating loyalty to the movement. During this stage there are two kinds of leaders: the prophet who formulates and promulgates the social myth in general terms, and the reformer who attacks specific wrongs and develops a clearly defined program.

Third is the *formal stage* of the formulation of issues and the formation of publics. The movement in this period goes beyond collective excitement and social contagion to appeal to the essential desires of the people. Issues emerge which are disputed and discussed by publics, the dominant social form. Violent and organized conflict directed toward definite objectives appears, followed by the formulation of policies and programs which become a formal part of the behavior of the participants. Group morale and ideology become highly developed, with statesmen skilled in policy formulation as leaders.

Fourth is the *institutional stage* of legalization and societal organization. A new society, formed as the out group, has legalized its power and become the new in group; it has become institutionalized. The movement depends increasingly more on discussion and deliberation and less on collective behavior as a way of fixing policies. In this stage leadership is of the administrator-executive type.

One of the more recent typologies of the natural history of social movements is that of Armand Mauss (1975:61–6) who identified five stages through which they move: (1) incipiency, (2) coalescence, (3) institutionalization, (4) fragmentation, and (5) demise. Figure 10.2 provides a graphic illustration of the process.

In the *incipiency* stage there is public concern about some situation defined as a problem. Members of the public, who are not organized, read and write about the problem, have occasional meetings, and engage in similar activities. The response of the host society is usually indulgent, unless the beginning movement is seen as very threatening. However, the host society does attempt to restore general agreement by using various techniques of conciliation. Serious members may respond to these conciliatory efforts by trying to test the boundaries of indulgence, which may arouse some hostility in the society

FIGURE 10.2: Normal Pattern for the Natural History of a Social Movement

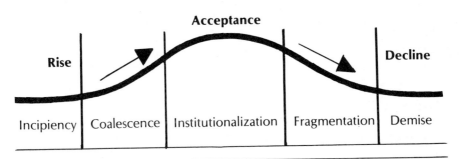

Source: Mauss (1975: 66).

toward the social movement. Societal efforts to control the movement through conciliation may work for a long time.

The *coalescence* stage is characterized by the formation of formal and informal movement organizations. They appear in response to repressive action by the opposition or as a consequence of a lack of corrective action from the society. Short of strong repressive measures or virtual capitulation by society, the movement at this point is very difficult to stop.

The third stage, *institutionalization*, occurs when standardized patterns have been developed to cope with the movement. This is the time of the movement's greatest success; it is organized, has a large membership base and resources, and influences the political processes of society. There may still be repression, but it is reserved for the fanatics who do not respond to co-optation. The whole society takes the movement seriously.

Fragmentation of the movement takes place in the fourth stage. It occurs after a time of success, primarily through the process of co-optation. Many of the earlier supporters of the movement will think that matters have so improved that they can give their attention to other matters. Those remaining in the movement often struggle among themselves and establish splinter organizations. The leadership changes, too, as charismatic leaders are replaced with more bureaucratic ones.

The last stage is *demise*, which is often not recognized within the movement. Instead members of the movement may see the situation as a victory or only a momentary pause. Through the process of co-optation only a few groups of deeply devoted people remain active and they are likely to be subjected to severe and generally approved repressive measures. Such repression may drive the remaining membership underground and to extreme tactics.

Now that some of the types and stages of social movements have been reviewed, we can begin to consider the conditions leading to social movements.

Preconditions of Social Movements

A number of concepts have been used to account for the conditions that give rise to social movements. Among these are "structural conduciveness and structural strain," "rising expectations and relative deprivation," "oppression, colonialism, and mass society." Some of these have already been mentioned in the discussion of crowds in Chapter VII. In this case the same concepts are often employed to explain related but different phenomena in collective behavior.

Structural Conduciveness: General Comments

This discussion is derived from the first stage, structural conduciveness, of the value-added model of collective behavior (Smelser, 1962). We recall from Chapter II that for a particular form of collective behavior to occur, the structure of a society or group must be conducive to it. Earlier it was mentioned that riots are sometimes triggered by rumors that circulate when conventional news media are inadequate or curtailed by circumstances. Similarly, it is possible to see that a social structure could discourage or encourage particular kinds of social movements. Some societies are much more tolerant of dissent than others. Those that permit little dissent may either eliminate social movements or drive them underground and force the development of "secret societies" or terrorism. Smelser points out that a society which encourages the development of new knowledge indirectly encourages social movements designed to change a situation previously taken for granted. He mentions the case of the development of medical knowledge for controlling venereal disease (1962:287). In this instance, knowledge led to a worldwide health movement, which is still underway, to wipe venereal disease from the face of the earth. The idea of structural conduciveness can be illustrated in more detail by referring to the student protest movement of the 1960s and early 1970s.

Structural Conduciveness: The Student Movement

The student movement began as a reform movement based on an "idealistic humanism." The Port Huron Statement of 1962, the working papers of the

Student for a Democratic Society (SDS)—one of the many organizations in the movement, proclaimed its goal to be the establishment of a true "democracy of individual participation." In 1964, the Berkeley Free Speech Movement attempted to maintain and expand the rights of students to pamphleteer and raise money for political causes on the campus of the University of California. By that time it was clear that the bureaucratic structures of the establishment had been identified as a focal point for the movement's opposition. The partisans of the student protest movements were convinced that establishment bureaucracies unduly restricted individual freedoms and denied individuals' participation in decisions affecting their lives. University administrations and the Selective Service, were castigated as prime examples of the bureaucratic apparatus intended to manipulate people. The war in Viet Nam intensified student opposition toward the end of the 1960s and radicalized leadership groups within the general movement. Former President Nixon's "Cambodian incursion," for example, precipitated a massive protest demonstration in Washington D.C. Approximately 250,000 people converged on the Nation's capitol city. Aside from such highly visible events, there were many other factors that promoted the development of the student protest movement.

Flacks' (1971) analysis of the period shows how the structure of society in the United States was conducive to the development of the student protest movement. First, he points out that youth is a social as well as biological stage of life. Definitions of what ages constitute youth and adult statuses vary considerably from one culture to another. In many cultures the transition from childhood to adulthood is extremely rapid, but in the United States the transition is much more prolonged. The youth in our country, people over 16 years of age who have not entered the labor force, (Flacks 1971:9) are a familiar aspect of life. At the time of his writing, Flacks pointed out that less than half of those between 16 and 21 years of age were full-time members of the labor force. A large proportion of these were still in school, only a fraction were in the armed services, and substantial numbers were unemployed. Of those between 21 and 24 years of age, 25 percent were still in school. In Flacks' view this separation of a large proportion of the persons under 25 years of age from the mainstream of society, a development of the previous ten years, was one of the most important social changes since World War II. "There have been 'youths' throughout history, but as far as one can tell, never has such a large proportion of the young population been so 'youth'-ful" (Flacks 1971:10).

The number of young people still in school during the 1960s was especially significant because the educational goals and structures of American universities were in themselves conducive to the development of the student protest movement. Advanced societies require a large number of persons competent to perform complex tasks. Among the primary sources of such people are

Free Speech demonstrators surround a campus police car during a rally at the University of California, Berkeley in 1964.

universities and colleges, which along with other goals associated with liberal humanism, are expected to prepare people for the occupational world. The structure of the university also provided students with wide latitude in the use of their time. Furthermore, university structure was conducive to the student protest movement because it encouraged young people to experiment and question in all areas of life. However, as Flacks (1971:41) pointed out:

> from the viewpoint of the official culture, the student is expected to strike an extremely delicate balance with respect to such freedom. In the immediate university situation, he is supposed to separate his free, searching, experimental role from his formal educational activity. With respect to academic activity, he is expected to be disciplined, vigorous, routinized, and submissive. Furthermore, he is expected to understand that student freedom is a special privilege that is restricted to those who were chosen for student status and restricted to the university years. From the perspective of the official culture, the student who would try to extend

the freedom of university life to people outside the university or maintain it for himself upon leaving the university setting would be making a serious error.

During the 1960s and early 1970s thousands of students did try to extend the freedom of university life to the outside world, while critics of higher education frequently blamed the universities and colleges themselves for fermenting student dissent. But the structural conduciveness of a given situation is likely to be complex and worth close examination; indeed, a review of research reveals that the extent to which faculties supported student protests varied with a number of important factors.

Lazarsfeld and Theilens (1958) and Cole and Adamsons (1969) provided information on the relationship between political orientation and the academic man and his behavioral and attitudinal responses toward certain issues during times of crisis. The liberal faculty member, as one would expect, was more likely to be tolerant or supportive of student demonstrations during the previous decade than the conservative faculty member was (also see Cole and Adamsons, 1969). Similar research reported by Bart (1970), Downing and Salomone (1969), and Shuman and Laumann (1967) demonstrated that junior faculty members tended to be more liberal in political orientation than senior faculty members. This is consistent with Stouffer's earlier (1955) conclusion that there is a tendency for educated persons to become less tolerant with age.

Some intriguing findings reported by Abramson and Wences (1970, and Wences and Abramson 1970) indicated that faculty tolerance of political nonconformity was also closely related to the length of time a faculty member had been a resident at a particular university. Abramsom and Wences interpreted the *longevity factor* as an indicator of a local orientation and relative satisfaction with community values. A second study replicated and extended their findings by showing the effect of longevity when controlling for political orientation, age, and job satisfaction (Pugh et al. 1972). As shown in Table 10.1 the gamma coefficient between longevity and faculty support of student dissent increased slightly (−.27 vs. −.29) when controlling for age and was not eliminated by controlling for either job satisfaction or political orientation. As in the earlier studies reported by Abramson and Wences, controlling for longevity eliminated an inverse relationship between academic rank and faculty support of student dissent. Consequently, the difference between junior and senior faculty reported in earlier studies was merely an artifact of the circumstance that senior faculty are longer and more conservative residents of university communities than are their junior colleagues.

In addition to political orientation and longevity, it appears that faculty support of student dissent in the 1960s varied by academic discipline. Contem-

Table 10.1: Faculty Support for Student Dissent by Longevity, Standardized on Age, Job Satisfaction, and Political Orientation

	Percent Support of Student Dissent			
Unstandardized	Low	Moderate	High	N
1–2 years	32	30	38	60
3–5 years	53	25	23	53
6 years or more	57	20	23	65
		Gamma = –.27		
Standardized On Age				
1–2 years	36	29	34	60
3–5 years	53	24	23	53
6 years or more	61	23	16	64
		Gamma = –.29		
Standardized On Job Satisfaction				
1–2 years	34	35	30	30
3–5 years	51	26	23	50
6 years or more	56	20	23	64
		Gamma = –.18		
Standardized On Political Orientation				
1–2 years	34	28	38	56
3–5 years	56	27	17	53
6 years or more	51	20	29	65
		Gamma = –.16		

Source: Pugh, et al. (1972:527).

porary research tended to confirm the common assumption that campus unrest was especially high among students associated with the social sciences and humanities. This may have been true, to some extent, because the faculties working in these areas were the most supportive and tolerant of student protest. The relationship between academic area and faculty support of student dissent is illustrated in Table 10.2. The findings indicate that the marked association between academic affiliation and tolerance is not eliminated when controlling for longevity. The data also show that academic affiliation is a strong predictor of tolerance for student dissent when controlling for political orientation. Apparently, departmental affiliation had a contextual influence that overrode individual characteristics such as political attitudes and relative satisfaction with community values. It is likely that peer group pressure promoted the expression of liberal attitudes in actual support of dissent, and dissuaded the more conservative faculty members in the humanities and social sciences from actively opposing student demonstrations.

In Tables 10.1 and 10.2 it is noteworthy that faculty support of the student protest movement was operationalized in terms of actual cooperation with students. If a faculty member had continued his classes when many did not

Table 10.2: Faculty Support for Student Dissent by Academic Field, Unstandarized and Standardized on Longevity and Political Orientation

	Percent Faculty Support of Student Dissent		
Unstandardized	*Low*	*Moderate*	*High*
Education	71	15	14
Business Administration	53	28	19
Natural Sciences	44	33	22
Humanities	29	24	47
Social Sciences	18	39	43
Standardized			
On Longevity			
Education	69	17	15
Business Administration	56	26	18
Natural Sciences	45	30	25
Humanities	30	26	44
Social Sciences	22	38	40
Standardized On			
Political Orientation			
Education	62	22	16
Business Administration	50	28	23
Natural Sciences	45	27	28
Humanities	33	25	42
Social Sciences	14	36	50

Source: Pugh, et al. (1972:530).

during the crisis of the spring of 1970 or had given no form of cooperation to various student demonstrations, then that person had a "low degree of support"; if a faculty member had either signed antiwar petitions or had excused students from classes so that they might attend protest rallies, then that person was considered "moderately supportive" of student protest; and if a faculty member had supported antiwar demonstrations by canceling classes for at least a week or had given money for students to attend the mass demonstration in Washington D.C., then that person was considered "highly supportive" of the student protest movement. The distinction regarding actual cooperation shows that faculty support of the student protest movement went well beyond the limits of liberal rhetoric.

Social Stress: General Comments

There is consensus that social movements tend to occur as a response to stressful changes in a group's environment. But the language used to describe the nature of these changes varies greatly and the data used to support various hypotheses are often difficult to interpret. Some scholars see social movements as a reaction to *historical trends,* others emphasize the *immediate impacts* of political upheaval, oppression and economic exploitation. For example, Roberts and Kloss have argued that the eighteenth and nineteenth century labor movements in the United States, as in Europe, were in "dialectical opposition" to industrialization (1974:118). Anthropologists, on the other hand, emphasize the short-run impact of "cultural imperialism" on indigenous peoples. In either case, the essential point is that social movements are a response to *absolute misery and suffering.* But some scholars have taken a different position. They argue that the level of suffering and misery associated with oppression is so demanding that its victims have little time for anything but immediate problems of survival. From this second general perspective it is argued that totally oppressed and exploited groups rarely mount significant social movements, and such movements are more likely to occur following a period of *rising expectations and relative deprivation.*

Choosing between these general positions is difficult. The choice is made more difficult, as Olsen (1963:529–52) points out, because a situation interpreted as a response to relative deprivation may instead be a reaction to absolute misery and suffering. Analyses based on aggregate national income data may obscure the fact that overall economic growth can be accompanied by serious losses for large segments of a population. People having outdated skills and abilities, industries with obsolete technology, and persons in declining economic areas may undergo considerable suffering while overall indicators of national prosperity are improving.

The interpretation of data bearing on the hypothetical relationship between rising expectations and the development of social movements is also more difficult than one might expect. The basic idea is that people are more likely to rebel or begin social movements when conditions are improving rather than when they are at their worst. But here it is important to note that the reality of the situation, that is, whether or not things are actually getting better or worse, may not be so important as people's perceptions of them. People can believe things are getting better or worse even when they are not. Difficulties of this kind continue to spark debate and need to be kept in mind when considering stress as a precondition of social movements.

The possible origins of stress are many and only a few can be considered in detail. Our attention is focused on three potential sources of stress: (1) stress resulting from relative deprivation, (2) stress resulting from the conditions of a mass society, and (3) stress resulting from the failure of tension management within a society. These three broad categories, not all inclusive, illustrate the importance of stress as a precondition of social movements.

Social Stress: Relative Deprivation

The idea of *relative deprivation* is one of the most popular current explanations of the rise of social movements. It is similar to but not identical with the concept of rising expectations. According to the hypothesis, when people see a discrepancy, either real or perceived, between what they are getting and what they believe they should be getting, they may begin a social movement designed to correct the situation. This sense of discrepancy may come when people compare themselves to others who are significant to them or when they compare their current situation to the social conditions of their immediate past. The relevance of the comparison standard is crucial to an understanding of when people are likely to feel deprived. It is easy to see that students who complain about the quality and quantity of food served in university cafeterias are not comparing themselves with persons living in Bangladesh or in other regions where food of any quality or quantity is in short supply. The perception of relative deprivation often implies a strong feeling of injustice and creates a sense of urgency.

According to Aberle (1967) people can experience relative deprivation when a discrepancy occurs along any of four principal dimensions. Groups of people can feel deprived of (1) *material goods* and (2) *social recognition* or *self-esteem.* They can also feel deprived because of the imposition of certain kinds of (3) *behavioral restrictions.* Polygamous Indians were greatly aggrieved when forced to give up their practice of multiple marriage on government reservations. Some groups of people may feel deprived because of (4) *unequal opportunities* to achieve valued social statuses. Occupational discrimination against women and ethnic minorities, for example, has been a particularly acute problem in the United States.

How people will react to the various kinds of relative deprivations is difficult to predict. A social movement is not the only possible outcome. In some cases people may decide to *work harder* and reduce the gap between what they have and what they feel they should have. In other cases people may *reduce their expectations* or "anticipated actualities" as a way of eliminating any discrepancy between what they have and what they want. But sometimes neither of these reactions is practical. It can be a bitter discovery to learn that hard work doesn't always get what you want, just as it can be a small comfort to eat hotdogs instead of steak. And a subjugated group can either *withdraw* or it can *fight* with its enemy, but as before, these reactions are not always practical. By the early 1890s for example, American Indians could not withdraw to new hunting grounds and fighting could only mean certain annihilation.

Aberle has also proposed that a group's reaction to social deprivation is dependent, at least in part, on the severity of relative deprivation and on the group's perception of whether they are collectively capable of controlling a situation. High relative deprivation is likely to result in either *transformative* or *redemptive* social movements, whereas low relative deprivation is hypothetically most likely to result in *alterative* or *reformative* social movements. If the source of a group's problem is amenable to its control, the collectivity is likely to adopt empirically oriented solutions, but when a collectivity sees a problem beyond the limits of its control, it is most likely to adopt solutions based in magic or religious ritual. The Ghost Dance Religion practiced in tribes of North American Indians is a religious solution for severe relative deprivation. In fact, the Ghost Dance offers a rare opportunity to test the general hypothesis that relative deprivation is a precondition of social movements (Carroll 1975).

Relative Deprivation: The Ghost Dance

The Ghost Dance originated around 1889 when an Indian "messiah" named Wovoka prophesied an imminent cataclysmic upheaval, symbolized as a great whirlwind, that would destroy white society and inaugurate an Indian millenium or paradise on earth. An interesting account of Wovoka's doctrine comes from an ethnographer named James Mooney (1965). Mooney was sent by the United States government to investigate the new Indian religion because some people felt that Wovoka's doctrine was the cause of renewed unrest. The popular press of the time had warned of a new "Indian Outbreak" among the Sioux in particular. The tragedy at Wounded Knee was indeed a culmination of events that were influenced by the Ghost Dance.

Mooney travelled over 32,000 miles between 1890 and 1892 in an effort to interview persons living in over 20 different tribes. He quickly discovered that newspaper correspondents who had written about the messiah had never really talked with him and that the Indians themselves regarded the prophet as "almost a myth, something intangible, to be talked about but not seen." (Mooney 1965:7) Tenacious efforts to find Wovoka brought Mooney to the Walker Indian Reservation in Western Neveda on New Year's Day, 1892.

Wovoka's prophecy had two key features. First, he predicted that the dead ancestors of Indians would be resurrected on an earthly paradise in which everyone is happy and forever young. Second, he predicted a cataclysmic event from which his followers would be spared, but all others, especially white men, would be destroyed. In Wovoka's revelation, God commanded him to tell his people that they must be good, love one another, and give up quarrelling, warfare, and stealing. Only if they followed these instructions would they be reunited with friends in a world without death, sickness, and old age. A prominent feature of the new millenium, according to Wovoka, would be the return of the buffalo. For the Plains Indians, a buffalo was more than just an animal. The buffalo was a symbol of prosperity, of freedom, and of the Indians supremacy in their aboriginal habitat. At no time in their past experience had the buffalo ever completely vanished; now it was only a question of waiting for their return from some "distant lands."

To hasten this grand occasion Wovoka was shown a dance and commanded by God to bring it back to his people. By performing this dance at irregular intervals, for five consecutive days each time, the Indians could secure happiness and prompt the events ushering in a new millenium. The Ghost Dance was usually begun in the middle of the afternoon or after sundown. A large area was carefully cleared, usually in the vicinity of a sweat house. The participants, both young and old, would then form a large circle ranging in size from 50 to 500 people. They faced toward the center of the ring and circled slowly from right to left dragging their right feet behind them. In large gatherings each complete revolution of the circle was accompanied by a single chant initiated by a medicine man.

The dancing continued in an increasingly dusty circle for hour after hour, and as participants fell to the ground they were replaced by new recruits. The medicine men, who were positioned inside of the circle on the alert for signs of impending exhaustion, waved an "eagle feather" in the face of each participant just before the point of collapse. The hypnotic waving of the eagle feather, combined with the physical condition of the dancers and their psychological expectations, was frequently sufficient to induce a trance-like state in which visions of the messiah and the ghosts of friends and relatives were common. During the dance ritual, the Indians wore specially painted "ghost shirts" that they believed were endowed with magical powers which would protect them from danger and stop the white man's bullets. It was the tragic disconfirmation of this belief at Wounded Knee that led to the decline of the Ghost Dance among the Sioux. But by then the new religion had already spread to many tribes on the North American plains and its popularity persisted for some time.

Anthropological records indicate that nearly 40 tribes knew about the Ghost Dance before 1892. But the Ghost Dance was not popular among all of these groups. Consequently, the problem is to explain why it was adopted in some tribes but not in others. An obvious possibility is that only the most severely deprived tribes would accept the new religion. But all the knowledgeable tribes were "deprived" in the years just before 1890 and we have no way of knowing which were more deprived than others. All of the tribes who knew about the Ghost Dance, for example, were dependent upon the buffalo, but it is not known which tribes were more dependent than others. What is known, however, is when the buffalo herds were eradicated in different regions of the western plains. And this became the basis for Carroll's (1975) test of hypothesis that *relative deprivation is a precondition of transformative social movements.*

Carroll reasoned that "the absolute level of deprivation is less important than the perceived discrepancy between societal conditions in the recent past and in the present" (1975:393). In his study, Carroll assumed that the greater the amount of time elapsed between a tribe's loss of its buffalo herd and 1890, the less its collective sense of relative deprivation. Presumably the passage of time would give people an opportunity to forget the past and adjust to a new reality. The more recent a tribe's loss of its buffalo herd, the greater its sense of relative deprivation, and the greater its likelihood of being receptive to the Ghost Dance.

In the second half of the nineteenth century there were two major herds of buffalo on the North American plains; a southern and a northern herd. In the 1870s the southern herd was reduced from about three million to roughly ten thousand animals. The northern herd, according to a leading specialist, remained intact until about 1880. It was exterminated in the years between 1880 and 1883 (Roe 1970). Knowing a tribe's geographical location in relationship to these two herds can therefore be used to give some idea of the amount of time elapsed since a tribe's loss of the buffalo. Tribes located near the northern herd in 1890 would have experienced a "recent" loss, whereas those who had been dependent on the southern herd would not have experienced a recent loss. Of the 40 or so tribes that knew about the Ghost Dance, Carroll found that he had adequate data on 37 cases. As shown in Table 10.3, 25 of these groups were highly receptive to the Ghost Dance and 12 were not. None of the 12 tribes rated low on acceptance had recently been deprived of the buffalo. For this reason, Carroll concluded that the tribes living in areas where the buffalo had more recently been exterminated were, in fact, more likely to adopt the Ghost Dance than others. Nevertheless, it should be emphasized that 18 out of 25 tribes in which the new religion was popular had not experienced a recent deprivation of buffalo. Although the results of Carroll's test are consistent with his hypothesis, they are far from conclusive as others have been quick to point out (Brown 1976). The significance of the study is in its innovative approach to a difficult quantitative problem. Carroll's data are consistent with findings from other studies (e.g., Aberle 1967, Worsely 1957).

Social Stress: Mass Society

Another explanation holds that a particular state of the social system, a *mass society*, is associated with severe social stress which is often accompanied by extremist movements. A mass society is one in which elites are easily accessible to nonelites and nonelites are readily available for mobilization by elites

Table 10.3:   Relationship Between Recency of Deprivation Occasioned by the Loss of the Buffalo and Acceptance of the Ghost Dance

Deprivation	Acceptance	
	High	Low
Recent	7	0
Not Recent	18	12

(Q=+1.00, p=.05)
Source: Carroll (1975:395).

(Kornhauser 1959:30). The availability of nonelites depends on the extent to which they lack attachments to intermediate groups such as those in the local community, voluntary associations and occupational groups. In a mass society, traditional groups and institutions have lost their hold over the loyalties and behavior of individuals. That is, the intermediate relationships found in work groups, voluntary associations, and similar organizations are weak or nonexistent. When such mediating relationships are weak or absent, people are likely to be alienated from society. They see little meaning in life and feel adrift in the world. Consequently, they are ready and available candidates for social movements and those with the weaker attachments to intermediate groups are the first to join (Kornhauser 1959).

Mass societies then provide fertile ground for extremist social movements. But, on the other hand, a society characterized by considerable multiple group membership will be less likely to have extremist social movements as such memberships will check the rise of a single organization which attempts to gain the absolute devotion of its followers.

The mass society approach has been sugject to criticism by Oberschall (1973:104–13) who refers to a number of recent extremist social movements which fail to support it. Included are McCarthyism, the Radical Right movement of the 1960s, the flouridation controversies and even the spread of Nazism. Oberschall points out that intermediate groups also have considerable mobilizing potential. Intermediate groups do not necessarily balance out one another, but may be organized on a class basis with potential for rapid mobilization.

Social Stress: Tension Management Systems

In Mauss' view (1975), societies are *tension management systems* in which there are always normative discrepancies, dysfunctions, and other strains caused by both large and small changes. Social movements coalesce around points of strain in an attempt to correct publically defined social problems. Some societies, especially large and heterogenous ones, have more points of strain than others. However, it is difficult, if not impossible to predict which social problems will prompt social movements. Moreover, Blumer (1971) suggests that social problems themselves result from a process of collective definition rather than simply being the result of intrinsic malfunctioning. Some social conditions become problems only after they have been defined in that way:

> the rise and fall of social problems *is* related to change in the social structure and to changes in the economic and technological realms, but not in the way that objectivist theories maintain. Our argument is that social problems arise during these times of social change, not so much because of concomitant conditions like strain, disorganization, anomie, and the like, but simply because more people have more time, more resources and more energy to address social conditions, to define some of them as problematic and to engage in the processes of collective behavior which will produce social problem movements. (Mauss 1975:-44).

Predicting Social Movements From Stress Conditions

Scholars have given careful thought to the stress conditions leading to social movements. All of the views discussed above, and others, have both their advocates and attackers. Each, in spite of criticisms, has something of value to offer the student even though none has gained complete dominance over the others. Each, too, has some predictive value. But, can we predict social movements? Can we specify that certain stress conditions will be followed by a certain type of social movement with specific goals which will follow a particular natural history.

Chalmers Johnson (1966:119–34) has argued it is impossible to construct statistical measures which will lead to a precise prediction of a revolutionary movement. He has suggested the construction of an index of disequilibrium which can, however, point to the potential of such activity. One useful indicator is suicide rates which can be inversely related to social integration. Another indicator of disequilibrium is increased production and acceptance of competing ideological views expressed in an increase in the ratio between the armed forces and the total population, especially with no obvious external threat. That is, the greater the number under arms in proportion to the total population, the more likelihood there is a potential social movement or revolutionary situation. Another measure might be gross crime rates and political crime rates.

As Johnson observes, there are severe difficulties measuring social movements and the results are likely to be predictive in only a loose sense. However, since Johnson wrote, social indicators have been developed which might permit the identification of extreme situational stress for certain persons within society. Furthermore, during the urban disorder of the late 1960s and early 1970s, the United States government established a crisis center to predict places where violence was most likely.

Oberschall (1973:71–2) has suggested that when conflicts are delayed, as when a military crisis pulls everyone together for victory, they usually reappear later in more extreme form. He also pointed out "accelerators" of social movements, such as mass communication, international travel, the development of economic systems which transcend national boundaries, global political alliances and links, and the foreign education of many future political leaders. Oberschall says particular places—"focal points" such as Paris—are traditional starting places for movements (1973:138–40). Those involved in social movements, both for and against them, tend to look upon focal points as cues to what may happen next.

Summary and Conclusions

One of the major concerns in the field of collective behavior has been to describe social movements in all their variability. Typologies of social movements developed by Herbert Blumer, Roberta Ash Garner, and David F. Aberle, were reviewed as were the "natural histories" of Rex D. Hopper and Armand Mauss. The typological approach and the natural history method can be used simultaneously in describing a particular social movement.

The literature on preconditions of social movements include two broad areas: (1) *structural conduciveness*, and (2) *social stress*. The idea of structural conduciveness is illustrated by the student protest movement of the 1960s and early 1970s. Flacks saw youth as having special status in American society and the university as a conducive context for protest movements. Scholars have used somewhat different vocabularies to describe stress conditions underlying the development of social movements. The ideas of misery, oppression, and social deprivation are prominent although the concept of *relative deprivation* has been especially influential in recent research. The hypothetical relationship between the rise of social movements and relative deprivation is a possible explanation for the Ghost Dance religion that took hold on the North American Plains in the last decade of the 1800s.

Social stress can be considered as a product of *mass society*. When intermediate social relationships are weak or absent, people feel cut adrift or alienated from society. The relationship between alienation and participation in social movements will be given more detailed attention in chapter XI. Another source of social stress is the breakdown of a society's tension management system. Social movements may either coalesce around a recognized social problem or they may define a social problem that needs correction.

Stress conditions cannot precisely predict social movements; there are many indicators and suggestions for predicting social movements in the literature, but knowledge is not developed sufficiently to accurately predict certain types of social movements.

A precondition for the rise of the women's movement in the 1960s and '70s was an awareness of the role of women in history.

A sign of the times in an era of anti-Viet Nam protests.

CHAPTER XI

Mobilization

I t is sometimes difficult to give a precise time or identify a specific event that marks the beginning of a social movement. Did the civil rights movement in the United States begin with the abolitionists of the nineteenth century or the founding of the National Association for the Advancement of Colored People (NAACP) in the early twentieth century, or with the Supreme Court decision of 1954, the Montgomery Bus Boycott led by Dr. Martin Luther King in 1958, or did it really begin with the lunch counter sit-ins at Greensborough, North Carolina in February, 1960? All of these events are significant benchmarks, but none is the indisputable beginning of the civil rights movement. And if it is sometimes difficult to pinpoint the beginning of a social movement, it is often much more difficult to explain how social movements are mobilized—to account for why some grow and develop while others do not.

This chapter reviews some of the most important contingencies involved in the *mobilization* of social movements. It begins with consideration of ideologies because they play an important part in the growth and development of social movements. After a brief outline of differences in *leadership* and *membership* patterns, the focal point of the chapter is the *recruitment* and *conversion* process. Emphasis is on the question of who joins social movements and on the problem of accounting for extreme commitment. Finally the emergence of *organizational patterns* in social movements concludes the chapter.

Ideology

Ideology has three major functions in social movements: (1) rationalization, (2) justification, and (3) motivation. These characteristics are important in differentiating between movements that do and do not attract mass support (Marx and Wood 1975:282–4). The three functions exist even though there may be a wide gap between leadership and membership views of ideology, and even though members of the same movement may follow a number of different ideologies. Along the same line, Roberts and Kloss (1974:16–8) argue that social movements whose ideologies are not in harmony with western "master trends"—industrialism, bureaucracy, and cultural imperialism—are likely to fail. These master trends generate enormous power and influence for some and great unrest and discontent for others. Each, too, has an "oppressive nature" and a "liberating potential." For example, failure would be expected of a movement which opposed any further use of industrialization and technology, while a movement wanting a more "humane" use of it would have a better chance of achieving its goals.

Rationalization: Ideology provides a basis for collective action; an ideology must *explain* the existence of a social movement. Consequently, an ideology generally includes three broad components (Killian 1964:434–7). First, it includes a version of history that shows how the goals of a movement are in basic harmony with the traditions of society. Second, there is a vision of the future which provides a description of the desirable state of affairs. It is assumed that if ideological guidelines are followed and the movement is successful, some idealized state of affairs will be achieved. Should the movement fail, there will be continued difficulties or worse. Third, an ideology specifies the heroes who have struggled nobly in the past and who will continue to do so in the present, and the villains who are responsible for the problems a movement is trying to correct. Ideology is a crucial aspect of social movements because it gives meaning to strains and dissatisfactions (Marx and Wood 1975:382, Oberschall 1973:178); it shows the gap between the ideal and the reality of social life.

One of the basic distinctions made about ideologies concerns their scope. Killian (1964) points out that an ideology may focus on only a part of the social order. This is similar to Smelser's (1962) conception of the norm-oriented movement which is restricted to a desire for change in only a part of the society. Others are much more comprehensive (Killian 1964) or value oriented (Smelser 1972) in that they advocate change in many or all of the most important institutions.

There are also differences in the changes called for by various ideologies. They can be reactionary, aiming to restore some previous state of affairs perceived as desirable; or they can be conservative, designed to preserve the situation as it is. Often the conservative movement rises in opposition to a *progressive movement* designed to achieve some change in society (Killian 1964).

As a social movement develops strength, it is likely to be viewed as threaten-

Mail order Bride

Lunch counter sit-ins such as this one in 1960 helped to get the civil rights movement going in the United States.

ing by some, who may then form a countermovement with its own critical ideology. These ideological attacks raise questions which must be answered by the original movement. This leads to a complication and elaboration of what may have begun as a simple ideology. Ideologies and counterideologies may then grow so extensive and complex that few are able to fully understand them.

Justification: The second major function of ideology is to provide a justification for action. Naturally, the rationale used to explain the existence of a social movement frequently supplies its justification. Neither the explanations nor the justifications offered by ideology are necessarily rational in the sense that most people would readily accept their credibility. Some bizzare beliefs have provided people with justification for extremely *antisocial* behavior.

On August 9, 1969, Charles Manson sent four of his followers on a "mission" that would horrify the people of Los Angeles. In the dark of night, Tex Watson, Susan Atkins, Patricia Krenwinkel, and Linda Kasabian descended on the residence of actress Sharon Tate and her guests (Bugliosi 1974). Watson cut the telephone wires to the house and the members of Manson's "family" then scaled the wall surrounding the home and jumped to the ground. Once inside the yard, Watson suddenly noticed a pair of headlights in the driveway. He ordered the women to lay down and ran to the automobile which had stopped near the estate's gate-control mechanism. The first victim of the evening, Steve Parent, was shot four times. Manson's family then continued on its murder spree. At the main house, Watson slit a screen on one of the front windows, then went to the front door and let Atkins and Krenwinkel inside. Linda Kasabian waited outside listening for the sound of any approaching cars.

Once inside the house the three members of Manson's family spread out in an effort to locate and bring together all of its occupants. Watson found Voytek Frykowski lying on a couch and told him: "I'm the Devil and I'm here to do the Devil's business." Moments later Susan Atkins and Patricia Krenwinkel reported the whereabouts of the other occupants. Watson ordered them all brought to the living room. Patricia Krenwinkel returned with Abigail Folger, the coffee heiress, and Susan Atkins returned with Sharon Tate and hairstylist Jay Sebring. Ordered to lie on their stomachs, Sebring objected because Tate was over eight months pregnant, and Watson shot him. After taking their money, he tied rope around Sebring's neck and then the necks of Sharon and Abigail. Watson then threw the rope over a beam of the ceiling and began to pull on it. One of the victims asked what was going to happen, and he replied without a trace of feeling, "You are all going to die." Frykowski was stabbed 51 times, shot twice, and struck violently over the head 13 times; Tate was stabbed 16 times (Bugliosi 1974).

Charles Manson was the leader of a cult of murderers that may have killed 40 people. The ideology that he developed was a combination of the Bible, the Beatles, and Scientology. Manson believed that the Beatles were the prophets in the Bible whom God had given the power of "fire and brimstone." The Beatles had the lyrics of their songs; the power of the spoken word. Manson was particularly enthralled by several songs from the "White Album," especially the cuts entitled "Piggies," "Revolution 1," "Revolution 9," and "Helter Skelter." He loved to sermonize about a "land of milk and honey" where the family would be safe from Helter Skelter—that is, safe from an imminent black revolution. Armageddon was at hand; it was time for the "blackies" to take over "the reins of power." But because Manson believed that the blackies would prove to be incompetent, he told his followers that he and his people would eventually regain the ascendency. The self-proclaimed "Infinite Being" promised to take his people to safety in a "hole in the ground" where they could await their moment of ultimate triumph.

All of this sounds ridiculous, but not to Manson's cult at Spahn Ranch which believed in him and the necessity of his message. His followers scrawled slogans from the "White Album" on the walls of their victims' homes and justified the Tate and LaBianca murders as necessary to spark the Black Revolt: Helter Skelter had to be started for the incompetent blacks. Then the blacks would come out of the ghettos, "stabbing, killing, mutilating bodies, and smearing blood on the walls." The prosecuting district attorney was able to convince a jury that Manson had succeeded in indoctrinating these ideas. The heart of the case against Manson, who did not participate in the killings himself, was his complete control over the minds of his followers (Bugliosi 1974:233).

Motivation: The third important aspect of ideology is its *appeal* to potential partisans. The ideas and beliefs expressed in ideology predispose people to behave in particular ways and encourage commitment to a social movement. The persistence of the Peyote Cult among North American Indians can be accounted for, at least to some extent, by analyzing the appeal of its ideology (Aberle 1967). The Ghost Dance and the Peyote Cult originated at about the same time, but only the Peyote Cult has continued to exist as a significant cultural form. Today it is organized as the Native American Church of North America.

The Peyote Cult was probably invented at the Kiowa, Comanche, and Wichita Agency in 1885. By 1889 it had spread to 16 tribes, by 1955 it was practiced in 61 tribes, and by 1966 the peyote religion had spread to 77 tribes. Peyote is a small, hairy cactus that looks something like the buttons on an overcoat when dried. It grows in areas of Texas and Mexico and is an integral component of the peyote ritual. The ritual itself usually begins at sundown and lasts all night. Participants assemble in a round house and a meeting is conducted by four major officiants. The "road chief" is in overall charge of the ceremony and usually announces the purpose of the meeting. Meetings are generally called whenever a member of the Church has a special problem or when someone is ill. A "drummer chief" does the drumming for songs, and a third official takes care of the fire and is called the "fire chief." The fourth ceremonial official, called the "cedar chief," sprinkles dried cedar incense on the fire at appropriate points in the ritual.

The road chief and the fire chief typically sit opposite a door that faces east. In front of them is a raised crescent moon shaped out of dirt that serves as an altar on which there is an especially large peyote button. It is the focus of prayer and singing because it is believed to be a "material embodiment" of spiritual power. The peyotists believe in the existence of a divine power that is an invisible force influencing things and events, and that man must have this power in order to be successful and healthy. Furthermore, they believe that this supernatural power can be transferred from one thing to another under the proper ceremonial conditions. For these reasons, a specially prepared peyote button is always eaten by the person for whose benefit the meeting has been called. An additional button is passed around from time to time for everyone attending the meeting.

Peyote tastes bitter and often causes an unpleasant sense of nausea that can be followed by a mild state of euphoria. LaBarre's (1959) account of the Peyote

Cult originally stressed the importance of hallucinations as part of the religious experience of its followers. Now it seems more likely that auditory hallucinations and visions are relatively rare (Aberle 1967). In any case, "the peyote experience" is interpreted as a communication with God. It involves self-reflection and deep introspection in the context of group communion; its goal is a sense of internal peace and a desire for self-improvement. Self-improvement can be achieved by following the "Peyote Way," an ethic that stresses brotherly love, care of the family, self-reliance, and the avoidance of alcohol. But what is the actual appeal in all of this?

First, according to Aberle's analysis, the ideology of the Peyote Cult is a strong antidote for *anomie*. The "Peyote Way" gives people rules to follow and creates internalized sanctions for honesty and social responsibility. Moreover, the ideology of the Peyote Cult can enhance a person's sense of self-esteem, since the peyote experience is considered a mystical path to knowledge possessed only by Indians. A third factor contributing to the appeal of the Peyote Cult is the noncompetitive and cooperative nature of its ideology. It stresses personal development and fulfillment, rather than competition with whites, and a renewed sense of ingroup responsibility combined with an emphasis on accommodation with white society. Finally, the ideology of the Peyote Cult emphasizes the importance of associational ties within a community and recognizes the pivotal role of the family.

Even though ideologies are considered to be a crucial component of social movements, Marx and Wood (1975:382) argue that they are not necessarily useful in understanding the dynamics of social movements. Ideology may not be the most important variable in explaining types of movements or the motives of individual joiners. Also, it may be incorrect to assume there is a close fit between official ideology and the beliefs of the followers of a movement, nor do rank and file members necessarily share similar beliefs. A number of studies have shown considerable diversity in ideological beliefs among members of the same social movement. The study of ideology is therefore no substitute for close investigation of actual membership and leadership patterns. Ideology is an incomplete explanation of how social movements work.

Leadership and Membership

Who leads social movements? The answer is complicated because the kinds of persons who lead are likely to differ from stage to stage in the development of a social movement. Leadership patterns characteristic of the early stages of development may be different from those found when a social movement is about to become a fully institutionalized organization. In addition, as social movements change, different types of leadership may be needed and emerge as a consequence. Beyond these complications it is clear that some social movements are dominated by a single leader whereas others are directed by a group of equal leaders or by a principal leader and his lieutenants. In spite of these difficulties several typologies of leaders have been developed (e.g., Hopper 1950, Smelser 1962). A recent typology is that of Killian (1964).

The *charismatic leader* is thought to be most characteristic of the early dvelopment of the social movement. He or she is bold, compulsive, and able to make a stirring appeal to the emotions. Indeed the charismatic leader leads by force and strength of personality rather than by institutionalized patterns. To those committed to the movement such a leader has heroic proportions. And in some cases charismatic leaders will actually claim to have supernatural powers.

The death or departure of a charismatic leader is likely to be followed by considerable change in a social movement. It may suffer a decline as some members who were attracted by the leader's personal characteristics leave. Factionalism previously suppressed by the charismatic leader may lead to great change and even destruction of the movement. Another possibility is that the departure of the charismatic leader will be followed by more professional or executive leadership. This process has been called the routinization of charisma (Weber 1968). Routinization of charisma leads to the appearance of an administrative leader associated with the development of bureaucratic organization. Such leaders tend to be pragmatic and willing to compromise ideological principles (Killian 1964). Zald and Ash (1966) believe that the routinization of charisma is likely to conserve a dominant core while producing increasingly radical splinter groups.

Social movements also have an *intellectual leadership* composed of people who elaborate the values and develop the ideologies of the movement. Usually they are not activists. Instead, they give the appearance of being reasonable, logical, and well-informed individuals. Such people exercise enormous importance in the development of social movements. L. P. Edwards (1927) has even suggested that if intellectuals revolt against the prevailing system then a revolution is almost certain to follow.

The leaders of social movements, of whatever type, are probably not highly disturbed persons, or "nuts" and "crackpots" as they are often described. That such terms are applied to them is more likely a reflection of hostility toward them (Mauss 1975:53). In Oberschall's view, leaders of social movements are characterized by the same qualities that provide good leadership in conventional situations. It appears that the upper and middle class strata usually supply the leadership to all types of social movements; indeed a substantial proportion of all kinds of social movements, far above their percentage of the population at large, may come from the upper and middle class strata (Oberschall 1973:155). In any case, the leaders of social movements are exposed to a number of risks. At least in the early stages of the movement, they are without officially designated authority and income. Much of their effectiveness then depends on the use of techniques of persuasion, motivation, and reinforcement (Mauss 1975:51–2).

The *agitator* has been characterized as one type of social movement leader. The question remains: is it possible for agitators to create and generate discontent where there was none before, or are they able to seize and direct, at least partially, the discontent which is already present, thus helping to generate a social movement? Milgram and Toch (1969) suggest that, while persons perhaps can be trained to agitate and there may be occasional "outside agitators" in some collective event, leadership is always local.

Persons who have an interest in maintaining the status quo are likely to believe the agitator is able to generate a social movement in a situation previously characterized by contentment. Such a position, as was suggested in Chapter VIII, can lead those in authority to see no real reason to change conditions. On the other hand, if agitators are believed to focus discontent that is already present, there may be quite a different response from authorities.

Membership Patterns

Leaders of social movements are likely to share many characteristics with persons occupying leadership positions in more institutionalized organizations. But are the members of social movements unrepresentative of most people? We can begin our discussion of this question by considering how social movement membership distinctions have been made.

One basic distinction is that between social movements that are *exclusive* and admit only persons with certain characteristics and those that are *inclusive* and admit everyone who wishes to join (Zald and Ash 1966:330–1). The exclusive social movement confines membership to persons who have or will attain certain characteristics. The desired characteristics often involve attributes such as language, political commitment, religious faith, and racial or ethnic background (Milgram and Toch 1969:596). Some exclusive social movements have a long period of training and apprenticeship before full-fledged membership is granted. Even after persons are admitted, testing of devotion and commitment may continue.

In the case of inclusive movements almost everyone may be admitted and encouraged to join. Membership may require little commitment and involve little or no period of indoctrination. There may be no specific duties, only a requirement of general support, and members may belong to other organizations if they wish.

Mauss (1975) has suggested that membership might be understood in terms of rings. In the outermost ring, most distant from the leadership, is that part of the general public which has a sympathetic leaning or inclination toward the movement and its ideology. The sympathetic members are often considered by more deeply committed members to be fair weather friends, but they do offer tacit if not active support.

The second membership ring Mauss calls "active membership." It is made up of persons with definite but not exclusive interest in the movement. The active members may be interested in other causes and may be willing to compromise the goals and aims of the movement. As Marx and Wood (1975:-386) point out, most people do not devote their entire lives to a social movement. However, during exceptional periods large numbers can be involved and supportive.

The third innermost ring of membership, which includes the principal leaders, is composed of those most intensely committed. To them the goals of the movement are an exclusive concern and they are least willing to compromise their ideoloy.

Recruitment and Conversion

Who Joins: We don't know why some rather than other people join social movements. However, a number of hypotheses have been examined regarding specific social movements. Even though the results of these studies may not apply in all cases, they are significant because they frequently contradict commonsense notions. Five prominent hypotheses have been selected for discussion. Not all of these hypotheses are confirmed by empirical evidence, yet all have enjoyed considerable acceptance at one time or another. The first three are specific to the problem of explaining who joined the student protest movement of the 1960s and early 1970s.

It has been commonly assumed that protest movements on the "radical left" tend to recruit their partisans from the underprivileged working class, whereas protest movements on the "radical right" tend to recruit their partisans from the upper strata of society (Bendix and Lipset 1966). This assumption suggested the hypothesis that participants in the student protest movement would come disproportionately from a lower socioeconommic status background than nonparticipants. A corollary hypothesis was that student protesters were poorly equipped for academic achievement in higher education and were consequently "maladjusted." Both of these hypotheses were popular in some quarters of the general public because they were consistent with the ideological position that higher education is "not meant for everyone" and that "mass education" can only produce further conflict and disruption. The difficulty was that neither hypothesis could be empirically verified.

From the beginning of the student protest movement, data collected on a number of university campuses indicated that *activists tended to be recruited disproportionately from upper status families.* One study compared activists in the Berkeley Free Speech Movement (FSM) with a cross section of nonactivists on the same campus (Watts and Whittaker 1966). As shown in Table 11.1 it was found that the parents of FSM activists represented an "academic elite." Nearly 26 percent of the activists' fathers had achieved an advanced academic degree (M.A. or Ph.D.) compared to 11 percent of the fathers of nonactivists. Richard Flacks (1967a) found a very similar pattern at the University of Chicago. Students who had participated in a sit-in reported higher family incomes, higher educational levels for both their fathers and mothers, and greater identification with the "upper–middle class" than was true among students who had not participated in the sit-in. The finding that student protesters came disproportionately from upper class rather than lower class backgrounds is replicated in several other studies (Watts, Lynch, and Whittaker 1969; Westby and Braungart 1966, 1970). Although there is at least one study (Dunlap 1970) that found no difference in the family backgrounds of activists and nonactivists, there is no clear evidence that student protesters were ever more likely to be recruited from lower class families.

**Table 11.1:   Education Level Attained
by Parents of FSM Activists**

Sample	*Father*		*Mother*	
Highest Year Completed in School	Percent Cross Section (N=39)	Percent FSM (N=39)	Percent Cross Section (N=39)	Percent FSM (N=39)
12th Grade or Less	36.7	28.4	49.0	40.7
1 to 3 Years of College	13.0	18.3	22.8	15.1
A.B. Degree (Including those with some graduate work but no advanced degree)	27.3	17.7	24.1	27.3
Professional Degree (Law, M.D., D.D.S., etc.)	12.2	10.1	0.0	0.6
Academic Degree (M.A., Ph.D.)	10.8 *	25.5	4.1 *	16.3
Overall Significance Level	$X^2=15.13$	$P<.01$	$X^2=15.32$	$P<.01$

*Denotes significant single comparisons
Source: Watts and Whittaker (1966:53).

It was equally impossible to confirm the subsidiary hypothesis that student protesters lacked interest in higher education or were not capable of doing well. In fact, a few studies found that activists were significantly brighter than their nonactivist counterparts (Block, Haan, and Smith 1968; Flacks 1967a; Heist 1966). A survey of students arrested in connection with a sit-in during the Berkeley Free Speech Movement revealed that:

> Most are earnest students of considerably better than average academic standing . . . Of the undergraduates arrested, nearly half had better than "B" averages . . . Twenty were Phi Beta Kappas, eight were Woodrow Wilson Fellows; twenty have published articles in scholarly journals; fifty-three were National Merit Scholarship winners or finalists, and two hundred sixty have received other academic awards (Draper 1965:14).

The second major hypothesis advanced to account for the membership of the student protest movement argued that activists were "rebelling against the parental generation" (Feuer 1969). The idea that a "generation gap" was an underlying cause of the student protest movement was opposed by a third major hypothesis that argued that activists were enacting the liberal, humanitarian values they had learned at home (Derber and Flacks 1967; Flacks 1967a, 1967b; Keniston 1967). The "parental socialization" hypothesis stressed agreement between students and their parents, whereas the "generational rebellion" hypothesis emphasized disagreement between parents and students. These two hypotheses are alternatives to each other in that data confirming one would necessarily disprove the other.

The bulk of the available evidence suggests that the "parental socialization hypothesis" receives the most support. Student activists tended to be recruited from families in which the parents were liberal rather than conservative. One study (Dunlap 1970) compared the party preferences of the parents of students who were active with SDS or the YAF against each other, and against the party preferences of parents of a cross section of students who were active in neither of these campus organizations. The data shown in Table 11.2 indicate that students who protested under the banner of the SDS were more likely to have Democratic parents than were those involved with YAF. The Young Americans for Freedom (YAF) was a radical right wing organization and so it was not surprising to find that the parents of these students were more conservative and were more likely to be Republicans than Democrats. The parental socialization hypothesis received its clearest support from the data for mothers rather than fathers.

Dunlap's data from the University of Oregon echoed the results reported earlier by Flacks (1967a) at the University of Chicago. Flacks found that left wing activists were less likely to have Republican fathers than were nonactivists (13% vs. 40%). He refined the parental socialization hypothesis by specifying that left wing activists were generally more liberal than their parents even

Table 11.2: Parental Party Preference of Radical and Conservative Student Activists

| | Fathers | | | | | |
| | S.D.S. | | Cross-Section | | Y.A.F. | |
Party Preference	%	N	%	N	%	N
Republican	37	(7)	47	(90)	68	(15)
Democratic	53	(10)	49	(94)	18	(4)
Other	11	(2)†	4	(8)	14	(3)§
Total	101*	(19)‡	100	(192)‡	100	(22)‡

| | Mothers | | | | | |
| | S.D.S. | | Cross-Section | | Y.A.F. | |
	%	N	%	N	%	N
Republican	32	(6)	49	(94)	78	(18)
Democratic	68	(13)	45	(86)	9	(2)
Other	—	—	6	(12)	13	(3)§
Total	100	(19)‡	100	(192)‡	100	(23)

*Rounding Error
†Includes one "Independent" and one "Socialist"
‡Some Cases Not Classifiable
§Includes two "Independents" and one "American Independent Party"
Source: Dunlap (1970:175).

though their parents tended to be more liberal than other parents. In this case, it could be argued that student activism represented an extension of parental values. The data shown in Table 11.3 from still another university campus illustrate the tendency of activists to see themselves as slightly more than, or at least as liberal as, their parents (Pugh et al. 1971).

Table 11.3: Participation in Antiwar Demonstrations by Generational Continuity in Political Orientations

Student—Parent Political Orientation	Percent Protestors	Percent Nonprotestors	N
Student More Liberal Than Parents	18	82	367
Student Equally Liberal As Parents	14	86	59
Student No Definite Political Position	9	91	129
Parents No Definite Political Position	5	95	20
Student Equally Conservative As Parents	3	97	124

Source: Pugh, et al. (1971:22).

A fourth major hypothesis bearing on the recruitment of activists into the student protest movement focused attention on *alienation*. The idea was simply that activism was an expression of alienation among young people. There is some evidence to support this contention. Protest activity was much more prominent at large universities where bureaucratic procedures were more impersonal and threatening (Scott and El-Assal 1969). Survey results from the

Berkeley campus of the University of California show that student activists scored higher on Srole's Anomie Scale (1956) than did nonactivists (Watts, Lynch, and Whittaker 1969). The difficulty with the Berkeley data is that it has never been clear what the Srole scale is measuring. To the extent that it measures a sense of "powerlessness," the finding that activists score high is inconsistent with participation in student protest activity (Watts et al. 1969:4). People who feel "helpless" should see little point in trying to correct a situation with which they disagree. But if the Srole Anomie Scale taps *dissatisfaction rather than helplessness* the Berkeley data would be easily interpretable. Keniston has argued that alienation is more likely to produce countercultures than protest movements (1967). If his position is correct, the Berkeley activists probably felt dissatisfied, not helpless.

The final hypothesis regarding the recruitment process in the development of social movements is based on *relative deprivation*, discussed in Chapter VII where it was applied to the analysis of crowds. The assumption is that social movements are likely to recruit followers from among those people who have experienced relative deprivation, and the greater a person's sense of relative deprivation, the greater the likelihood of recruitment. In testable form the hypothesis usually states that the proportion of people experiencing relative deprivation will be higher among members of movements than that found among a comparable cross section of nonmembers. This is exactly what Aberle (1967) found when he compared peyotists and nonpeyotists among the Navaho.

The history of the American Navaho Indian after the 1860s is unlike the history of most North American tribes. Most tribes experienced continuous loss of land as the Federal Government repeatedly decreased the size of reservations. But the Navaho reservation actually increased in size in the years after their imprisonment at Fort Sumner between 1864 and 1868. And both the Navaho population and their livestock number also increased. To some extent the Navaho owed their success to the arid land that they had been forced to live on. Nobody wanted it. Things changed, however, toward the end of 1930s. By that time Navaho land was heavily overgrazed and the Federal Government initiated a policy of livestock reduction. In 1933 roughly 40,000 people owned about one million sheep, goats, and cattle; in 1953 the comparable figures were 74,000 people and one-half million sheep, goats, and cattle. For the Navaho this reduction in livestock, while their population continued to increase in size, was their most devastating experience since the years of imprisonment.

The figures shown in Table 11.4 compare peyotists and nonpeyotists living in two separate communities on the Navaho reservation: Aneth (A) and Mexican Springs (MS). The first row indicates that peyotists held much larger median numbers of livestock before reduction than that held by nonpeyotists. So peyotists had the greatest amount to lose when the government implemented its new policy. The median number of sheep, goats and cattle (SG and C) lost by 9 peyotists living in Mexican Springs was 439 compared to a median figure of 139 for 26 nonpeyotists. The second row is based on self-reported data, and the third row is based on official records. In either case, there is little doubt that the peyotists must have experienced the greatest "negative discrepancy" between what they thought should be theirs and the number of livestock they actually had. A correlation coeefficient calculated between "first use of peyote" and loss of livestock in Mexican Springs was quite strong (rho = .53). And finally, it is also noteworthy that there were no significant social movements among the Navaho until the emergence of the *peyote cult* which followed livestock reduction. (Aberle 1967).

Table 11.4: Differences Between Peyotists and Nonpeyotists on Livestock Measures

Stock Measure	Community	*Peyote* Median	N	*Nonpeyote* Median	N	Z	P	Combined P
SG&C Holdings Before	A	400	17	139	6	1.50	.07	
Reduction	MS	575	9	175	26	2.74	.01	.01
Reported Loss, SG&C	A	340	17	137	6	1.29	.10	
	MS	332	9	143	26	2.32	.01	.01
Official Loss, SG&C	A	340	17	136	6	1.20	.10	
	MS	439	9	139	26	2.70	.01	.01

Notes: All z-scores are normal deviate approximations for the summed ranks test. All p-values are one-tailed. All livestock figures are converted to sheep units. Adapted from: Aberle, (1967:262).

Recruitment Strategies: Now that a number of hypotheses regarding who is most likely to join a social movement have been discussed, we can consider how people are persuaded to join. Several approaches have been identified (Wilson 1973:167–73). One is a *morality* strategy which places reliance upon moral obligations. A second approach involves a *utilitarian* strategy in which payments or other inducements are offered to members. And as a third approach, *coercion* can be used to force people to join. Regardless of recruitment strategy, effective commitment is best obtained only through *long-term involvement* on the part of the membership (Marx and Wood 1975:401). It is sometimes possible to have membership passed from parents to children. That is, children can become members of social movements through *socialization* over a relatively long period of time (Milgram and Toch 1969:590–2). Nevertheless, Milgram and Toch (1969:592) point out that adult *conversion* is more common than socialization since most social movements are not so permanent as to allow for long-term processes.

The conversion experience may be related to a contradiction between general cultural values, often very deep seated, and the values and norms of the social movement, which may also be an important part of the culture. For example, patterns of behavior expected on the basis of sex are introduced early in the socialization process and are continually reinforced. These patterns are discriminatory toward females and are in conflict with values placed upon equality. But it is not easy to alter attitudes learned over a long period of time and it may well require a process of conversion. Even so, conversion is probably not a sudden "turnabout" in thinking. One study of conversion in a Billy Graham Crusade found that the process is a "socially programmed event" in which people *affirm* their values rather than *change* them suddenly (Wimberley et al. 1975).

Developing Commitment

Once an individual has become a member of a social movement, how is commitment developed? Obviously persons whose membership is confined to Mauss' outer two rings never become wholly or deeply committed to a social movement. Many movements are pluralistic in character and never seek deep commitment from their membership. This is not the case with leaders and those in the innermost ring who can become so committed that they are willing, even eager, to die for their movement. We learn, almost weekly, of persons throwing away their lives in terrorist actions all over the world. But extreme commitment is not a new thing, as we think of the Christian martyrs who died gladly for their faith.

A great many things can contribute to the development of extreme commitment to a social movement. Some of the most important factors are: (1) isolation from "outside" social relationships, (2) "inside" reward contingencies, (3) the intrinsic rewards of various activities, and (4) the development of morale. In the first case, some social movements demand so much time of their members that they prevent the development or maintenance of outside social relationships (Coser 1974). Becoming a member can mean a complete *reorientation of friendship patterns.*

The Unification Church, led by Reverend Moon, provides a contemporary example. Membership is total and the training process is demanding. The new member spends many hours in intense activity and has contact with no one outside the movement; even when the training period is over, contact with nonmembers is minimal. Probably one of the most important reasons the "Moonies" have generated so much hostility, leading almost to a countermovement, is that the parents of members have been so deeply cut off from their children.

Gusfield (1968) believes that commitment is fostered through a member's participation in a network of *interpersonal relationships.* People who join movements develop new friendships with other members. These friendships become increasingly important as alternative relationships with nonmembers become more limited. If there are frequent contacts with nonmembers—through recruitment or proselytizing efforts, for example—the movement's ideology may be such that any event serves to confirm its truth (Lofland 1965:212–44.) If the value of social rewards (fun, respect, money, drugs, etc.) found within a movement is high, the value of friendships within the movement will be still higher. Consequently, leaders of social movements that restrict contact with outsiders can be especially powerful when they are able to manipulate strong reward contingencies within a group of followers. And at the same time, the members of such groups will find themselves deeply committed to those groups. Disagreement with movement leaders would risk breaking important friendships and losing rewards just when a person's friends outside the movement and alternative sources of pleasure are at a minimum. Charles Manson used these techniques to control his family.

It was commonly assumed that Manson's control over his family was based on drugs; however, sex, which was allocated within the cult as if it were a bag of jelly beans, was more important. Most of Manson's family were females and he initiated them into the group through day-long sexual encounters. He even directed exotic group orgies in which he determined both the partners and the positions that would be used. Members of the family who were in his disfavor were always excluded from these orgies (Bugliosi, 1974:433). Exclusion from the group was a particularly strong sanction because it meant more than just the loss of sexual opportunities.

Manson's idea of love was a central feature of the ethic that he preached. He said that love is love and that it cannot be defined. But his family interpreted this to mean that "Charlie is love"; and that love meant doing things for each other, particularly for Manson. Exclusion from the orgies therefore represented a withdrawal of the family's "love" for an individual. It also may have meant a loss of personal identity. When people joined Manson's group they were always given new names like Sadie Mae Glutz who was really Susan Denise Atkins. Manson did this to "break down" the middle class inhibitions of his followers and "reorient" their thinking about themselves in a context that deemphasized past experience. But this use of aliases also meant that the new identities he was attempting to create were closely tied to participation in the family. Exclusion from the carefully orchestrated sex orgies could have been an existential catastrophe for any of his followers.

The one drug that Manson did use to control his family was LSD. He would

Charles Manson at the time of his arrest in late 1969.

personally distribute it to every member of the family, making sure that he took less for himself than he gave to any of the others. Once they started "tripping" he would carefully begin to "unprogram" their minds from conventional thinking. Manson told them, in fact, that they should give up thinking and repudiate their own ego-controls. Borrowing ideas from Scientology, he told his group that they were to "clear" their minds and that if they reached "theta clear" they would be able to "straighten up" their lives. An important aspect of Manson's reprogramming strategy was his extraction of small favors from group members.

Manson would explain that love meant doing things for each other; "If you love me, and I love you, you should light my cigarette." But small favors always led to bigger and bigger favors; from lighting cigarettes to killing people! One of Manson's favorite requests sent his family out on late night adventures. These forays into the night were referred to as "creepy-crawley expeditions." He would tell his followers to go into town, break into a suburban home, quietly move throughout the house, moving little objects around, and then leave without waking the residents. Shortly before she was killed by members of Manson's family, Rosemary LaBianca confided in a close friend that "someone is coming in our house while we were away. Things have been gone through and the dogs are outside when they should be inside" (Bugliosi 1974:34). Creepy-crawley expeditions were useful to Manson not only because they served as a dress rehearsal for the murders that he had planned, but because they also frightened the members of his family.

Manson manipulated the fear of his followers and used it to achieve compliance to his requests. He constantly probed for an individual's deepest anxieties and preached about death. Death, he said, was only a change in the state of the soul. But even if a person's spirit can't die, his followers must have understood that leaving the family was a fatal decision. People had disappeared in the desert.

A third factor promoting commitment to a social movement is the intrinsic *reward* derived from participation in its activities. One question that has intrigued scholars is whether the peyote ritual has any real power to make people feel better. There is evidence that peyote has some curative capacity. It is a mild analgesic (Aberle 1967), and an old and somewhat creaky participant might forget his arthritic joints during the course of an all-night ceremony. Peyote may also inhibit the growth of a wide spectrum of bacteria and therefore help in preventing some forms of sickness (LaBarre 1959:255). Aside from the chemical properties of peyote, it is eaten in a therapeutic context in which it is *expected* to do good things. The expectation alone might lead people to feel better after participation in the peyote ritual.

The fourth factor contributing to the commitment of members to social movements is the development of a sense of *morale* or *esprit de corps* (Blumer 1951). Esprit de corps develops from intensive in-group interactions, especially when these informal relationships are confined to a relatively small group or an elite inner circle. Participation in formal ceremonial behavior is also important. Large ceremonial gatherings with speeches, music, uniforms, awards of medals and other honors, and carefully designed physical settings can generate enormous in-group feelings.

Morale or deep commitment has certain characteristics (Blumer 1951). People with high morale are convinced of the absolute truth and rightousness of their movement. They also deeply believe that the goals of the movement will be achieved one day. Along with this is the view that the movement has a sacred or nearly sacred mission to accomplish its goals. It is here that a charismatic leader may play an extremely important part, even if he or she is no longer living. Martyrs, too, can be extremely important in the development of morale.

As mentioned above, not all members of social movements are deeply committed nor does membership necessarily produce deep commitment. In the beginning, joiners may be quite tentative about their membership. As time goes by, the average member may become more and more intimately associated with the movement through the processes described above, such as spending more time and energy, receiving more support and authority from leaders and members, having their needs and purposes becoming more and more tied to the movement, and having a continual reinforcement of their beliefs (Milgram and Toch 1969:593).

Membership, even deeply committed membership, in a movement is not necessarily permanent. People leave as well as join social movements. It is not unusual to find people enthusiastic supporters at one time and later extremely hostile toward the same movement. People may leave a movement because its demands come in to conflict with the values, especially ones held before joining, of the member. Persons whose conceptions of the movement are shaped by their own experiences and needs instead of those of the leaders and members may also drop out. Another reason for leaving is the development of attitudes and needs which cannot find expression in the movement (Milgram and Toch 1969:594). As with becoming a member, loss of commitment is usually gradual rather than sudden. It is not always easy, either socially or psychologically, to become a member or leave a social movement. *The God That Failed* (1949) describes the difficulties some of the persons leaving the communist movement experienced.

Organization

Social movements are organized, but not in the same way as highly bureaucratic systems. They are in a state of flux and their organization changes from day to day. Turner and Killian (1972) suggest that emergent norm theory provides an explanation for the development of organization within social movements (Turner and Killian 1972).

Early in its life cycle, a social movement can be a *simple collectivity* rather than an organized group. Over time it adds group properties as it develops its own traditions, values, and normative structures. If it survives, a social movement becomes more and more institutionalized (Killian 1964:26–9).

In order to survive, social movements must adapt to their host society or succeed in changing it. When they are successful they become social institutions in their own right. Toch (1965) believes that the process of institutionalization is marked by increasing concern for self-perpetuation—the "three Ps": prosperity, power, and popularity—and decreasing concern for ideological goals. A movement is therefore faced with a dilemma: while it needs organization to survive, the existence of organization can frustrate the attainment of its goals.

This widely accepted point of view stems from the work of Robert Michels (1949). He argued that overwhelming oligarchic tendencies always arise in organizations devoted to democratic values. Movements develop organizational demands as a consequence of their growth; the necessity to make quick decisions, to communicate effectively, to establish a complex division of labor, and to meet the needs of full-time labor leads to the development of stable leadership. The leaders become professional and attain skill and knowledge. Thus, as the movement organization becomes routinized and bureaucratic characteristics appear, its leaders begin to have a stake in preserving the organization itself regardless of its democratic bias and its ability to attain its goals. According to Michels, there is an iron law of oligarchy holding that a movement will lose its original democratic character, develop conservative leadership, and become an oligarchy interested primarily in preserving itself.

Recent research (Zald and Ash 1966) indicates the complexity of a social movement's *organizational dilemma*. Its leaders may become more attached to their offices than to the goals of the movement under several conditions. A condition that favors such a situation occurs when a movement develops a basis of financial stability which is independent of its membership. Also favoring oligarchism is a situation in which both the leaders and followers develop commitment to personal goals such as social position or a stable family life. It is also possible that the cooperation of leaders with other movement organizations may lead to a transformation of goals. Zald and Ash (1966) point out that under certain conditions the leadership of social movements can become less rather than more conservative. If a movement's leadership is committed to more radical goals than its membership, then membership apathy and oligarchical tendencies can lead to greater rather than less radicalism. In short, goal transformation may take several directions. Goals may shift toward the extreme left or toward greater conservatism (as the Michaels theory predicts), or unattainable goals can be replaced by more easily achieved goals.

As an example, the organizations which made up the civil rights movement in the United States were oligarchical in structure for a very long time and interested in achieving their goals through reform efforts within the structure of the general society. But after the early 1960s and especially the "Mississippi Summer of 1964," the leadership and members of the civil rights movement assumed a more extreme and radical cast then had been the case before. There was a shift from a set of rather conservative civil rights organizations to ones, such as the Black Panthers, that were much more radical in character.

Within a broad social movement there are often submovements, frequently called "movement organizations" or MOs. Consider, for example, that all of the following groups are or were an active part of the contemporary civil rights movements in the United States: the Black Muslims, the Black Panthers, the Congress of Racial Equality (CORE), the National Association for the Advancement of Colored People (NAACP), the National Urban League, the Southern Christian Leadership Conference (SCLC), and the Student NonViolent Coordinating Committee (SNCC). This is, by no means, a complete list.

The relationships between organizations within the same social movement may take several forms (Zald and Ash 1966). The interaction between movement organizations may be cooperative, but it is rare for movement organizations to cooperate fully with one another except during full-scale revolutions or total movement activities such as staging a large demonstration. Sometimes movement organizations form a coalition in which they pool and coordinate their resources, but continue to maintain their own organizational activities.

Summary and Conclusions

The chapter begins with consideration of three principal functions of *ideology* for the mobilization of social movements. Ideology is used to *rationalize, justify, and motivate behavior.* It is therefore one of the factors that distinguishes between movements that do and do not attract mass support. Ideology is crucial to the growth of social movements because it gives meaning to the strains and dissatisfactions experienced by potential recruits; at the same time, it offers a vision of some idealized future. Belief in ideology is usually more important than its logical persuasiveness or sense of reality.

The answer to the question "who joins social movements?" is complicated by a number of factors. The leaders of the early stages of social movement may be quite different from those found at later stages. While some movements are led by a single individual, others are led by a group of people or by a principal leader and his lieutenants. The *charismatic leader* is thought to be most characteristic of the early development of a social movement. Indeed the charismatic leader leads by force and strength of personality rather than by institutionalized authority. Administrative leadership of social movements is associated with the departure of charismatic leaders and the development of *bureaucratic forms.* The *agitator* has also received attention as a type of social movement leader, but there is little evidence that "outside" agitators play a significant role.

One of the basic distinctions made with regard to membership patterns distinguishes between *exclusive* and *inclusive* social movements. Exclusive social movements admit only persons with certain characteristics and those that are inclusive admit everyone who wishes to join. The question of why some people join social movements rather than others is one about which we have relatively little general knowledge. But a number of hypotheses relevant to specific social movements have been researched.

The classic hypothesis that protest movements on the "radical left" tend to recruit partisans from the underprivileged "working class" has not been confirmed with regard to participation in the student protest movement. Student activists were disproportionately recruited from the upper strata of society rather than the lower. In addition, student activists were not maladjusted low achievers on university campuses across the country. In fact, student activists were as bright, if not brigher than nonprotesters, and many of them were clearly superior students.

Another hypothetical cause underlying the student protest movement was also disproved by the available data. The student protest movement was not an expression of "generational rebellion." In fact, most studies found that there was substantial agreement between student activists and their parents, and their parents in turn were more liberal and humanistically oriented than the parents of other students, supporting the "parental socialization hypothesis." Student activists put into action values that they had learned at home.

The single hypothesis regarding recruitment into social movements that has received consistent support in a great variety of studies is based on the notion of *relative deprivation.* People who experience the greatest amount of relative deprivation are apparently the most likely recruits for social movements. The perceived gap between what people feel they should have and what they actually have is a critical determinant of their response.

Once people have joined a social movement, a great many factors contribute to the development of their *commitment* to the movement. *Isolation* from outside relationships, *in-group reward contingencies,* the intrinsic *reward values* of certain in-group activities, and the development of *esprit de corps* all help to produce commitment. Leaders of social movements that restrict contact with outsiders can be especially powerful if they are also in a position to manipulate strong reinforcement contingencies within a group of followers.

Finally, social movements are organized in their later stages of development, but not in the same way as highly bureaucratic systems. The process of *institutionalization,* the development of bureaucratic forms, may be associated with a concern for self-perpetuation. Indeed the most telling sign of a completely successful movement is its institutionalization and assimilation into society at large.

Student activists tend to put into action values that they have learned at home from their parents.

Yasir Arafat, leader of the Palestine Liberation Organization, addresses the United Nations General Assembly in November 1974.

CHAPTER XII

Success and Failure

W hat happens to social movements? Their fate depends on the operation of many variables including their strategy and tactics, the reactions of social control authorities and the public, and internal problems within the movement itself. Social movements may exist for many years, even centuries; they may completely disappear or become quiescent; or they may fail to gain any of their goals, or enjoy partial or complete success. A social movement may have considerable impact upon its host society, sometimes upon other societies as well. Several of these possibilities are considered below.

Strategies and Tactics of Social Movements

An enormous variety of strategies and tactics have been employed by social movements at one time or another. Turner (1970:148–9) suggested that they may be divided into three broad categories: bargaining, coercion, and persuasion. *Bargaining* takes place when the social movement controls or has something of value which is desirable to another group. Leaders of the social movement offer to exchange the valued possession for acceptance of their demands. For example, the leaders of the civil rights movement may be willing to deliver votes in return for concessions or support.

Coercion, the second category, may be considered to be negative bargaining. When coercion is employed, the social movement manipulates the situation of the target group so the target group, not the movement, will bear the cost or punishment which results from the refusal to give in to the movement's wishes. Coercion may be expressed in activities which range over a continuum. At the lower extreme the coercive activities embarrass or inconvenience the target group; at the higher extreme the movement is engaged in civil disobedience.

Finally, *persuasion* is symbolic manipulation. In this situation the social movement has neither substantial rewards or punishments with which to bargain. Instead, the social movement usually tries to show that its values are consistent with the values held by the target group.

Both Alinsky (1971 and Wilson (1973) pointed out that no particular set of strategies and tactics guarantees success for the social movement. However, Wilson (1973:236) identified three characteristics associated with successful social movements. First, strategies and tactics are most effective when they have breadth. It is best to apply pressure to several points through various means rather than to rely upon only one means such as demonstrations or petitions which have a narrow focus. Second, simplicity is desirable in order to keep activities within the capabilities of the movement's membership. Extremely elaborate and complex activities often break down in confusion and disarray. Third, flexibility is also important. The successful social movement avoids irrevocable commitment to any single strategy or tactic; it never commits all its resources to a single campaign. Maintaining flexibility permits the social movement the opportunity to respond to the opposition's counteractivities.

The goals of a social movement bear upon the strategies and tactics it uses to attain them. If a social movement's goals are for some reform within the boundaries of the broad society, then its strategies and tactics are likely to be within the general norms of the society. But if its goals are revolutionary or radical, its strategies and tactics may be innovative, extreme, and very much outside the usual normative boundaries.

Another important variable which influences the choice of strategies and tactics is the *strength of the movement* itself. Clearly the strong social movement has more alternatives than the weak one. Early in its development, for example, the leaders of the Palestinian Liberation Organization (PLO) may have believed that one of the most effective strategies open to them was terrorism. Now that the PLO has achieved widespread international recognition and respectability and there is a Palestinian government in exile, it is in a position to disavow the use of terror, and indeed, has begun to do so.

The strength of a movement may be difficult to determine, since its measure can involve a number of different variables. While the number of members is important, it may not always be as important as depth of their commitment. There is a considerable difference between those willing or even eager to die for a social movement and those whose commitment is limited to the contribution of an occasional five-dollar check. Strength is also associated with the power and prestige of the members. An indication of the importance of this variable may be gained through examination of the ideological statements of social movements frequently published, as paid advertisements, in mass media publications like the *New York Times*. These statements often include a long list of distinguished members and supporters. Also important are the financial conditions of the movement, the support of involved publics, interest groups, and other social movements. Organization is important, as a well-organized movement is likely to be more successful than a poorly organized one. At a given point in time, the strength of a social movement reflects a combination of the preceding variables (Marx and Wood 1975:401).

The choice of strategies and tactics also depends on the *host societies' reaction* to the social movement. In order to avoid backlash, social movement activities must not antagonize important segments of the society. At the same time, they must continue to interest and attract the movement's membership. Should the society be extremely negative, the movement might be driven underground and its members resort to tactics more extreme than those employed when the movement was able to operate openly. Many social movements generate public controversy which is accompanied by polarization of previously uncommitted parts of the society. Such polarization often leads to more extreme tactics by both movements and countermovements. Many social movements begin by attempting to achieve their goals within the normative system of the host society, but as host society reaction becomes more negative, the movement's choice of tactics may become more extreme. This problem will be discussed in more detail later in this chapter.

Sometimes leaders of social movements will attempt to provoke social control authorities to attack the movement, especially if it is seeking goals consistent with broader social values. An attack by the authorities may increase general sympathy if its efforts are met with violations of the members' rights by police forces sworn to uphold them. During the anti-Viet Nam movement of the 1960s and early 1970s, efforts to repress the movement were often seized upon and treated as theater. These theatrical events often had the effect of making control authorities appear absurd and outrageous (Free 1970, Rubin 1970). They also led to attacks by confused authorities, which radicalized previously uncommitted persons.

Social movements may employ *ambiguity* as a tactic (Wilson 1973). Ambiguous tactics are often those which border on illegality. In the United States, large demonstrations and mass marches are legal under the laws which protect the right of free expression. But such events can be disruptive and violate the rights of others who are trying to move from place to place. In the same way, very literal and strict adherence to procedures and rules can slow down or even stop the operation of large systems, as is demonstrated when air traffic controllers, who usually do not follow regulations with absolute precision, use this tactic as a means of achieving their ends.

Social movements may use *threats* which, even if not carried out, may be important in negotiations for social change. They function to coerce the persons in power to give concessions in the hope of deferring mass protest (Marx and Wood 1975:386). As an example we can consider a selection from Saul Alinsky's *Rules for Radicals* (Alinsky 1971), a current textbook of social movement tactics. The case below is a description of a technique employed by the Woodlaw Association, a black ghetto social movement in Chicago during the 1960s, whose goals were to preserve and control the neighborhood. When it seemed to members of the organization that the city administration was not going to respond as they wished, a new approach was developed:

> O'Hare Airport became the target. To begin with, O'Hare is the World's busiest airport. Think for a moment of the common experience of jet travelers. Your stewardess brings your lunch or dinner. After eating, most people want to go to the lavatory. However, this is often inconvenient because your tray and those of your seat partner are loaded down with dishes. So you wait until the stewardess has removed the trays. By that time those who are seated closest to the lavatory, have gone up and the "occupied" sign is on. So you wait. And these days of jet travel the seatbelt sign is soon flashed, as the airplane starts its landing approach. You decide to wait until after landing and use the facilities in the terminal. This is obvious to anyone who watches the unloading of passengers at various gates in any airport—many of the passengers are making a beeline for the men's or the ladies' room.
>
> With this in mind, the tactic becomes obvious—we tie up the lavatories. In the restrooms you drop a dime, enter, push the lock on the door—and you can stay there all day. Therefore, the occupation of the sit-down toilets presents no problem. It would take just a relatively few people to walk into these cubicles, armed with books and newspapers, lock the doors and tie up all the facilities. What are the police going to do? Break in and demand evidence of legitimate occupancy? Therefore, the ladies restrooms could be occupied, completely; the only problem in the men's lavatories would be stand-up urinals. This, too, could be taken care of, by having groups busy themselves around the airport and then move in on the stand-up urinals to line up four or five deep whenever a flight arrived. An intelligence study was launched to learn how many sit-down toilets for both men and women, as well as stand-up urinals, there were in the entire O'Hare airport complex and how many men and women would be necessary for the nations first "shit-in."
>
> The consequences of this kind of action would be catastrophic in many ways. People would be desperate for a place to relieve themselves. One can see children yelling at their parents, "Mommy I've got to go," and desperate mothers surrendering "all right—well, do it, do it. Do it right here." O'Hare would soon become a shambles. The whole scene would become unbelievable and the laughter and ridicule would be nationwide. It would probably get a front page story in the London *Times*. It would

be a source of great mortification and embarrassment to the city administration. It might even create the kind of emergency in which planes
would have to be held up while passengers got back aboard to use the
planes' toilet facilities.

The threat of this tactic was leaked (again there may be a Freudian slip
here, and again, so what?) back to the administration, and within forty-
eight hours the Woodlawn Organization found itself in conference with
the authorities who said that they were certainly going to live up to their
commitments and they could never understand where anyone got the
idea that a promise made by Chicago's City Hall would not be observed.
At no point then, or since, has there ever been any open mention of the
threat of the O'Hare tactic. Very few of the members of the Woodlawn
Organization knew how close they were to writing history (Alinsky
1971:142–4).

Public Reactions and Social Control Strategies

It is difficult to separate consideration of the strategies and tactics used by
social movements from the general public's and authority's reaction to them.
A social movement which achieves even minimal attention has thereby gained
some sort of response from the general society of which it is a part. The
response can be, of course, either positive or negative. Few, for example, have
been opposed to eradicating such diseases as infantile paralysis. In these situations control authorities are likely to be helpful to the activities of the movement. They may provide meeting places or offer traffic control at meeting
places; often prominent persons in the mainstream of society may provide
public support.

Turner (1969) considered what conditions make the public view acts of
disruption and violence as social protest, crime and deviance, or rebellion and
revolution. Turner (1969:816) suggests that protest is action which: (1) is an
expression of some grievance or a conviction of wrong or injustice, (2) is
calling attention to a situation in which the people involved cannot change
themselves, (3) is designed to call attention to the grievance, (4) is designed
to provoke change on the part of a target group, and (5) is characterized by
a combination of sympathy and fear which is designed to move the target
group to correct the situation. Rebellion and revolution, on the other hand, are
action, not communication, with the purpose of destroying the existing system,
while crime and deviance are considered primarily as individual acts which
have an illegal, harmful, or nonconforming character (Turner 1969:816).

As Turner observes (1969:817) the interpretation of an event by the public
and those participating in it may be different. If the action does not match the

public's concept of protest then it will be defined as something else. In order to appear as protest, at least in the United States, the protestors must give the appearance of being an important part of a powerless and deserving group which has suffered well-documented injustices. Those groups that are clearly advantaged in comparison to the protestors are usually more willing to grant the claim of injustice than those with less advantage. For example, "the great middle segment of American population finds it easier to identify black ghetto disturbances as social protest than to interpret college student demonstrations in the same sense" (Turner 1969:820). The disturbance must be openly, not secretly, planned, or spontaneous. If there is serious injury or damage it must seem unintentional. If there is a carnival atmosphere, and it appears that the participants get personal gain, the action is likely to be defined as criminal or deviant.

Many social movement actions involve both threat and appeal, a combination which can help overcome resistance to acknowledging the protest. An event is more likely to be considered protest if the appeal aspect carries more weight than the threat. Too much threat might lead to an interpretation of the event as one of rebellion or revolution. In such a case, location can be important. White suburban dwellers may be more influenced by the appeal aspect of a ghetto disturbance than people who live closer to it.

Third parties often become involved in the activities of social movements and may find it easier than the target group to give the action a protest definition. This is likely to happen when there is strong pressure for the third party to take sides, and when taking either side is a costly prospect. By deeming the event protest, the third party may be able to maintain its neutrality through acknowledging a real grievance and condemning improper means. The third party may make a partisan interpretation when they are close to the aggrieved group, or when the circumstances favor coalitions.

The official definition of the event as crime, deviance, rebellion, or revolution is more likely when the general community view is homogeneous, and when the authorities know that they have the recourses to make effective their control efforts. Lacking these, the target group is likely to choose the protest definition as it gives them a chance to engage in less costly conciliation. In the long run, however, the protest definition is unstable and is likely to change if disturbances continue.

Social movements often generate opposition from significant parts of the society and its authorities. When a movement is opposed, the host society faces the problem of controlling it without creating an even more serious problem. Will the assassination of a particular charismatic leader crush a movement or will it create a martyr and generate sympathy for the movement, thus contributing to its growth? The consequences of control actions can be difficult to predict.

One reaction on the part of the host society, especially early in the movement's development, is to ignore it as much as possible, or to deny it any hearing at all. Members of social movements, on the other hand, often seek any publicity or attention, even if it is negative, as they may think any recognition is better than none. There is a widespread belief that knowledge of social movement activity spreads rapidly through the mass media and that it serves to encourage people in other places to take similar action. Associated with this is the notion that if the mass media do not report such activity it will remain localized. It has been alleged that, during the urban disturbances of the 1960s and early 1970s, widespread media coverage of urban disturbances gave people in other cities the idea of doing the same thing.

In Oberschall's (1973:243) view, *recognition* is a basic condition for the institutionalization of conflict between control authorities and social movements. When there is conflict, the authorities have to decide whether to attempt to repress the movement or negotiate with it. A decision to negotiate means the movement has gained some legitimacy although the authorities may not agree with its ideas. It can have the effect of institutionalizing and placing under normative regulation the conflict generated by the movement. Refusal to negotiate can, on the other hand, lead to serious uninstitutionalized conflict. Oberschall (1973:243–4) says:

> The employers who refused to allow their employees to be represented by a trade union in collective bargaining on the terms of the labor contract, the Southern City Council that refused to negotiate with the NAACP or any other body of black citizens who came forward as spokesmen of the black community to demand desegregation of black accommodations, the refusal of the U.S. and South Vietnamese governments to consider the National Liberation Front as anything else but a front set up by the North Vietnamese, are all instances of the complexity and fundamental importance of the recognition issue in social conflict.

Ridicule is a common and often devastating technique used both by control authorities and by social movements. Alinsky (1971) argues that one of the most effective things social movements can do is make people laugh at authorities. It is easy to see that one of the consequences of carrying out the O'Hare airport operation described earlier would have been worldwide amusement directed toward both airport and municipal authorities. Those hostile toward a social movement or toward the authorities make up unfavorable and absurd names for them, tell jokes, and sing funny songs about their opponents (Denisoff and Peterson 1972).

Another control technique is *co-optation*, the process which attempts to meet the movements criticisms through a propaganda program which points to aspects of the movement's goals which are shared by the whole society, and tries to persuade members of the movement to become part of the establishment. Those in power can accomplish this by forming a committee, composed of representatives from "all sides of the question" including social movement members. Members of social movements who accept such positions often moderate their views and sometimes become members of the "opposition." Other members may consider them "cop-outs" or "sell-outs." Associated with cooptation may be repression or what Mauss (1975:60) calls the "double death squeeze," that is the response of society may include efforts to employ cooptation, some steps toward meeting the movement's goals, and *repression* (the use of various social control techniques) at the same time. This is not a new or unusual response. Ash Garner (1977:47–52) presents data on seven seventeenth century agrarian revolts in colonial America. The response, with variations, was to incorporate some of the demands into the political system, extend amnesty to the followers, and often to execute the leaders.

An effort to control the social movement through *minimal reform* may also be attempted by control authorities. The demands of the social movement may be met in part. Such a policy may satisfy the moderate followers so they will be unwilling to support the extreme demands of the most committed members. This is illustrated by the Townsend movement (Cantril 1941). Dr. Townsend founded and led a movement whose ideology was that the economic problems of the United States during the 1930s and 1940s would be solved if the government gave $200 a month to everyone over 65 years of age. The next month the recipient had only to show that he or she had spent the first $200 to receive the next $200. Townsend thought this would lead to full production, employment, and consumption as money circulated again. The Townsend movement grew rapidly and seemed, for a time, to be within reach of achieving its program. But its influence declined as a consequence, among other things, of increased old-age benefits in many states. This led many members to drop out of the movement.

The most extreme control technique is to employ *violence* to repress a social movement. The use of force is frequently successful, but it can also lead to radicalization and counterviolence. There is evidence that force did not deter the protest activities of student demonstrators during the late 1960s and early 1970s (Lewis and Adamek 1974, Adamek and Lewis 1973). Violence can even strengthen a social movement, or it can drive a movement underground, leaving the remaining membership with the idea that the only action left to them is terrorism. Control authorities also face the difficulty of ensuring that the use of violence will continue to be directed against members of the social movement rather than against themselves. There are cases in which troops refused to control demonstrations or even changed sides. Furthermore, extreme violence often leaves bitter and long-lasting memories among all participants.

The *radicalization* of a social movement is a process involving the movement, its leaders, and the control agents. According to Marx and Wood (1975:-399), the police helped to make true their own assessment of the Black Panthers as a violent and revolutionary group. This appraisal and the accompanying harassment gave the Black Panthers decreasing choice in their actions and forced them to assume a more violent posture.

Sometimes authorities attempt to control by placing an agent provocateur within the social movement. As is now well known, such persons were widely employed during civil rights, youth, and anti–Vietnam War movements of the late 1960s and early 1970s. This was by no means a new technique of control. The task of the agent provocateur is to generate difficulties for the movement through such techniques as pushing members to engage in illegal activities (such as violence), informing, or generating suspicion and distrust within the movement. These activities can be very successful: fear of the presence of such persons creates demoralization and paranoia within the movement, vital information can be given to authorities, and the agent provocateur may be able to create destructive splits and divisions. Yet, the activities of such persons may actually aid a social movement. They may bring additional resources (provided by authorities), spark new leadership, help create martyrs, and—if the agent provocateur is exposed—cast doubt upon the legitimacy and honesty of the authorities (Marx 1974).

Internal Problems and the Disappearance of Social Movements

Toch (1965:271–2) identified several factors which contribute to the natural death of social movements. One of these is *inflexibility*. The leaders or members of a social movement may become so committed to the goals and ideology of the movement that they refuse to change or moderate their views to meet alterations in the society. Gusfield's (1955:221–52) paper on the Women's Christian Temperance Union (WCTU) provides an interesting example of this process. The temperance movement, of which the WCTU was a part, was a powerful and successful force in the United States for well over a hundred years. It contributed heavily to the passage of the prohibition amendment to the United States Constitution and helped make the consumption of alcohol a moral issue. There is a remnant of the temperance movement today, but it

Women in Fredericktown, Ohio take direct action against the evils of liquor in 1879.

can hardly be considered powerful or successful. The WCTU has lost its appeal to the middle class, once the primary source of its membership and support, through its insistence on emphasizing the absolute prohibition of alcohol rather than changing to an emphasis upon moderate usage and the treatment of alcoholism as a disease rather than as a moral failure. Some younger members have wanted to moderate the WCTU's position, but they have found that the more rigid leadership perpetuates itself (Gusfield 1957). Today alcohol use is so deeply imbedded in American society that an insistence upon absolute abstinence can hardly have widespead appeal.

Another source of failure is the *institutionalization* of the movement. To some this might be considered a success, but Toch (1965:219–21) suggests that this process often leads to a concern with the perpetuation of the movement rather than concern with its goals. The "three Ps"—prosperity, power and popularity—become important. As time passes, there is less and less concern with the ideology of the movement, except for those aspects which seem to contribute to its survival. The movement may become progressively more oriented toward people who have no real needs but who can help with the three Ps. Those people who continue to insist on the goals specified in the old ideology are often considered unrealistic troublemakers who refuse to understand what is really going on in the world. An institutionalizing social movement becomes geared to current social institutions, and develops a vested interest in maintaining them since they are tied in with its own survival.

It is possible for social movements to *outlive their original demands.* In such situations the organized social movement may exist long after losing its real impetus and general support. Messinger (1955) argues that such was the case with the Townsend movement of the 1930s. Its ideology was simple, and the members expected that its goals would be achieved through national rather than local effort. The Townsend movement began to lose its relevance with the moderation of the depression. As the states began to improve their own pension and old-age welfare systems, the movement was forced to shift its concern from a national effort to local and state matters. Some members wanted to support the state activity while others believed it was a violation of the movement's ideology to do so. The necessity to adapt contributed to a sharp decline in membership, as did general improvements in the conditions of the aged and the total society. The adaptation made by the Townsend movement was primarily one of changing to social clubs which attempted to finance themselves by selling health foods, vitamins, minerals and various kinds of pills.

Another cause of decline and failure is that the movement may contain *destructive internal contradictions.* The youth movement of the 1960s and early 1970s placed a strong ideological emphasis upon voluntarism combined with an antiorganizational bias, often expressed in the phrase "do your own thing." It has been observed that a social movement's success depends upon some sort of organization. Even though the organization is emergent and changing continuously, it is difficult to imagine the accomplishment of even simple goals without some division of labor, a system of authority, and continuity. The youth movement's strong hostility toward all forms of authority kept it from persisting for long or establishing its plans on a permanent basis. But it also faced another problem.

Highly stressed values of the youth movement were openness and generosity, expressed through such actions as sharing food, shelter, and clothing. It was expected that openness and generosity would be returned in full measure. But the youth movement failed to protect itself against the predators on its fringe. There appeared many individuals, especially in centers of youth culture such as the Haight-Asbury section of San Francisco, interested in taking free food, clothing, shelter, and so on without making any contribution in return (Howard 1974).

Flacks (1971) noted that youth, as a stage in the life cycle, is soon over, and that the cohesive brotherly and sisterly feelings emphasized during the height of the youth movement are hard to maintain for a long period of time. A social

movement can change a society only when it meets the aspirations and interests of the people as a whole, or at least a large part of them. But the youth
movement was actively hostile to older persons. Few older persons considered
the slogan "never trust anyone over thirty" a warm invitation to join.

Another set of variables which can result in either success or failure of a
movement are *unanticipated contingencies:* those events which are unplanned
and unexpected, and appear to be beyond the control of people in a society.
The early pacifist movement following World War II was influenced by unanticipated contingencies. Both the growth of severe tension between the United
States and the Soviet Union after the war and the Marshall Plan presented
members of the peace movement with a dilemma. Only the most committed
pacifists were able to oppose the Marshall Plan because of its military aspects.
Many others approved of the rebuilding aspect of the Marshall Plan. But the
unanticipated development of a "cold war" between the U.S.A. and the
U.S.S.R. led many "peace activists" to rethink their position, thus weakening
the movement (Wittner 1969).

In the case of the youth movement, the unexpected cycle of depression and
inflation which followed the Viet Nam war contributed to its demise. During
its peak, many middle-class members, sometimes called "dropouts," believed
they could easily rejoin the occupational mainstream whenever they wished.
The unanticipated difficulty of getting jobs made this assumption increasingly
doubtful, however, and probably reduced the number of persons interested in
dropping out.

Finally, social movements sometimes fail because they are *unsuccessful in
achieving their goals* or because *anticipated events do not occur.* In the fall of
1975 authorities at Waldport, Oregon investigated reports that about 20 persons in the region had sold all of their property shortly before disappearing
from the area. It was alleged that a Martian had told these people that they
would be taken to another world and a better life. The leaders of the cult who
were called Bo and Peep, also known as "The Two," had promised that those
"who dared to give up everything" would be transported to a new "spiritual
plane" aboard a UFO from outer space. There was supposedly a place in
Colorado where the converts could be prepared for the arrival of the space-
craft. The followers of The Two were required to "throw off" their families and
possessions and travel about the country in search of a higher state of spiritual
knowledge. There were reports that "a hippie had given away his guitar" and
that one man had sold his fishing boat for five dollars. The Oregon state police
reported that a man had given away "150 acres, all his farm equipment, and
three children" (The Toledo Blade 1976a:4). But by the winter of 1976 disillu-
sioned followers of the "Great Lost UFO Cult" had turned up at a rustic
halfway house in the seclusion of Topanga Canyon near Los Angeles.

It is important to recognize that the preceding variables seldom operate in isolation. Rather they are likely to occur in combination. Historical review of particular social movements usually shows the presence of many such variables. It is also clear that the precise contribution of any of these variables is extremely difficult to determine.

Demise

When a movement is in a state of demise or disappearance, the situation is seldom recognized as such by its members (Mauss, 1975:65). The condition may be defined instead as a success or only a temporary setback. It is difficult to say precisely when a movement has failed and when it is only quiescent; many social movement organizations exist for long periods during which they exhibit relatively little activity.

However, many social movements do flare up to some high point of recognition and influence and then, perhaps for the reasons described above, decline, become quiescent, or disappear. When are they completely gone or quiescent? Is there really nothing significant left of the WCTU, the Townsend movement, or the counterculture, all of which seemed so powerful only a short time ago?

Although the youth movement seems quiescent today, there are still some flickers of activity. Of the thousands of counterculture communes that may have been established during the peak years of the counterculture, some still survive in both rural and urban places. It is too soon to say if there will be many, or any, long term successes, although it does seem that many of the new communes lack the characteristics of success, especially deep commitment of the utopian societies described by Kanter and discussed below (Kephart 1976: 263–302).

These and other movements remain active at least in the memories of the participants. When "old veterans" come together they enjoy talking over their past experiences. They also carry with them experiences such as knowing how to organize demonstrations. These veterans and their skills can provide active help to a new movement growing from the old. They can also serve an uplift function; some of the older survivors of the sufferage movement have filled this role for the new women's liberation movement. Occasionally movements in a long period of quiescence flare up again, though not in precisely the same form; old survivors may reappear to serve as heroes and heroines, as in the case of the women's liberation movement and survivors of the sufferage movement.

A social movement organization which seems to be failing may attempt to revitalize itself through a search for new direction or through increased efforts to recruit new members (Festinger et al. 1956). It may turn to more radical means to achieve goals if its leadership believes conventional paths to goal attainment are closed. Or the social movement might decrease the importance of the primary goals or change the focus of discontent to something more easily achieved (Worsley 1957).

Successful Social Movements

Sometimes social movements are successful, although success is rarely so complete that everything in a movement's program is achieved. Yet many reform movements do get some of their programs adopted, and occasionally there is a revolutionary takeover by a social movement. In order to continue, a social movement must seem to have some chance of success to its members; at least some of the goals must appear to have a reasonable chance of attainment. Once the goals have been achieved, the movement must cease to exist or it must establish new goals (Zald and Ash 1966).

Since members and leaders often have a vested interest in the continuation of the movement, they may formulate a new set of goals. The old March of Dimes organization was designed to help conquer infantile paralysis, and it succeeded. Rather than go out of existence, the organization shifted its goals to an attack on birth defects and hereditary diseases. As long as there are serious diseases, the discovery of a control for any particular disease presents no threat to the existence of the organization. Many organizations, both those with emergent and those with more stable characteristics, have two kinds of goals: those which can be realized in a relatively short time and those which can never be realized. A principal goal of a state university is to educate the eligible citizens of the state and qualified out-of-state persons. This goal can never be fully realized as such citizens will continue to arrive for education year after year. But, on the short term basis, each class can and does receive whatever kind of education is in fashion at the time.

Another measure of the success of a social movement may simply be continuing in existence over a long period of time. This is especially applicable to the commune movement which, in various forms, has been attractive for hundreds of years. Kanter (1972) in her study of utopian communes in the nineteenth century in the United States found some that lasted for over 100 years while others failed in less than a year. In her view the primary distinguishing variable was deep commitment. Communes whose members were deeply committed were more likely to continue than those whose members were not so committed. A number of mechanisms worked to create and deepen commitment. One of these was sacrifice. In order to belong, members had to give up something: alcohol, tobacco, coffee, tea, rich food, sex; the sacrifice increased the motivation to continue. Another was to provide the individual with a stake in the community through investment of some sort. Sometimes this required giving property which was not returned if the individual left. Also employed was renunciation of relationships, outside and inside, which might be disruptive to communal cohesion. Communion among members, including communal sharing and work, served to deepen commitment. An individual's commitment was also deepened through mortification or denigration of self which provided a new identity based on a group membership. Transcendence, the feeling of power and meaning residing in the community, was also effective. Feelings of transcendence came through communal ideology, the leadership, a sense of mystery which was often spiritual, and fixing routine to the tiniest detail (Kanter 1972:75–125).

Revolutionary social movements can be successful in introducing vast changes over the entire institutional system including the family, religion, economics, and the government. The winners, after they come to power, often tend to become more moderate and develop an interest in restoring the usual services of everyday life. Successful revolutionary social movements may also cause great suffering. If there is a counterrevolution or the most radical members of the revolutionary movement come to power, there may be a period of terror or even systematic genocide of some part of the population. The successful revolutionaries often persecute the people previously defined as enemies. The terror period has an enormous impact on the population and is long remembered. The successful revolutionary movement may be followed by a new tyranny despite the promise in its ideology of a new age of freedom. Over a long period of time some of the changes instituted by a revolutionary movement revert to the old ways or are otherwise eroded, while other revolutionary changes may be preserved. The revolutionary ideology is likely to continue to form a theoretical foundation although it may diverge considerably from reality.

The Impact of Social Movements

Even though the study of the consequences of social movements is not as well developed as that of some other aspects (Marx and Wood 1975:403–6), it is clear that major changes come through social movements. Social movements rarely leave their host society unchanged; often they have an impact on other societies as well. The consequences of social movements can be disastrous and bloody or highly beneficial. Regardless of how important or trivial social movements are perceived to be, they are likely to have some consequences, and it is clear that social movements and their consequences are not confined to national boundaries. Few today can escape being influenced by the clash between the two primary ideological systems of capitalism and communism. It is a continual preoccupation of politicians in the United States who refer to it as a competition or race encompassing arms, space, agricultural production, and consumer goods.

Further impacts of social movements are suggested by Mauss (1975:69–70); a social movement may leave residues at the popular culture level, the normative level, and in the area of laws and law enforcement. At the popular culture level, the residues are likely to take the form of jokes, songs, hair styles, and fashions of dress. Although the youth movement of the 1960s and early 1970s is in a state of quiescence or demise today, many of its superficial characteristics are very much present. Some of the superficial aspects were taken up in money-making activities: second hand clothing stores, back packs, and hiking boots became big business. At the normative level, too, residues of even unsuccessful social movements can be found. One consequence of the civil rights movement has been to define racial jokes as being in "bad taste." It has also generated a heightened sense of self and racial pride in its adherents, evidenced in the slogan "Say it loud, say it proud, I am black, and I am beautiful." Heightened self-respect often generated respect for the social movement's members from its opponents. The Zero Population Growth (ZPG) movement, while it can hardly be considered a complete success, has contributed to the feeling of many that having large families should be avoided.

In the United States there is a tendency to attempt to solve problems posed by social movements through laws and their enforcement. The activities of the women's liberation movement have resulted in the passage of an enormous amount of legislation, with more likely to come. This has introduced significant changes into the occupational structure of the United States. Few people in the 1960s pictured women cadets at the military academies in the 1970s.

In the area of laws and law enforcement, unanticipated consequences may and often do appear. Efforts to solve problems may fail and may even generate new social difficulties or be followed by entirely unexpected results. A case often mentioned is the passage of the Eighteenth Amendment to the Constitution of the United States in 1919 which prohibited the consumption of alcohol as a beverage. Since this amendment did not enjoy total support, many people continued to consume alcohol. There developed an extensive illegal apparatus to supply alcohol to those who wanted it. Even though prohibition was repealed in 1933, the illegal organization which developed then remains a problem today. Some have considered the law and law enforcement reaction to illegal drug usage a similar situation. It may be said that much contemporary illegal drug usage stems primarily from the youth movement of the 1960s and early 1970s although a great deal of the prohibitive legislation was passed earlier. The enforcement of anti-drug use laws has been accompanied by the development of an extensive illegal supply system and an ever growing contempt for law enforcement agencies among those who use drugs. Often a social movement leaves the seeds of another movement which reappears at a later time. The contemporary women's movement grew from earlier efforts and, in this sense, has a long history.

Conclusion

Social movements employ strategies that range from the mildest efforts to terrorism. These activities were said to fall into the broad categories of *symbolic manipulation, bargaining, and coercion.* Their use and effectiveness depends upon a number of variables including the strength of the movement and the efforts of the host society to control the movement. If the goals of a social movement are generally approved by the host society, it may actually offer help to the movement. However, if there is significant opposition, the host society may apply control measures to halt or destroy it. These measures may range from ignoring and refusing to recognize the existence of the movement to the applying deadly force against it.

Many social movements disappear for such reasons as *inflexibility, institutionalization, outliving their original demands, internal contradictions, unexpected contingencies, and repression.* Sometimes it is difficult to determine whether a movement has actually failed or is only in a period of quiescence, after which it may develop new power and influence.

Sometimes social movements are successful, though they probably never achieve all their goals. Some are able to introduce reforms and others succeed in completely overthrowing a system.

All movements are likely to have some kind of impact upon their host societies. These changes may be as trivial as the introduction of new fads, argot, and jokes; or they may be enormously extensive, resulting in an entirely new social system which affects the whole world.

Does the graffiti on this elevated subway station in West Philadelphia represent another form of collective behavior?

Postscript

This concluding statement is neither a summary of the preceding chapters nor a catalog of theoretical generalizations and empirical findings. We want instead to bring the text to an end by restating some of its major themes and objectives. Since we know that patience can be exhausted, we have tried to be as brief as possible.

The concept of situational stress was used to organize the diversity of topics found in the field of collective behavior. But it does have faults. First, the idea of stress is frequently used at different levels of analysis. Second, it is frequently used both as a stimulus and as a response. And third, it is generally used without much concern for measurement problems (Mileti, Drabek, and Haas 1975:6–7). Nevertheless, we believe that situational stress is a valuable integrative concept for the field of collective behavior: especially when its various uses are properly distinguished.

At a sociological level of analysis, situational stress has been used here as a stimulus condition for the emergence of collective behavior. It refers to natural or social conditions that place excess demands on the capacity of groups to achieve collective goals. As the title of the text suggests, we felt it useful to view collective behavior as an adaptive response of social groups. It seemed to us that collective behavior is often a search for new situational definitions and organizational structures; structures that meet the unfulfilled goals of individuals in groups and cope more successfully with the realities of changing natural and social environments. It was for this reason that we began each of the major divisions of the text with a chapter emphasizing the natural and social preconditions of collective behavior.

At a psychological level of analysis, situational stress was treated as an experience of individuals. It was considered an experience that is a response to external circumstances and a motivational factor in human action. Relative deprivation, for example, is a person's experience of perceived inequities within a group or society. It can motivate certain actions, but it is not necessarily an exact analogue of objective indicators of social inequity. We tried to make these distinctions clear throughout the text without diverting attention from the substantive topics of collective behavior.

Collective behavior was defined as a relatively unorganized pattern of social interaction in human groups. It is an emergent social process because it involves forms of social interaction in groups that cannot be explained solely on the basis of psychological propositions about individuals acting in isolation from other people. The behavior of individuals is influenced by the groups of which they are a part and a person's range of behavioral options is restricted by social and natural circumstances that set the range of available choices. The study of collective behavior reveals some of the processes which help to explain why people sometimes find themselves doing things they did not intend and saying things they do not believe. Participants in collective behavior often wonder how they could have gotten involved, and we have considered the same puzzle.

Social life is not as simple as it often seems and common sense has a habit of letting us down when we need it the most. We have tried to show that many of the common sense explanations of collective behavior are not substantiated by empirical evidence. There is a strong tendency to blame the failures and misbehavior of other people on alleged individual weaknesses and personal deficiencies. Considerable discussion was focused on empirical studies of urban rioters in the 1960s to show how misleading this tendency can be. The *riff-raff* theory of riot participation was wrong, and yet even today it is still accepted by the general public and by many government officials.

Throughout this text we have left questions unanswered. There was little choice. The study of collective behavior is still in its infancy even though it is one of the oldest concerns of the social sciences. It has never received the same theoretical and research attention as many other fields. Its potential contribution to our understanding of human behavior can be realized only with further development of the discipline. And we believe that the field has entered a growth phase. The old stereotypes of collective behavior are making way for new conceptualizations and for a *new view of collective behavior* which emphasizes, rather than obscures, its continuities with organized social action. There is a new *eclectic approach* in the field which is free to draw upon the totality of the social sciences. Collective behavior has suffered as a discipline for too long as a result of its self-imposed isolation from the general fields of anthropology, psychology, and sociology. The general theories and methodologies developed within those areas are applicable to the study of collective behavior.

All of these changes have followed a period of skeptical reassessment in the field. A reassessment wich led some to advise the abandonment of the discipline. But this crisis in confidence has passed and research is continuing with a renewed commitment, a commitment based in part on the recognition of the field's practical significance. It would be a serious mistake to suppose that the field of collective behavior deals with the study of unique historical events. Collective behavior is an ongoing and recurring part of social life. Disasters will continue to occur, crowd violence is with us today, and new social movements are always on the horizon.

As we said in the beginning of this text, collective behavior offers an opportunity to study the limits of social action in human groups. The study of collective behavior contributes to our understanding of both social conflict and social change. Finally, this text has been an opportunity to say something about the behavior of people in groups, about the nature of individual existence in a social world. We hope to have encouraged a more sympathetic view of human weakness and a keener appreciation of human greatness.

*

References

Aberle, David F.
    1967   The Peyote Religion Among the Navaho. Second Printing. Chicago: Wenner-Gren Foundation for Anthropological Research and Aldine Publishing Co.

Abramson, Harold and Rosalio Wences
    1970   "Campus dissent and academic punishment: the response of college professors to local political activism." Paper presented at the Annual Meeting of the American Sociological Association, Washington, D.C.

Adamek, R. J. and J. M. Lewis
    1973   "Social control violence and radicalization: the Kent State case." Social Forces 51:342–7.

Adams, D.
    1970   "The Red Cross: organizational sources of operational problems." American Behavioral Scientist 13:392–403.

Alinsky, Saul O.
    1971   Rules for Radicals: A Practical Primer for Realistic Radicals. New York: Vintage Books.

Allport, Floyd H.
    1924   Social Psychology. Boston: Houghton.

Allport, Gordon W. and Leo J. Postman
    1947   The Psychology of Rumor. New York: Henry Holt.

Altman, James W., Robert W. Smith, Rheda L. Meyers, Frank S. McKenna, and Sara Bryson
    1960   Psychological and Social Adjustment in a Simulated Shelter. Pittsburg: American Institute for Research.

Anderson, William A.
    1969a   "Disaster warning and communication processes in two communities." The Journal of Communication 19:92–104.
    1969b   "Social structure and the role of the military in natural diaster." Sociology and Social Research 50:242–52.
    1970   "Military organizations in natural disaster: established and emergent norms." American Behavioral Scientist 13:415–22.

Anderson, Jon W.
  1968   "Cultural adaptation to threatened disaster." Human Organization 27:298–307.

Asch, Solomon E.
  1956   "Studies of independence and conformity. A minority of one against a unanimous majority." Psychological Monographs 70:9.

Aveni, Adrian F.
  1977   "The not-so-lonely crowd: friendship groups in collective behavior." Sociometry 40:96–99.

Ball-Rokeach, Sandra J.
  1973   "From pervasive ambiguity to a definition of the situation." Sociometry 56:378–89.

Baron, R.
  1970   "Anonymity, deindividuation and aggression." Unpublished doctoral dissertation, University of Minnesota.

Bart, Pauline
  1970   "The role of the sociologist on public issues: an exercise in the sociology of knowledge." The American Sociologist 5:339–44.

Barton, Allen H.
  1969   Communities in Disaster: A Sociological Analysis of Collective Stress Situations. New York: Anchor Books.

Bendix, Reinhard and Seymour M. Lipset
  1966   "The field of political sociology." Pp. 9–47 in Lewis A. Coser (ed.), Political Sociology. New York: Harper Torchbooks.

Berk, Richard A.
  1974a   "A gaming approach to crowd behavior." American Sociological Review 39:355–73.
  1974b   Collective Behavior. Dubuque, Iowa: Wm. C. Brown Company Publishers.

Berk, R. A. and H. E. Aldrich
  1972   "Patterns of vandalism during civil disorders as an indicator of selection of targets." American Sociological Review 37:533–46.

Bernard, Viola W., Perry Ottenberg, and Fritz Redl
  1971   "Dehumanization: a composite psychological defense in relation to modern war." Pp. 16–30 in Robert Perrucci and Marc Pilisak (eds.), The Triple Revolution Emerging. Boston: Little, Brown and Company.

Blauner, Robert
  1966   "Whitewash over Watts." Trans-Action 3:3–9.

Block, J. H., N. Haan, and N. B. Smith
  1968   "Activism and apathy in contemporary adolescents." In J. F. Adams (ed.), Contributions to Understanding of Adolescence. Boston: Allyn and Bacon.

Blumer, Herbert
　1951　"Collective behavior." Pp. 167–222 in Alfred McClung Lee (ed.), Prin-
　　　　ciples of Sociology. New York: Barnes and Noble.
　1971　"Social problems as collective behavior" Social Problems 18:298–306.
　1975　"Outline of collective behavior." Pp. 22–45 in Robert R. Evans (ed.), Read-
　　　　ings in Collective Behavior. Second ed. Chicago: Rand McNally.

Bogart, Leo
　1950　"The spread of news on a local circuit: a case history." Public Opinion
　　　　Quarterly 14:769–72.

Brissett, Dennis
　1968　"Collective behavior: the sense of a rubric." American Journal of Sociology
　　　　74:70–8.

Brouillete, John R.
　1970　"The department of public works: adaptation to disaster." American Behav-
　　　　ioral Scientist 13:369–79.

Brown, Kaye
　1976　"Quantitative testing and revitalization behavior: on Carroll's explanation
　　　　of the Ghost Dance." American Sociological Review 41:740–3.

Brown, Michael and Amy Goldin
　1973　Collective Behavior. Pacific Palisades, California: Goodyear.

Brown, Richard Maxwell
　1969　"Historical patterns of violence in America." Pp. 45–84 in Hugh Davis
　　　　Graham and Ted Robert Gurr (eds.), The History of Violence in America.
　　　　New York: Bantam Books.

Brown, Roger W.
　1965　"Mass phenomena." Pp. 833–76 in Gardner Lindzey (ed.), Handbook of
　　　　Social Psychology. vol. 2. New York: The Free Press.

Bucher, Rue
　1957　"Blame and hostility in disasters." American Journal of Sociology 62:467–
　　　　75.

Buckley, Tom
　1975　"About New York: once there was an elephant." The New York Times
　　　　(May 5):26.

Buckner, H. T.
　1965　"A theory of rumor transmission." Public Opinion Quarterly 29:54–70.

Bugliosi, Vincent with Curt Gentry
　1974　Helter Skelter. New York: Bantam Books.

Burton, Richard
　1974　"To play Churchill is to hate him." The New York Times (November
　　　　24):23.

Bushnell, John H.
  1969   "Hupa reaction to the Trinity River Floods: post-hoc response to aboriginal belief." Anthropolitical Quarterly 42:316–24.

Calhoun, J.
  1962   "Population density and social pathology." Scientific American 206:139–48.

Campbell, Donald T.
  1958   "Common fate, similarity and other indices of the status of aggregates of persons as social entities." Behavioral Science 3:8–25.

Cannetti, Elias
  1962   Crowds and Power. New York: The Viking Press.

Cantril, Hadley
  1940   The Invasion From Mars: A Study in the Psychology of Panic. Princeton: Princeton University Press. (Republished, New York: Harper Torchbooks, 1966.)
  1941   The Psychology of Social Movements. New York: Wiley and Sons.

Caplan, Nathan S. and Jeffery M. Paige
  1968   "A study of ghetto rioters." Scientific American 219:15–21.

Carroll, Michael P.
  1975   "Revitalization movements and social structure: some quantitative tests." American Sociological Review 40:395.

CB–10–4 News
  1977   May

Chapman, Dwight W.
  1962   "A brief introduction to contemporary disaster research." Pp. 3–22 in George W. Baker and Dwight W. Chapman (eds.), Man and Society in Disaster. New York: Basic Books.

Chase, Stuart
  1925   The Tragedy of Waste. New York: Grosset and Dunlap.

Chorus, A.
  1953   "The basic law of rumor." The Journal of Abnormal and Social Psychology 48:313–14.

Church, June S.
  1974   "The Buffalo Creek disaster: extent and range of emotion and/or behavioral problems." Omega 5:61–3.

Clark, Richard X.
  1973   The Brothers of Attica. New York: Links Books.

Cohen, Albert K.
  1965   "The sociology of the deviant act." American Sociological Review 30:5–14.

Cole, Stephen and Hannelore Adamsons
  1969   "Determinants of faculty support for student demonstrations." Sociology
          of Education 42:315–29.

Coleman, J. S. and J. James
  1961   "The equilibrium size distribution of freely-forming groups." Sociometry
          24:36–45.

Coser, Lewis A.
  1974   Greedy Institutions: Patterns of Undivided Commitment. New York: The
          Free Press.

Couch, Carl J.
  1968   "Collective behavior: an examination of some stereotypes." Social Prob-
          lems 15:310–22.
  1970   "Dimensions of association in collective behavior episodes." Sociometry
          33:457–460.

Crussman, Richard, editor
  1949   The God That Failed. New York: Harper and Row.

Currie, Elliot and Jerome Skolnick
  1970   "A critical note on conceptions of collective behavior." Annals of the
          American Academy of Political and Social Sciences 391:34–45.

Danzig, Elliot R., Paul W. Thayer, and Lila R. Galanter
  1958   The Effects of a Threatening Rumor on a Disaster-Stricken Community.
          Washington, D.C.: National Academy of Sciences.

Darley, J. J. and B. Latane
  1968   "Bystander intervention in emergencies: diffusion of responsibility." Jour-
          nal of Personality and Social Psychology 8:377–83.

Davies, James C.
  1962   "Toward a theory of revolution." American Sociological Review 27:5–19.
  1969   "The J-curve of rising and declining satisfactions as a cause of some great
          revolutions and a contained rebellion." Pp. 690–730 in H. D. Graham and
          T. R. Gurr (eds.), Violence in America. New York: Bantam Books.

Davis, Kingsley
  1945   "The world demographic transition." Annals of the American Academy of
          Political and Social Sciences 237:1–11.

Davis, Kingsley and E. Jones
  1960   "Changes in interpersonal perception as a means of reducing cognitive
          dissonance." Journal of Abnormal and Social Psychology 61:402–10.

Dellinger, R. W.
  1977   "Looters." Human Behavior. December:42–5.

Denisoff, R. Serge and Richard A. Peterson, ed.
  1972   The Sounds of Social Change. Chicago: Markham.

Denisoff, R. Serge and Ralph Wahrman
  1975   An Introduction to Sociology. New York: Macmillan Publishing Co.

Derber, Charles and Richard Flacks
  1967   "An exploration of the value system of radical student activists and their parents." Paper presented at the Annual Meeting of the American Sociological Association, San Francisco.

Desroches, Fred
  1970   "Disaster hits Pike County, Kentucky, hard." CB 10–4 News, Inc. 2:1.
  1971   "The April 1971 Kingston Penitentiary riot." Canadian Journal of Sociology 16:317–31.

Downing, L. A. and J. J. Salomone
  1969   "Professors of the silent generation." Trans-Action 6:43–5.

Drabek, Thomas
  1968a   Disaster in Aisle 13. Columbus: College of Administrative Science–Ohio State University.
  1968b   "Social processes in disaster: family evacuation." Social Problems 16:336–49.

Drabek, Thomas and Keith Boggs
  1968   "Families in disaster: reactions and relatives." Journal of Marriage and the Family 30:443–51."

Drabek, Thomas E. and J. E. Haas
  1969   "How police confront disaster." Trans-Action 6:33–8.

Drabek, Thomas and William H. Key
  1976   "The impact of disaster on primary group linkages." Mass Emergencies 1:89–106.

Drabek, Thomas E. and Enrico L. Quarantelli
  1967   "Scapegoats, villains, and disasters." Trans-Action 4:12–7.

Draper, H.
  1965   Berkeley: The New Student Revolt. New York: Grove Press.

Dunbar, Walter
  1973   "Why Attica?" Pp. 9–14 in Prevention of Violence in Correctional Institutions. U.S. Department of Justice.

Dunlap, Riley
  1970   "Radical and conservative student activists: a comparison of family backgrounds." Pacific Sociological Review 13:171–81.

Dynes, Russell R.
  1970   "Organizational involvement and changes in community structure in disaster." American Behavioral Scientist 13:430–9.
  1975   "The comparative study of disaster: a social organization approach." Mass Emergencies 1:21–32.

Dynes, Russell R. and E. L. Quarantelli
    1968a   "Group behavior under stress: a required convergence of organizational and collective behavior perspectives." Sociology and Social Research 52:416–29.
    1968b   Redefinition of property norms in community emergencies." International Journal of Legal Research 3:100–112.

Edwards, Lyford P.
    1927   The Natural History of Revolution. Chicago: University of Chicago Press.

Engel, G. L.
    1962   Psychological Development in Health and Disease. Philadelphia: Saunders.

Erikson, Kai T.
    1976   Everything in Its Path: Destruction of Community in the Buffalo Creek Flood. New York: Simon and Schuster.

Erikson, Patricia, Thomas E. Drabek, William H. Key, and Juanita L. Crowe
    1976   "Families in disaster: patterns of recovery." Mass Emergencies 1:208–21.

Fanon, Frantz
    1960   The Wretched of the Earth. New York: Grove Press.

Festinger, Leon
    1950   "Informal social communication." Psychological Review 57:271–82.
    1954   "A theory of social comparison processes." Human Relations 7:117–40.

Festinger, Leon, Dorwin Cartwright, Kathleen Barber, Juliet Fleischl, Josephine Gottsdanker, Annette Keyser, and Gloria Leavitt
    1948   "A study of rumor: its origin and spread." Human Relations 1:464–86.

Festinger, Leon, A. Pepitone, and T. Newcomb
    1952   "Some consequences of deindividuation in a group." Journal of Abnormal and Social Psychology 47:382–9.

Festinger, Leon, H. W. Riecken, Jr., and S. Schachter
    1956   When Prophecy Fails. Minneapolis: University of Minnesota Press.

Feuer, Lewis S.
    1969   The Conflict of the Generations: The Character and Significance of Student Movements. New York: Basic Books.

Flacks, Richard
    1967a   "The liberated generation: an exploration of the roots of student protest." The Journal of Social Issues 23:52–75.
    1967b   "Student activists: result not revolt." Psychology Today 1:18–23,61.
    1971   Youth and Social Change. Chicago: Markham.

Flynn, E. E.
    1973   "Sources of collective violence in correctional institutions." Pp. 15–32 in Prevention of Violence in Correctional Institutions, U.S. Department of Justice (LEAA).

Fogelson, Robert M.
   1971   Violence As Protest. Garden City, New York: Anchor Books, Doubleday
           and Co., Inc.

Form, William H. and C. P. Loomis
   1956   "The persistence and emergence of social and cultural systems in disasters."
           American Sociological Review 21:180-5.

Form, William H. and Sigmund Nosow
   1958   Community in Disaster. New York: Harper and Bros.

Foreman, Paul B.
   1953 "Panic theory." Sociology and Social Research 37:295-304.

Foy, Eddie and Alvin F. Harlow
   1928   Clowning Through Life. New York: E. P. Dutton and Co.

Free
   1970   Revolution for the Hell of It. New York: Pocket Books.

Freedman, J., A. Levy and A. Buchanan
   1972   "Crowding and human aggressiveness." Journal of Experimental Social
           Psychology 8:528-48.

Freud, Sigmund
   1922   Group Psychology and the Analysis of the Ego. London: The Hogarth
           Press.

Friedsam, Hiram J.
   1961   "Reactions of older persons to disaster-caused losses: an hypothesis of
           relative deprivation" Gerontologist 1:34-37.
   1962   "Older persons in disaster" Pp. 151-184 in George W. Baker and Dwight
           W. Chapman (eds.) Man and Society in Disaster. New York: Basic Books.

Fritz, Charles E.
   1960   "Some implications from disaster research for a national shelter program."
           Pp. 139-56 in George W. Baker and John H. Rohrer (eds.), Symposium on
           Human Problems in the Utilization of Fallout Shelters. Washington, D.C.:
           National Academy of Sciences, National Research Council.
   1961   "Disaster." Pp. 651-94 in Robert K. Merton and Robert A. Nisbet (eds.),
           Contemporary Social Problems. New York: Harcourt, Brace, Jovanovich.

Fritz, Charles E. and Eli S. Marks
   1954   "The NORC studies of human behavior in disaster." Journal of Social
           Issues 10:26-41.

Fritz, Charles E. and J. H. Mathewson
   1957   Convergence Behavior in Disasters: A Problem in Social Control. Washing-
           ton, D.C.: National Academy of Sciences, National Research Council.

Garner, Roberta Ash
   1977   Social Movements in America. Second ed., Chicago: Rand McNally.

Garson, G. David
  1972a "The disruption of prison administration: an investigation of alternative theories of the relationship among administrators, reforms, and involuntary social service clients." Law and Society Review 6:531–62.
  1972b "Force versus restraint in prison riots." Crime and Delinquency 18:411–21.

Gergen, K. and M. Gergen
  1971 "Encounter: research catalyst for general theories of social behavior." Unpublished manuscript cited in P. N. Middlebrook, Social Psychology and Modern Life. New York: Alfred A. Knopf.

Gibbs, Jack C.
  1965 "Norms: the problem of definition and classification." American Journal of Sociology 70:586–94.

Gordon, Mitchell
  1963 Sick Cities. Baltimore: Penguin Books.

Grebler, Leo
  1956 "Continuities in the rebuilding of bombed cities in Western Europe." American Journal of Sociology 61:463–9.

Grinspoon, Lester
  1964 "Fallout shelters and the unacceptability of disquieting facts." Pp. 117–30 in George W. Grosser, Henry Wechsler, and Milton Greenblat (eds.), The Threat of Impending Disaster. Cambridge, Massachusetts: The Massachusetts Institute of Technology Press.

Gurr, Ted R.
  1968 "Urban disorder: perspectives from the comparative study of civil strife." Pp. 445–52 in Louis H. Masotti and Don R. Brown (eds.), Riots and Rebellion: Civil Violence in the Urban Community. Beverly Hills: Sage Publications.

Gusfield, Joseph R.
  1955 "Social structure and moral reform: a study of the Woman's Christian Temperance Union." American Journal of Sociology 61:221–32.
  1957 "The problem of generations in an organizational structure." Social Forces 35:323–30.
  1968 "The study of social movements." Vol. 14 in The International Encyclopedia of the Social Sciences. New York: Crowell, Collier, and Macmillan.

Haas, J. Eugene and Thomas E. Drabek
  1973 Complex Organizations: A Sociological Perspective. New York: Macmillan Publishing Co.

Haas, J. Eugene and Dennis S. Mileti
  1976 Socioeconomic Impact of Earthquake Prediction on Government, Business, and Community. Boulder: Institute of Behavioral Science, The University of Colorado.

Haas, J. Eugene, Robert W. Kates and Martin J. Bowden (eds.)
  1977   Reconstruction Following Disaster. Cambridge: MIT Press.

Hartmann, G. W.
  1948   "The black hole of Calcutta: fact or fiction?" Journal of Social Psychology 27:17–35.

Hartung, F. E. and M. Floch
  1956   "A social-psychological analysis of prison riots." Journal of Criminal Law, Criminology and Police Science 47:51–7.

Heist, P.
  1966   "The dynamics of student discontent and protest." Paper presented at the Annual Meeting of the American Psychological Association, New York.

Heussentamm, F. K.
  1971   "Bumper stickers and the cops." Trans-Action 8:32–3.

Hoffer, Eric
  1951   The True Believer: Thoughts on the Nature of Mass Movements. New York: Harper.

Homans, George
  1950   The Human Group. New York: Harcourt, Brace and Company, Inc.

Hopper, Rex D.
  1950   "The revolutionary process." Social Forces 28:270–9.

Howard, John R.
  1974   The Cutting Edge: Social Movements and Social Change in America. New York: J. B. Lippincott.

Hudson, Bradford B.
  1954   "Anxiety in response to the unfamiliar." Journal of Social Issues 10:53–60.

Huie, W. B.
  1965   Three Lives for Mississippi. New York: WCC Books.

Iklé, Fred Charles
  1954   "The social versus the physical effects from nuclear bombing." The Scientific Monthly 78:182–7.

Jacobs, Norman
  1965   "The phantom slasher of Taipei: mass hysteria in a non-Western society." Social Problems 12:318–8.

Jacobs, Paul
  1971   "The McCone commission." Pp. 286–306 in Anthony Platt (ed.), The Politics of Riot Commissions. New York: Macmillan.

Janis, Irving L.
  1962   "Psychological effects of warnings." Pp. 55–92 in George W. Baker and Dwight W. Chapman (eds.), Man and Society in Disaster. New York: Basic Books.

Janos, Leo
1974 "The gathered tribes." Time (September 23):64,69.

Janowitz, Morris
1964 "Converging theoretical perspectives." Sociological Quarterly 5:113–32.

Jeffries, Vincent, Ralph H. Turner, and Richard T. Morris
1971 "The public perception of the Watts riot as a social protest." American Sociological Review 36:443–51.

John, Frederick
1973 "The Martians are coming." The Toledo Blade (October 28):40–4.

Johnson, Alvin
1918 "Short change" New Republic 14:381–383.

Johnson, Chalmers A.
1966 Revolutionary Change. Boston: Little, Brown and Company.

Johnson, Donald M.
1945 "The 'Phantom Anesthetist' of Matoon: a field study of mass hysteria." Journal of Abnormal and Social Psychology 40:175–86.

Johnson, Norris R.
1974 "Collective behavior as group induced shift." Sociological Inquiry 44:105–10.

Johnson, Norris R., James G. Stemler, and Deborah Hunter
1977 "Crowd behavior as 'risky shift': a laboratory experiment." Sociometry 40:183–87.

Johnson, Norris R. and William E. Feinberg
1977 "A computer simulation of the emergence of consensus in crowds." American Sociological Review 42:505–21.

Kanter, Rosabeth Moss
1972 Commitment and Community: Communes and Utopias in Sociological Perspective. Cambridge, Massachusetts: Harvard University Press.

Katz, Daniel and Robert L. Kahn
1966 The Social Psychology of Organizations. New York: John Wiley and Sons, Inc.

Katz, Elihu
1957 "The two-step flow of communication: an up-to-date report on an hypothesis." Public Opinion Quarterly 21:61–78.

Kelley, H. H. and J. W. Thibaut
1969 "Group problem solving." Pp. 1–101 in Gardner Lindzey and Elliot Aronson (eds.), The Handbook of Social Psychology, Vol. 4. Reading, Massachusetts: Addison-Wesley.

Kelman, H. and L. Lawrence
1972 "Violent man: American response to the trial of Lt. William L. Calley." Psychology Today 6:41–5, 78–82.

Keniston, Kenneth
  1967   "The sources of student dissent." Journal of Social Issues 23:108–37.

Kennedy, Will C.
  1970   "Police departments: organization and tasks in disaster." American Behavioral Scientist 13:354–61.

Kephart, William M.
  1976   Extraordinary Groups: The Sociology of Unconventional Life Styles. New York: St. Martins Press.

Kerckhoff, Alan C. and Kurt W. Back
  1968   The June Bug. New York: Appleton, Century, Crofts.

Kerckhoff, Alan C., Kurt W. Back, and N. Miller
  1965   "Sociometric patterns in hysterical contagion." Sociometry 28:2–15.

Killian, Lewis M.
  1952   "The significance of multiple-group membership in disaster." American Journal of Sociology 57:309–14.
  1964   "Social movements." Pp. 426–55 in R. E. L. Faris (ed.), Handbook of Modern Sociology. Chicago: Rand McNally.
  1968   The Impossible Revolution? Black Power and the American Dream. New York: Random House, Inc.

Kilpatrick, F. P.
  1957   "Problems of perception in extreme situations." Human Organization 16:20 –2.

Kinston, Warren and Rachel Rosser
  1974   "Disaster: effects on mental and physical state." Journal of Psychosomatic Research 18:437–56.

Klapp, Orrin E.
  1972   Currents of Unrest: An Introduction to Collective Behavior. New York: Holt, Rinehart and Winston, Inc.

Knopf, Terry Ann
  1975   Rumors, Race and Riots. New Brunswick, New Jersey: Transaction Books.

Kogan, N. and M. A. Wallach
  1967   "Effects of physical separation of group members upon group risk-taking." Human Relations 20:41–8.

Kornhauser, William
  1959   The Politics of Mass Society. Glencoe, Illinois: Free Press.

Kramer, Barry
  1973   "An age-old illness continues to crop up even in modern times." The Wall Street Journal (November 16).

LaBarre, Weston
  1959   The Peyote Cult. Hamden: Shoe String Press.

LaPiere, Richard Tracey
   1938   Collective Behavior. New York: McGraw-Hill Book Company, Inc.

Lang, Kurt and Gladys Engel Lang
   1961   Collective Dynamics. New York: Thomas Y. Crowell.

Larsen, Otto N.
   1954   "Rumors in a disaster." The Journal of Communication 14:111–23.

Lazarsfeld, Paul F. and Wagner Thielens, Jr.
   1958   The Academic Mind. Glencoe, Illinois: The Free Press.

Lazarus, Richard S.
   1968   "Stress." Pp. 337–48 in David L. Sills (ed.), International Encyclopedia of
           the Social Sciences. New York: Macmillan and The Free Press 15:337–48.

LeBon, Gustave
   1960   The Crowd: A Study of the Popular Mind. New York: Viking Press.

Lemons, Hoyt
   1957   "Physical characteristics of disasters: historical and statistical review." The
           Annals of the American Academy of Political and Social Science 309:1–14.

Lewis, Jerry M.
   1972   "A study of the Kent State incident using Smelser's theory of collective
           behavior." Sociological Inquiry 42:87–96.

Lewis, Jerry M. and R. J. Adamek
   1974   "Anti-R.O.T.C. sit-in: a sociological analysis." The Sociological Quarterly
           15:542–7.

Lewis, Jerry M. and John R. Carlson
   1977   "An assembly model applied to a political rally." Paper presented at the
           Annual Meeting of the North Central Sociological Association.

Lieberson, Stanley and Arnold R. Silverman
   1965   "The precipitating and underlying condition of race riots." American Soci-
           ological Review 30:887–98.

Lindskold, Svenn, Kevin P. Albert, Robert Baer, and Wayne C. Moore
   1976   "Territorial boundaries of interacting groups and passive audiences." Soci-
           ometry 39:71–6.

Locke, Hubert G.
   1969   The Detroit Riot of 1967. Detroit: Wayne State University.

Lowther, Mary P.
   1973   "The decline of public concern over the atom bomb." The Kansas Journal
           of Sociology 9:77–88.

Marx, Gary T.
   1970   "Issueless riots." The Annals of the American Academy of Political and
           Social Science 391:21–33.
   1974   "Thoughts on a neglected category of social movement participant: the
           agent provocateur and the informant." American Journal of Sociology 80:-
           403–42.

Marx, Gary T. and James L. Wood
  1975   "Strands of theory and research in collective behavior." Pp. 363–428 in
          Alex Inkeles, James Coleman, and Neil Smelser (eds.), Annual Review of
          Sociology, Vol. I. Palo Alto: Annual Reviews, Inc.

Masotti, Louis H. and Don R. Brown
  1968   Riots and Rebellion: Civil Violence in the Urban Community. Beverly Hills,
          California: Sage Publications

Mattick, Hans J.
  1975   "The prosaic sources of prison violence." Society 11:13–22.

Mauss, Armand L.
  1975   Social Problems as Social Movements. New York: J. B. Lippincott.

McCarthy, John D. and Mayer N. Zald
  1973   "The trend of social movements in America: professionalization and re-
          source mobilization." General Learning Press.

McLuckie, Benjamin F.
  1975   "Centralization and natural disaster response: a preliminary hypothesis and
          interpretations." Mass Emergencies 1:1–10.

McPhail, Clark
  1971   "Civil disorder participation: a critical examination of recent research."
          American Sociological Review 36:1058–73.

McPhail, Clark and David Miller
  1973   "The assembling process: a theoretical and empirical examination." Ameri-
          can Sociological Review 38:721–35.

Medalia, Nahum and Otto Larsen
  1958   "Diffusion and belief in a collective delusion: the Seattle windshield pitting
          epidemic." American Sociological Review 23:180–86.

Messinger, Sheldon L.
  1955   "Organizational transformation: a case study of a declining social move-
          ment." American Sociological Review 20:3–10.

Michels, Robert
  1949   Political Parties. Glencoe, Illinois: The Free Press.

Middlebrook, Patricia Niles
  1974   Social Psychology and Modern Life. New York: Alfred A. Knopf.

Mileti, Dennis S., Thomas E. Drabek J. Eugene Haas
  1975   Human Systems in Extreme Environments: A Sociological Perspective.
          Boulder: Institute of Behavioral Science, The University of Colorado.

Milgram, Stanley
  1963   "Behavioral study of obedience." Journal of Abnormal and Social Psychol-
          ogy 67:371–8.

Milgram, Stanley, Leonard Bickman, and Lawrence Berkowitz
1969   "Note on the drawing power of crowds of different size." Journal of Person-
        ality and Social Psychology 13:79–82.

Milgram, Stanley and Hans Toch
1969   "Collective behavior: crowds and social movements." Pp. 507–610 in Gard-
        ner Lindzey and Elliot Aronson (eds.), The Handbook of Social Psychol-
        ogy, Vol. 4. Reading, Massachusetts: Addison-Wesley.

Miller, Neal E. And John Dollard
1941   Social Learning and Imitation. New Haven: Yale University Press.

Mills, C. Wright
1958   The Causes of World War Three. New York: Ballentine Books.

Mintz, Alexander
1951   "Non-adaptive group behavior." The Journal of Abnormal and Social Psy-
        chology 46:150–9.

Mooney, James
1965   The Ghost Dance Religion and the Sioux Outbreak of 1890. Chicago: The
        University of Chicago Press.

Moore, Harry Estill
1958   Tornadoes over Texas: A Study of Waco and San Angelo in Disaster.
        Austin: University of Texas Press.

Moore, Harry E., Frederick L. Bates, Narvin V. Laymen, and Vernon J. Parenton
1963   Before the Wind: A Study of the Response to Hurricane Carla. Washington,
        D.C.: National Academy of Sciences, National Research Council.

Morin, E.
1971   Rumor in Orleans. Tr. P. Green. New York: Pantheon.

Mullins, Nicholas C.
1973   Theories and Theory Groups in Contemporary American Sociology. New
        York: Harper and Row.

Murton, Tom
1972   "Too good for Arkansas." Pp. 168–80 In Burton M. Atkins and Henry S.
        Glick (eds.), Prisons, Protest and Politics. Englewood Cliffs, New Jersey:
        Prentice-Hall, Inc.

National Advisory Commission on Civil Disorders, Otto Kerner Chairman.
1968   Washington, D.C.: U.S. Government Printing Office.

New York Times
1975a   April 13.
1975b   September 21.

Nkpa, Kwokocha K.
1975   "Rumor mongering in wartime." The Journal of Social Psychology 96:27–
        35.

Oberschall, Anthony
  1973   Social Conflict and Social Movements. Englewood Cliffs: Prentice-Hall.

Office of Civil Defense, Department of Defense
  1961   Fallout Protection: What to Know and Do About Nuclear Attack. Washington, D.C.: U.S. Government Printing Office.
  1968   In Time of Emergency: A Citizens Handbook on ... Nuclear Attack ... Natural Disasters. Washington, D.C.: U.S. Government Printing Office.

Office of Civil and Defense Mobilization, Department of Defense
  1959   The Family Fallout Shelter. Washington, D.C.: U.S. Government Printing Office.

The Official Report of the New York State Special Commission on Attica
  1972   New York: Bantam.

Ohlin, Lloyd
  1956   Sociology and the Field of Correction. New York: Russell Sage Foundation.

Olsen, Mancur, Jr.
  1963   "Rapid economic growth as a destabilizing force." Journal of Economic History 23:529–52.

Oswald, Russell G.
  1972   Attica—My Story. Garden City, New Jersey: Doubleday and Co., Inc.

Pallas, J. and B. Barber
  1972   "From riot to revolution." Issues in Criminology 7:1–19.

Park, Robert E. and Ernest W. Burgess
  1921   Introduction to the Science of Sociology. Chicago: The University of Chicago Press.

Parr, Arnold R.
  1970   "Organizational responses to community crises and group experience." American Behavioral Scientist 13:423–9.

Parsons, Talcott
  1937   The Structure of Social Action. New York: McGraw:Hill Book Company, Inc.
  1951   The Social System. New York: The Free Press of Glencoe, A Division of the Macmillan Company.

Petersen, William
  1975   Population. New York: Macmillan.

Pfautz, Harold W.
  1961   "Near-group theory and collective behavior: a critical reformulation." Social Problems 9:167–74.

Ponting, J. Rick
  1973   "Rumor control centers: their emergence and operations." American Behavioral Scientist 16:391–401.

Prassel, Frank Richard
    1970   "Rebellion in miniature, a sociological analysis of the prison riot." Paper read at the Annual Meeting of the Southwest Sociological Association.

Price, J.
    1971   "The effects of crowding on the social behavior of children." Unpublished doctoral dissertation, Columbia University.

Prince, Samuel H.
    1920   Catastrophe and Social Change. New York: Columbia University Press.

Pugh, M. D., Joseph B. Perry, Eldon E. Snyder and Elmer Spreitzer
    1971   "Participation in anti-war demonstrations: a test of the parental continuity hypothesis." Sociology and Social Research 56:19–28.

Pugh, M. D., Joseph B. Perry, Eldon E. Snyder and Elmer Spreitzer
    1972   "Faculty support of student dissent." Sociological Quarterly 13:525–32.

Quarantelli, Enrico L.
    1954   "The nature and condition of panic." American Journal of Sociology 60:267–75.
    1957   "The behavior of panic participants." Sociology and Social Research 41:187–94.
    1970   "The community general hospital: its immediate problems in disasters." American Behavioral Scientist 13:380–91.

Quarantelli, E. L. and Russell R. Dynes
    1970   "Property norms and looting: their patterns in community crises." Phylon 31:168–82.
    1976   "Community conflict: its absence and its presence in natural disasters." Mass Emergencies 1:139–52.

Quarantelli, E. L. and James R. Hundley, Jr.
    1969   "A test of some propositions about crowd formation and behavior." Pp. 370–86 in Robert R. Evans (ed.), Readings in Collective Behavior. Chicago: Rand McNally.

Quarantelli, Enrico L. and Jack M. Weller
    1974   "The structural problem of a sociological specialty: collective behavior's lack of a critical mass." The American Sociologist 9:59–68.

Raine, Walter J.
    1967   "Los Angeles riot study: the perception of police brutality in South Central Los Angeles." University of California, mimeograph.

Report of the Goldman Panel to Protect Prisoners' Constitutional Rights
    1971   New York: The Correctional Association of New York.

Roberts, Ron E. and Robert Marsh Kloss
    1974   Social Movements: Between the Balcony and the Barricade. St. Louis: C. V. Mosby.

Roe, Frank G.
 1970   The North American Buffalo: A Critical Study of the Species in its Wild State, Second ed. Toronto: University of Toronto Press.

Rosen, George
 1968   Madness in Society. London: Routledge and Kegan Paul.

Rosengren, Karl Erik, Peter Arvidson, and Dahn Sturesson
 1975   "The Barseback 'panic': A radio programme as a negative summary event." Acta Sociologica 18:303–321.

Rosenhan, D.
 1969   "Some origins of concern for others." In P. Mussen, J. Langer, and M. Covington (eds.), Trends and Issues in Developmental Psychology. New York: Holt, Rinehart and Winston.

Rosenthal, Marilynn
 1971   "Where rumor raged." Trans-Action 8:34–43.

Rosnow, Ralph
 1974   "On rumor." Journal of Communication 24:26–38.

Rosnow, Ralph and Gary Alan Fine
 1974   "Inside rumors." Human Behavior 3:64–8.
 1976   Rumors and Gossip. New York: Elsevier.

Ross, Edward A.
 1908   Social Psychology. New York: Macmillan.

Ross, James L.
 1970   "The Salvation Army: emergency operations." American Behavioral Scientist 13:404–14.

Rubin, Jerry
 1970   Do It: Scenarios of the Revolution. New York: Ballantine Books.

Rudé, George
 1959   The Crowd in the French Revolution. Oxford: Clarendon Press.

Schacter, Stanley and Harvey Burdick
 1955   "A field experiment on rumor transmission and distortion." Journal of Abnormal and Social Psychology 50:363–71.

Schacter, Stanley and R. E. Nisbett
 1966   "The cognitive manipulation of pain." Journal of Experimental Social Psychology 2:227–36.

Schacter, Stanley and J. Singer
 1962   "Cognitive, social and psychological determinants of emotional state." Psychological Review 69:379–99.

Schneider, D. M.
 1957   "Typhoons on Yap." Human Organization 16:10–15.

Schrag, Clarence
  1960   "The sociology of prison riots." Proceedings of the 19th Annual Congress of the American Correctional Association.
  1961   "Some foundations for a theory of corrections." Pp. 309–57 in Donald Cressey (ed.), The Prison. New York: Holt, Rinehart and Winston.

Scott, Joseph W. and Mohamed El-Assal
  1969   "Multiversity, university size, university quality and student protest: an empirical study." American Sociological Review 34:702–9.

Sears, David O. and T. M. Tomlinson
  1968   "Riot ideology in Los Angeles: a study of Negro attitudes." Social Science Quarterly 49:485–503.

Severe Storms: Prediction, Detection and Warning
  1977   Washington D.C.: National Academy of Sciences.

Sheinkopf, Kenneth G. and Mark R. Weintz
  1973   "The Beatles are dead! Long live the Beatles!" Popular Music and Society 2:321–6.

Sherif, Muzafer
  1936   The Psychology of Social Norms. New York: Harper and Row.

Shibutani, Tamotsu
  1966   Improvised News: A Sociological Study of Rumor. New York: The Bobbs-Merrill Co., Inc.

Shuman, H. and E. O. Laumann
  1967   "Do most professors support the war?" Trans-Action 4:32–5.

Singer, Benjamin D., Richard W. Osborn, and James A. Geschwender
  1970   Black Rioters: A Study of Social Factors and Communication in the Detroit Riot. Lexington, Massachusetts: D. C. Heath and Company.

Siporin, Max
  1966   "The experience of aiding the victims of Hurricane Betsey." The Social Service Review 40:378–89.

Skolnick, Jerome
  1969   The Politics of Protest. Washington, D.C.: U.S. Government Printing Office.

Smelser, Neil J.
  1962   Theory of Collective Behavior. New York: The Free Press.
  1964   "Theoretical issues of scope and problems." Sociological Quarterly 5:116–22.
  1970   "Two critics in search of a bias: a response to Currie and Skolnick." Annals of the American Academy of Political and Social Sciences 391:46–55.
  1972   "Some additional thoughts on collective behavior." Sociological Inquiry 42:97–101.

Smith, S. and W. Haythorne
  1972   "Effects of compatability, crowding, group size, and leadership seniority on stress, anxiety, hostility, and annoyance in isolated groups." Journal of Personality and Social Psychology 22:67–79.

Snyder, David and Charles Tilly
  1972   "Hardship and collective violence in France: 1830–1960." American Sociological Review 37:520–32.

Sorokin, Pitirim A.
  1942   Man and Society in Calamity: The Effect of War, Revolution, Famine, Pestilence Upon Human Mind, Social Organization and Cultural Life. New York: E. P. Dutton and Company.

Spilerman, Seymour
  1971   "The causes of racial disturbances: tests of an explanation." American Sociological Review 36:427–442.

Spitzer, Stephen P. and Norman K. Denzin
  1965   "Levels of knowledge in an emergent crisis." Social Forces 44:234–7.

Srole, L.
  1956   "Social interaction and certain corollaries: an exploratory study." American Sociological Review 21:709–16.

Stahl, Sidney and Marty Lebedun
  1974   "Mystery gas: an analysis of mass hysteria." Journal of Health and Social Behavior 15:44–50.

Stallings, A.
  1970   "Hospital adaptations to disaster: flow models of intensive technologies." Human Organization 29:294–302.

Stark, Margaret J. Abudu, Walter J. Raine, Stephen Burbeck, and Keith Davison
  1974   "Some empirical patterns in a riot process." American Sociological Review 39:865–76.

Stark, Rodney
  1972   Police Riots: Collective Violence and Law Enforcement. Belmont, California: Wadsworth.

Stoddard, Ellwyn R.
  1969   "Some latent consequences of bureaucratic efficiency in disaster relief." Human Organization 28:177–89.

Stoner, J. A. F.
  1961   "A comparison of individual and group decisions involving risks." Unpublished Masters Thesis, Cambridge, Massachusetts: Massachusetts Institute of Technology, School of Industrial Management.

Stouffer, Samuel A.
  1955   Communism, Conformity, and Civil Liberties. New York: Doubleday.

Strauss, Anselm L.
1944   "The literature on panic." Journal of Abnormal and Social Psychology 39:317–28.

Taylor, James B., Louis A. Zurcher, and William H. Key
1970   Tornado: A Community Responds to Disaster. Seattle: University of Washington Press.

The Toledo Blade
1975a   "Alleged Martian prompts land sale." (October 6):10.
1975b   "Amnesty for the Attica inmates." (September 25).
1976a   "Bo and Peep losing sheep to a UFO halfway house." (February 2):4.
1976b   "15 Mississippi pupils victims of mysterious fainting spells." (April 4):A-27.

Tierney, Kathleen J.
1977   "Emergent norm theory as theory: an analysis and critique of Turner's formulation." Paper presented at the Annual Meeting of the North Central Sociological Association.

Titmuss, Robert M.
1950   Problems of Social Policy. London: H. M. Stationery Office.

Toch, Hans
1965   The Social Psychology of Social Movements. Indianapolis: Bobbs-Merrill.

Turner, Ralph
1964a   "Collective behavior." Pp. 382–425 in R. E. L. Faris (ed.), Handbook on Modern Sociology. Chicago: Rand-McNally.
1964b   "New theoretical frameworks." The Sociological Quarterly 5:122–32.
1969   "The public perception of protest." American Sociological Review 34:815–31.
1970   "Determinants of social movement strategies." Pp. 145–64 in Tamotsu Shibutani (ed.), Human Nature and Collective Behavior. Englewood Cliffs: Prentice-Hall.
1976   "Earthquake prediction and public policy: distillations from a National Academy of Sciences report." Mass Emergencies 1:184–207.

Turner, Ralph and Lewis M. Killian, eds.
1957   Collective Behavior. Englewood Cliffs, New Jersey: Prentice-Hall.
1972   Collective Behavior. Second ed. Englewood Cliffs, New Jersey: Prentice-Hall.

Valins, Stuart
1966   "Cognitive effects of false heart rate feedback." Journal of Personality and Social Psychology 4:400–408.

Veltford, Helene Rank and George E. Lee
1943   "The Coconut Grove fire: a study of scapegoating." Journal of Abnormal and Social Psychology 38:138–54.

Wallace, Anthony F. C.
  1956   Tornado in Worcester: An Exploratory Study of Individual and Commu-
          nity Behavior in an Extreme Situation. Washington, D.C.: National Acade-
          my of Sciences, National Research Council.
  1957   "Mazeway disintegration: the individual's perception of socio-cultural dis-
          organization." Human Organization 16:23-4.

Wanderer, Jules
  1968   "1967 riots: a test of the congruity of events." Social Problems 16:193-7.

Warheit, George J.
  1970   "Fire departments: operations during major community emergencies."
          American Behavioral Scientist 13:362-8.

Watts, William A. and David Whittaker
  1966   "Some socio-psychological differences between highly-committed mem-
          bers of the Free Speech Movement and the student population at Berke-
          ley." Journal of Applied Behavioral Sciences 2:41-62.

Watts, William A., Steve Lynch, and David Whittaker
  1969   "Alienation and activism in today's college-age youth: socialization pat-
          terns and current family relationships." Journal of Counseling Psychology
          16:1-7.

Waxman, Jerry J.
  1973   "Local broadcast gatekeeping during natural disasters." Journalism Quar-
          terly 50:751-8.

Weber, Max
  1968   On Charisma and Institution Building. Chicago: The University of Chicago
          Press.

Webster, Murray, Jr.
  1973   "Psychological reductionism, methodological individualism, and large scale
          problems." American Sociological Review 38:258-73.
  1975   Actions and actors: Principles of Social Psychology. Cambridge, Massa-
          chusetts: Winthrop Publishers, Inc.

Weller, Jack M. and E. L. Quarantelli
  1973   "Neglected characteristics of collective behavior." American Journal of
          Sociology 79:665-85.

Wences, R. and H. Abramson
  1970   "Faculty opinion on the issues of job placement and dissent in the univer-
          sity." Social Problems 18:27-38.

Wenger, Dennis E., James D. Dykes, Thomas D. Sebok and Joan L. Neff
  1975   "Its a matter of myths: an empirical examination of individual insight into
          disaster response." Mass Emergencies 1:33-46.

Westby, David L. and Richard G. Braungart
  1966   "Class and politics in the family background of student political activists."
          American Sociological Review 31:690-2.
  1970   "The alienation of generations and status politics: alternative explanations
          of student political activism." In Robert S. Sigel (ed.), Learning About
          Politics: Studies in Political Socialization. New York: Random House.

Wheeler, L.
1966   "Toward a theory of behavioral contagion." Psychological Review 73:179–92.

White, Gilbert F. and J. Eugene Haas
1975   Assessment of Research on Natural Hazards. Cambridge: MIT Press.

Wicker, Tom
1975   A Time to Die. New York: Quadrangle/The New York Times Book Company.

Wilkinson, Paul
1971   Social Movement. New York: Prager.

Williams, Harry B.
1964   "Human factors in warning-and-response systems." Pp. 79–104 in George W. Grossner, Henry Wechsler, and Milton Greenblat (eds.), In the Threat of Impending Disaster. Cambridge, Massachusetts: The Massachusetts Institute of Technology Press.

Wilson, John
1973   Introduction to Social Movements. New York: Basic Books.

Wimberley, Ronald, Thomas C. Hood, C. M. Lipsey, Donald Clelland and Marguerite Hay
1975   "Conversion in a Billy Graham crusade: spontaneous event or ritual performance?" The Sociological Quarterly 16:162–170.

Wiseberg, Laurie
1976   "An international perspective on the African famines." Pp. 101–27 in Michael H. Glantz (ed.), The Politics of Natural Disaster. New York: Prager.

Withey, Stephen B.
1962   The U.S. and the U.S.S.R.: A Report of the Public's Perspectives on United States–Russian Relations in Late 1961. Ann Arbor: Institute for Social Research.

Wittner, Lawrence S.
1969   Rebels Against War: The American Peace Movement, 1941–1960. New York: Columbia University Press.

Wolfe, Alan
1973   The Seamy Side of Democracy: Repression in America. New York: David McKay Co.

Wolfenstein, Martha
1957   Disaster: A Psychological Essay. Glencoe, Illinois: The Free Press and the Falcon Wing Press.

Worsley, Peter M.
1957   The Trumpet Shall Sound: A Study of Cargo Cults in Melanesia. London: Macgibbon and Kee. (Reprinted 1968, New York: Schocken.)

Yanev, Peter
    1974   Peace of Mind in Earthquake County. San Francisco: San Francisco
            Chronicle.

Yutzy, Daniel
    1970   "Priorities in community response." American Behavioral Scientist 13:344
            –53.

Zald, Mayer and Roberta Ash
    1966   "Social movement organizations: growth, decay and change." Social Forces
            44:327–41.

Zimbardo, Philip G.
    1969   "The human choice: individuation, reason and order versus deindividua-
            tion, impulse and chaos." Pp. 237–307 in William J. Arnold and David
            Levine (eds.), Nebraska Symposium on Motivation. Lincoln: University of
            Nebraska Press.

Zygmunt, Joseph
    1972   "Movements and motives: some unresolved issues in the psychology of
            social movements." Human Relations 25:449–67.

Indexes

317

SUBJECT INDEX

Attica, 21, 145, 157-160, 193-219

Collective behavior
  Defined, 3
    and crowds, 12, 19-20
    and emotionality, 18
    and irrationality, 18-19
    and the mass, 22-23
    and the public, 22-23
    and situational stress, 13, 15-17
    and social context, 13-17
    and social groups, 4-6
    and social movements, 12
    and social organization, 6-12,
      13
    and stereotypes, 17-21
    and violence, 19-20
Collective hysteria
  Defined, 13
    and Baltimore students, 14-15
    and the June Bug, 13-14, 15
    and the Mattoon gasser, 11-12
    and Mississippi students, 14-15
    and mystery gas, 14
Crowds
  Blumer's crowd types, 143
  Crowd formation, 169-191
    and assembling instructions,
      174-175, 189
    and boundaries, 186-188
    and composition, 175-177
    and crowd crystals, 173
    and friendship patterns, 175
    and growth models, 170, 171,
      172
    and know-nothing hypothesis,
      174-175
    and mass discontent, 175-176
    and precipitating events, 158,
      162-164
    and proximate populations,
      169-172
    and riff-raff hypotheses, 177-
      183
    and social interaction in crowds,
      186-188
  Crowd violence at Attica, 193-219
    and assault plan, 211-214
    and deaths, 211
    and discipline, 212-213
    and emergent norms, 204-206

and excess fire power, 213
and final assault, 209-211
and Goldman Panel, 217
and inmate harassment, 195-196
and negotiation, 206, 207
and perceptual distortion, 211
and precipitating events at
  Attica, 199-202
and reprisals, 216-217
and rumors, 214-215
  Defined, 143

Deindividuation
  Defined, 67
    and anonymity-aggression hypo-
      thesis, 70-71, 215
    and behavioral outputs, 72-74
    and dehumanization, 72, 214
    and social inputs, 68-69
    and social responsibility, 71-72
    and subjective states, 69-72
Deprivation
  Absolute deprivation, 145-148
    and frustration-aggression hypo-
      thesis, 150, 164-165
    and overcrowding, 147
    and unemployment, 149, 179
  Relative deprivation, 148-155
    and civil rights, 148-152
    and French Revolution, 151-152,
      153, 155
    and Ghost Dance, 238-240, 241
    and J-curve of rising expecta-
      tions, 151-155
    and mass discontent, 175-176
    and Peyote Cult, 259-260
Disaster
  Defined, 82-83
  Impact, 101-117
    and behavior during impact,
      102-108
    and communication, 116-117
    and damage, 102
    and tornadoes, 102-103
    and typhoons, 105
  Recovery, 1
    and altruism, 124
    and assignment of blame, 137-
      138
    and conflicting roles, 122-123
    and controlling convergence,

and parole systems, 197-199
and prison conditions, 145-148,
158
and racial discrimination, 55,
155-158, 160-163, 196-197
and rumors, 116-117, 158-162
and storms, 79, 86, 87
and tornadoes, 77, 91-92, 100,
102-105
and threats, 84-98, 101
and unemployment, 149, 179
and urban migration, 158, 182
and warning, 84-98, 101, 119

and organized behavior, 33-36

Theory
Berk's rational calculus model,
25, 36-39
and high risk actions, 37
and risky shift, 37-38
Blumer's interactionist perspective, 25, 30-33
and circular reaction, 31
and collective excitement, 31,
32
and milling, 31
and recent criticism, 33
and social contagion, 31, 33
and social unrest, 30
LeBon's classical perspective,
25-30
and anonymity, 27
and emotion, 26, 27, 28, 29
and ideas, 27
and invincibility, 27
and law of mental unity, 26
and leaders, 28-29
and racial substratum, 26
and recent criticism, 29-30
Smelser's value-added model,
25, 39-43
and generalized belief, 40
and mobilization, 39, 40
and precipitating events, 40
and recent criticism, 41-43
and social control, 40
and structural conduciveness,
40, 203-204
and structural strain, 40, 41
Turner and Killian's emergent
norms, 25, 33-36
and ambiguous situations, 34
and crowd participants, 35
and crowd unanimity, 34
and recent criticism, 35-36

†